Religion and Society

International Studies in
Religion and Society

VOLUME 5

Religion and Society

An Agenda for the 21st Century

Edited by

Gerrie ter Haar and Yoshio Tsuruoka

BRILL

LEIDEN • BOSTON
2007

This book is printed on acid-free paper.

Library of Congress Cataloging-in-Publication Data

A C.I.P. record for this book is available from the Library of Congress

ISSN 1573-4293
ISBN 978 90 04 16123 8

PRINTED IN THE NETHERLANDS

CONTENTS

FOREWORD

The XIXth World Congress of the International Association for the History of Religions (IAHR), held from the 24th to 30th of March, 2005 in Tokyo, was attended by about 1800 researchers from 61 countries. Acting as the Chairperson of the Executive Committee of this Congress, I did not expect to have such a large number of participants, and I often got into a panic because our preparation did not keep pace with the schedule. In any event, we all were pleased to have so many participants. It was the second time that Japan had hosted the IAHR World Congress, the previous occasion being in 1958. The greatest difference with the 1958 Congress was that we had greater numbers of participants from Asia and Africa. This may reflect the changes that have occurred in the world of religious studies or in the world as a whole in the last half century. Such changes can also be sensed from the themes of the IAHR Congresses held during these years.

In the five years from the XVIIIth IAHR World Congress held in Durban, South Africa, in July 2000, to the XIXth Congress in Tokyo, Japan, in March 2005, the place of religion in the world underwent dramatic changes. The September 11 attacks that occurred in the United States in 2001, followed by the wars in Afghanistan and Iraq, are a vivid illustration of these changes. Political and economic factors should be analysed in detail to examine why such terrorist attacks and wars occurred. However, it should not be ignored that other factors such as culture and civilisation are intertwined with religion. No doubt, distrust among people due to religious differences has also contributed to making the political conflict more serious. The choice of *Religion: Conflict and Peace* as the overall theme of the XIXth IAHR World Congress in Tokyo was closely related to the situation of the world.

This book is compiled mainly from the papers presented at the plenary sessions of the Congress. In line with the Congress theme, a number of other topics that are considered as important for the contemporary study of religion were selected as sub-themes for discussion during the plenary sessions, with academic specialists serving as discussants. This book, therefore, reflects well the global expansion of the study of religion.

At the Congress, a number of sessions were prepared to provide participants with information on the present status of religious studies in the host country of Japan. Accordingly, the present study contains several articles on the history and condition of the study of religion in Japan. We hope that, through the case of Japan, the readers will understand that religious studies in the world are developing in diverse forms and directions. It is our sincere hope that this volume will contribute to the further progress of the study of religion in the world.

The publication of this book has been made possible through the cooperation of many people. I would like to express my appreciation to those who came from all corners of the world to Tokyo to deliver high-quality presentations and take part in the discussions, and to those who helped us in producing the book. I would like to take this opportunity again to express my gratitude to those who helped us with the organisation of the XIXth World Congress and those who rendered assistance in one way or another. Lastly, my greatest appreciation must be offered to Professor Gerrie ter Haar and Professor Yoshio Tsuruoka, who worked devotedly to arrange the Congress programme prior to the Congress, and to compile this book after the Congress.

Susumu Shimazono
April 2007

RELIGION IN THE TWENTY-FIRST CENTURY
A SHORT INTRODUCTION

Gerrie ter Haar and Yoshio Tsuruoka

In March 2005, Tokyo was the scene of an exceptional gathering, of hundreds of people who had come from all parts of the world to attend the largest-ever Congress of the International Association for the History of Religions (IAHR) for a whole week. The IAHR is a worldwide body that seeks to promote the activities of scholars contributing to the historical, social, and comparative study of religion. As such, the IAHR is the pre-eminent international forum for the critical, analytical and cross-cultural study of religion, in past and present. The organisation was founded in 1950 in Amsterdam and has grown over the years into a worldwide scholarly body that reflects the global diversity of its membership. The IAHR holds world congresses every five years, alternating between continents. In between congresses, conferences are held in as many parts of the world as possible to encourage international collaboration and intercultural exchange between scholars.[1]

From Amsterdam to Tokyo in 55 years has been a long time and a long way, during which the role of religion in public life has seen considerable changes. While in post-war Europe there has been a continuous trend towards secularisation, with religion being pushed to the margins of society, spiritually and intellectually, this has not been the case in most other parts of the world. Perhaps partly for this reason, the XIXth IAHR World Congress in Tokyo in 2005 was the biggest congress the IAHR has ever held in its 55 years of existence, with some 350 panels and a large number of symposia, round-tables and special sessions where more than 1,000 international scholars presented papers on a great diversity of subjects in the field of religion, with almost the same number of people attending the various meetings to listen to and discuss their findings. The programme covered an astonishing variety of subjects, as a simple reading of the congress programme demonstrates. The participants in the congress were equally diverse, as they came from

---

[1] More information about the IAHR is available at its website: www.iahr.dk.

over 60 different countries, and from all continents. This is testimony
to the progress of the IAHR in becoming a truly global organisation
for the study of religion. A telling sign in this regard, perhaps, was the
presence and participation in the congress proceedings of the United
Nations University, based in Tokyo.

The IAHR World Congress in Tokyo was held under the joint spon-
sorship of the Japanese Association for Religious Studies (JARS) and
the Science Council of Japan, in cooperation with other associations.
As Professor Shimazono indicates in his foreword to the present volume,
it was in fact the second congress to be sponsored by JARS, which
hosted also the IXth IAHR Congress in 1958. In addition, the year
2005 marked the 75th anniversary of the Japanese Association for
Religious Studies of as well the centennial of the inauguration of an
academic program of Religious Studies in the University of Tokyo.[2]

Religion and Society: An Agenda for the Twenty-first Century

The overall theme of the IAHR Congress in Tokyo was one of the most
urgent issues of our time—conflict and peace. Scholars of religions can
make an important contribution to debates on this subject by analysing
the role of religion in its various aspects and of individual religious
traditions in their various forms. This concerns ancient as well as living religions. Historical, sociological, anthropological, psychological,
textual, iconographical and philosophical approaches all have relevant
contributions to make.

Any scholarly analysis of the role of religion in conflict and peace is
bound to raise questions concerning religion and power. It must attempt
to explore the many facets of human conflict, social stability, and the
relationships between majorities and minorities, authorities and dissent-
ers, revolution and evolution, male and female, 'us' and 'them', and so
forth. It should assume that religion is a major social and cultural factor
or, as some would say, a social and cultural construction. Furthermore,
religion is associated with political power in either an implicit or an
explicit manner, which provides another important aspect of study.

Religion may serve as an identity marker in the maintenance of
ethnic, social or political stability, but it can also serve as an identity

---

[2] For further information, see the JARS website at http://www.soc.nii.ac.jp/jars/.

marker in conflicts of similar nature. Religion does not have to be the cause of, or a contributing factor to, violent conflict between social groups: religion and religious ideology can also serve to regulate social violence. At the time of the cold war, religion was often regarded as a constructive factor that could contribute to peace and stability. In recent decades, however, there has been a growing concern about its destructive side, as evidence seems to suggest that religion may intensify conflicts between civilisations. At the same time, there has been an increasing expectation that conflicts may be solved through a dialogue between civilisations.

Religion can promote discourses of oppression that regulate relations between genders, generations, classes, or other social groups. It can also provide models for an ideal society and for ideal relations between genders and groups. Religion can become a tool in the service of freedom, whether political or existential. Growing violence, political oppression and poverty may contribute to the emergence of new religious movements that are seen to promise a better future for those who are suffering, but that may themselves become the cause of serious new conflicts.

Religions often have traditions in which exemplary individuals, semi-mortal figures, or deities have attained victories for peace and emancipation. On the other hand, gods may be mirror images of their mortal servants, constantly at war with each other, spreading intrigue and misery in the divine and human worlds. The gods may serve as the ultimate justification for violence and hatred, or for peace and harmony between mortals. Some religious figures may invoke doom, exciting instability and frenzy, whereas others may serve as promoters of peace. All these matters were pursued at the congress in such a way as to deepen our knowledge and understanding of these issues.

The academic study of religion has drawn heavily on Western traditions of scholarship, that have themselves been shaped by the Enlightenment separation of church and state—as discussed in various parts of the book, in fact. The range of academic disciplines included under the rubric of the study of religion has spread worldwide, as a result of colonialism and the constitution of a truly global world of scholarship. However, the precise historical experience of every country and every region is unique, and many countries, including Japan, retain vibrant traditions of scholarship that are informed by the longer history of these countries. It has often been noted that the resurgence of religion in world politics that has been so noticeable since the late 1970s has surprised the many scholars who, steeped in a Western tradition of social science as a secular discipline, had expected religion to wither away as a public force. This raises the question of how scholars are to re-equip themselves to study religion in the twenty-first century. This is not the place to enter into any extensive speculation on the matter, other than to note that the role of non-Western scholars may be decisive in elaborating new methods that are adapted to current times. It is our hope that this book will make a significant contribution in this regard.

Contents of the Book

This book contains the revised papers of the congress's plenary sessions. These opened each day of the congress, addressing a theme of particular importance not only to scholars of religion but to the international community as a whole. They all addressed some of the most burning issues of our time and the role of religion therein. The opening session dealt with 'The Religious Dimension of War and Peace', the first of a series of topics to be considered by eminent scholars of diverse geographical origin and religious tradition. The following days were of no less interest in their choice of topics, including questions pertaining to the role of religion in matters of 'Technology, Life and Death'; 'Global Religions and Local Cultures', 'Boundaries and Segregations', and 'Method and Theory in the Study of Religion'. A separate day was set aside for presentations and debates about the study of religion in the host country, Japan. Japan has a long-standing history of Religious Studies (as it is generally called there), which is not widely known to outsiders. For that reason, a separate section in this volume is devoted to the way in which the study of some of the most important religious traditions in the world have been, and continue to be, studied in Japan. This seems all the more appropriate since Japan is home to the world's oldest and largest association for the study of religion.

The overall theme of the Tokyo Congress was Religion: Conflict and Peace. This is a highly topical subject, as religion is often seen today as a root cause of war. The question to be addressed by scholars is whether this is indeed so. Is religion an obstacle to, rather than an instrument for, peace? It is important to investigate in what ways religion may contribute to either war or peace, both at an ideological and a historical level. What meanings and values have religions attributed to the ideas of war and peace? And in what ways have they put such ideas into practice in past and present times? These are long disputed problems that need to be examined and considered anew at the beginning of the twenty-first century. In conformity with the overall Congress theme, Professor Mark Juergensmeyer, who is well-known for his pioneering work in this regard, set the tone for the scholarly debate with a keynote speech on 'Religious War, Terrorism, and Peace'.

Of a different, but no less important, order is the role of religion with regard to questions concerning the use of modern technology in respect to life and death. Religion can be seen as mediating between nature and humanity. In fact, religious traditions have produced various systems of ideas and practices according to which people live and die in their natural environment. Such systems inevitably reflect the technological resources of their time and place. Contemporary innovations in techno-sciences and -industries are not only destroying indigenous religious systems of knowledge, but also introducing new concerns relating to the human body, natural environments, humankind's and nature's life and death, that are often problematic. Addressing these unprecedented difficulties is one of the tasks confronting scholars today. In view of the long history of religions, it is also an urgent task for scholars of religion. Professor Ebrahim Moosa took this task upon himself in an exciting address about 'Neuropolitics and the Body'.

Some religions show a tendency to universal expansion, attempting to transcend the cultural and regional limits in which they originally emerged. At the same time, religious traditions are deeply rooted in par-ticular regional cultures. The so-called world religions have to integrate themselves in a local culture and become indigenous in a sense, if they are to actualise their universal aspirations. The combined processes of globalisation and localisation (sometimes referred to as 'glocalisation') of the contemporary world necessitate revising traditional dichotomies and terminologies, such as world religions and ethnic religions, monothe-isms and polytheisms, and others. This was done by another reputed scholar, Professor Talal Asad, who explained the relation between the global and the local from a particular angle in 'Explaining the Global Religious Revival: the Egyptian Case'.

In a different way, this debate was continued with a discussion on boundaries and segregations in religion(s). Religions offer epistemo-logical schemes to understand, evaluate, and order objects, events and humans in the world. Drawing clear lines between 'us' and 'others', inner and outer groups, etc. is one important function religion may assume. Today, however, the drawing of boundaries and the creation of segregation should be examined in relation to the universalist claims of human rights. In fact, religions have often recognised the importance of particular distinctions among humankind, for example those of men and women, and as a result they have legitimised certain forms of discrimination. In some cases, religious groups, despite advocating the fundamental equality of humankind, have nevertheless deemed certain people or groups to fall outside this category—to be inhuman, in other words—thus justifying aggression towards that which is deemed external to society. These aspects and functions of religion need reconsideration from a wide perspective. Such a perspective was offered from an unusual angle by Professor Suwanna Satha-Anand in her keynote speech on 'Fluid Boundaries, Institutional Segregation and Sexual Tolerance in Thai Buddhism'. Her address also raised a number of questions about the way in which the world's religious traditions are studied.

Methodological reflection is a continual task in the study of religion. The complex interplay between method and theory in the human and social sciences plays an integral role in academic reflection and scholarly debates related to it. In recent decades, it seems that under the influence of sister-disciplines as well as because of other factors, the study of religion has witnessed remarkable changes and developments in the fields of method and theory, in comparison with earlier eras. This matter was addressed by Professor Tomoko Masuzawa when she discussed the question of 'Theory without Method: Situating a Discourse Analysis on Religion', a profound critique of the dominant theoretical approaches in the study of religion, most of which have their origin in the West.

The book follows the original structure of the congress. Hence, it is divided into several parts, each addressing the themes outlined above. Each part contains a short introduction, followed by the keynote speeches referred to above, and two responsive papers by other experts in the areas under discussion. The last part of the book is devoted to the study of religion in Japan. The bibliography at the end of the book is also divided according to theme, and so are the biographical notes about the various contributors to the book. In compiling notes on authors, we have followed the Western convention of placing the personal name before the surname, although this practice is not customary in Japan and other parts of Asia. Concerning the bibliography, we equally follow Western convention in listing the author's surname first, followed by the personal name after a comma. The footnotes accompanying the text generally offer only summary details of the works cited; full details are included in the consolidated bibliography. It should be noted that in relevant cases the bibliographical references relating to the study of religion in Japan provide a transcription of the original Japanese title, with the English translation in brackets. The same applies to works originally published in Korean.

Religion, we may conclude, is set to be a major force in the twenty-first century. Here is a book that discusses every aspect of this fascinating subject, proposing an agenda for future study. It tells us what the world's leading scholars have to say in this respect. Issues of conflict and peace, ethical questions concerning the use of advanced technology, explanations of the global religious revival, and the role of women in religious leadership, as well as questions about how to study religion, are all discussed in this book. It is a volume that ranges exceptionally widely, in terms of the themes discussed, the variety of disciplines, and the participation of international scholars debating with each other. Such an international and inter-disciplinary debate can clear the way for a fresh approach to religion as one of the major issues of our time.

PART ONE

THE RELIGIOUS DIMENSION OF WAR AND PEACE

RELIGIOUS DIMENSIONS OF WAR AND PEACE
INTRODUCTION

Rosalind I. J. Hackett

The current era of global and local restructurings, as well as the development of what Saskia Sassen terms 'new geographies of centrality',[1] presents complex challenges for today's scholar of religion. New entanglements of religious ideas and political action, and changing formations and locations of religion require new interpretive perspectives. The rise of global media, and new discourses of difference, merit particular attention.

For those who specialise in the analysis of religiously-related violence and conflict, the global scenario is even more challenging. The new trope and phenomenon of terrorism represents innovative forms of asymmetrical warfare, as well as of mass mediation. Extremist factions and new movements can capture public attention in next to no time. The scholar of religion, still regrettably overlooked in many cases as informed resource, can provide the historical roots, comparative angle, content and contextual knowledge needed to analyse these new religious voices in the public sphere. Specialists in new religions, for example, have shed helpful light on processes of conversion, and radicalisation.[2]

Of particular import is the ability to assess the claims and the potency of religious rhetoric as resource for violent social transformation. In addition to discourse, the twenty-first century scholar of religion must be attuned to the power of images, and their strategic manipulation, in what Manuel Castells calls our 'global network society'.[3] Images of persecution, suffering, and demonisation can suffuse a group's self-understanding

---

[1] Saskia Sassen, 'Spatialities and temporalities of the global: elements for a theorization', *Public Culture*, vol. 12, no. 1, 2000, p. 225.

[2] See e.g. Thomas Robbins and Susan J. Palmer (eds.), *Millennium, Messiahs, and Mayhem: Contemporary Apocalyptic Movements*, New York: Routledge, 1997; Robert J. Lifton, *Destroying the World to Save It: Aum Shinrikyo, Apocalyptic Violence, and the New Global Terrorism*, New York: Henry Holt, 1999.

[3] Manuel Castells, *The Information Age: Economy, Society and Culture*, Oxford: Blackwell, 1997, pp. ii, 10–11.

and activism.[4] The rapidly expanding spectrum of small and large media, and new technologies of communication, necessitates a broader understanding of the media sphere.[5] It also calls for rethinking how violence and conflict are constituted and perceived. Recent moves by the British government to enact a bill to prohibit religious hatred are in part occasioned by the perceived upsurge in the propagation of negative representations of religious communities, notably the Muslim community, in the public sphere.[6] The United Nations Commission on Human Rights also acknowledges the heightened role of the media in inciting acts of violence and discrimination on religious grounds in its revised resolution on 'Combating Defamation of Religions.'[7]

More than ever before, mass mediated forms of expression such as magazine articles, public banners, and televised sermons can spark communal violence. This was the case of the 'Miss World riots' in Nigeria in 2002, for example, when a hapless young (Christian) journalist wrote that the Prophet Muhammad would have probably taken one of the contestants for a wife. Hundreds died in the ensuing riots between Muslims and Christians, and the contest was moved from Nigeria to London.

(Re)theorising religiously related violence and conflict also provokes new reflection on how religion is defined and articulated in the public sphere.[8] The different (legal, political, religious, cultural) understandings of what constitutes (good or legitimate) religion[9] can have profound

---

[4] Rosalind I. J. Hackett, 'Discourses of demonisation in Africa', *Diogenes*, vol. 50, no. 3, 2003, pp. 61–75.

[5] See Rosalind I. J. Hackett, 'Devil Bustin' satellites: how media liberalization in Africa generates religious intolerance and conflict, in R. I. J. Hackett, S. Mahmud and J. H. Smith (eds.), *Religion in African Conflicts and Peacebuilding Initiatives: Problems and Prospects for a Globalizing Africa*, University of Notre Dame Press (in press); also Faye Ginsberg, Lila Abu-Lughod and Brian Larkin (eds.), *Media Worlds: Anthropology on New Terrain*, Los Angeles and Berkeley: University of California Press, 2002.

[6] Racial and Religious Hatred Bill. http://www.publications.parliament.uk/pa/cm200506/cmbills/011/2006011.htm.

[7] 'Combating Defamation of Religions'. Commission on Human Rights Resolution 2003/4 E/CN.4/2004/L.5 April 13, 2004. http://www.unhchr.ch/Huridocda/Huridoca.nsf/(Symbol)/E.CN.4.RES.2003.4.En?Opendocument.

[8] Rosalind I. J. Hackett, 'A new axial moment for the study of religion?', *Temenos*, vol. 42, no. 2, 2006, pp. 111–29.

[9] Eileen Barker, 'Why the cults? New religions and freedom of religion and beliefs', in T. Lindholm, W. C. Durham and B. Tahzib-Lie (eds.), *Facilitating Freedom of Religion and Belief: Perspectives: Impulses and Recommendations from the Oslo Coalition*, Dordrecht: Kluwer, 2004, pp. 571–94.

consequences for minority groups in particular.[10] Bruce Lincoln laments the 'idealized and impoverished' understandings of religion that have been aired post-9/11.[11] Similarly, Robert Wuthnow avers that

> [t]he role of scientific studies [of religion] should not be, in the first instance, to discover what is common among the various traditions, but to understand what is different and to gauge reactions to those differences. *That task is especially important because of conflicts among religious traditions*, on the one hand, and because of the superficial assumptions one still encounters among naïve observers that 'all religions are the same' (emphasis added).[12]

However, Lincoln reminds us that these religious markers mask the fact that, like other cultural phenomena, religious communities and institutions 'wage their wars around rival claims to scarce resources: people, territory, wealth, positions of power, and economic advantage, but also such nonmaterial resources as dignity, prestige, and all manner of symbolic capita.'[13] Or, as sociologist John Hall tellingly states, 'There is no firewall between religion and other social phenomena', emphasising that: 'religion is more than symbolic currency, more than epiphenomena, more than merely a venue of violence; it becomes a vehicle for the expression of deeply and widely held social aspirations—of nationalism, anticolonialism, or civilizational struggle'.[14]

Finally, issues of religious conflict and violence frequently force scholars to address not just facts, but values.[15] Burton Mack posits that departments of religion should re-focus around the 'task of cultural criticism', with scholars of religion discussing 'the effective differences

---

[10] Nathan A. Adams, IV, 'A human rights imperative: extending religious liberty beyond the border', *Cornell International Law Journal*, vol. 33, no. 1, 2000, pp. 1–66; James T. Richardson, 'Discretion and discrimination in legal cases involving controversial religious groups and allegations of ritual abuse', in R. J. Ahdar (ed.), *Law and Religion*, Aldershot, UL: Ashgate, 2000, pp. 111–32; Winfred Fallers Sullivan, *The Impossibility of Religious Freedom*, Princeton University Press, 2005.

[11] Bruce Lincoln, *Holy Terrors: Thinking About Religion after September 11*, University of Chicago Press, 2003.

[12] Robert Wuthnow, 'Is there a place for "scientific" studies of religion?', *The Chronicle of Higher Education*, Jan. 2003, B10–B11.

[13] Lincoln, *Holy Terrors*, p. 74.

[14] John R. Hall, 'Religion and violence: social processes in comparative perspective', in M. Dillon (ed.), *Handbook for the Sociology of Religion*, New York: Cambridge University Press, p. 379.

[15] Wuthnow, 'Is there a place for "scientific" studies of religion?'.

different religions make [in society].'[16] All this serves to highlight the fact that, in anthropologist Michael Herzfeld's estimation, 'disinterested scholarship', as well as 'cultural relativism', are limited sources of refuge with their own problematic 'theodicies'.[17] Yet Robert Orsi advocates caution in responding to calls to the public sphere, lest we be drawn into projects of surveillance or reassurance, especially at times of 'political panic'.[18] The presentations in this section illustrate richly how the critique of three scholars of religion in the area of religious violence has illumined developments in a range of national, regional and global settings, for both colleagues and the wider public alike.

---

[16] Burton Mack, 'Caretakers and critics: on the social role of scholars who study religion', *Bulletin of the Council of Societies for the Study of Religion*, vol. 30, no. 2, 2001, pp. 32–8.

[17] Michael Herzfeld, *Anthropology: Theoretical Practice in Culture and Society*. Oxford: Blackwell, 2001, p. 238.

[18] Robert A. Orsi, 'Is the study of lived religion irrelevant to the world we live in?', *Journal for the Society for the Scientific Study of Religion*, vol. 42, no. 2, 2003, p. 174.

RELIGIOUS WAR, TERRORISM, AND PEACE

Mark Juergensmeyer

The assault on commuter trains in Madrid, the World Trade Centre attack in New York City, the release of nerve gas in subways in Tokyo—all of these are incidents of terrorism, and all of them linked with religion. Religion has been a factor in terrorism in virtually every religious tradition—not just Islam. A Christian terrorist, Timothy McVeigh, bombed the Oklahoma City Federal Building. A Jewish activist, Yigal Amir, assassinated Israel's Prime Minister Yitzhak Rabin. A Buddhist prophet, Shoko Asahara, orchestrated the unleashing of nerve gas in the Tokyo subways near the Japanese parliament buildings. Hindu and Sikh militants have targeted government buildings and political leaders in India. These and many other incidents force us to raise the question of whether religion leads to violence or peace.

But before we can speculate on how religion can contribute to peace, we too have to acknowledge the role that religion provides in terrorism and war. Most acts of religious terrorism in recent years are undertaken as part of a cosmic war—a great spiritual war between good and evil. This is true not only of the Muslim activists who believe in *jihad*, but also of Christian militants in the United States, Jewish activists in Israel, and the Aum Shinrikyo activists who unleashed nerve gas in Tokyo's subways. Those who believe in cosmic war think that is being waged not only in a spiritual sense but on a worldly plane. Often the evil forces are imagined to be Westernisation, or globalisation, or specifically George Bush and the U.S. government. At the same time the opposition to these acts of cosmic war, including the U.S. 'war on terrorism' and its invasion and occupation of Iraq, have been undertaken with a religious zeal as well.

In confronting these forms of religious violence in our contemporary life, three questions immediately arise. Why is religion involved in violence? Why is this happening now? And how can religion contribute less to violence than to peace?

Why religion?

Religious activists are puzzling anomalies in the secular world. Most religious people and their organisations are either firmly supportive of the secular state or quiescently uninterested in it. Osama bin Laden's al-Qaeda network, like most of the new religious activists, comprise a small group at the extreme end of a hostile subculture that itself is a small minority within the larger Muslim world. Osama bin Laden is no more representative of Islam than Timothy McVeigh is of Christianity, or Japan's Shoko Asahara is of Buddhism.

Still one cannot deny that the ideals and ideas of activists like Bin Laden are authentically and thoroughly religious. Moreover, even though their network consists of only a few thousand members, they have enjoyed an increase in popularity in the Muslim world after September 11, especially after the Afghan and Iraqi occupations by the U.S. military and its allies. The authority of religion has given Bin Laden's cadres the moral legitimacy of employing violence to assault the symbols of global economic and political power. Religion has also provided them the metaphor of cosmic war, an image of spiritual struggle that every religion contains within its repository of symbols—the fight between good and bad, truth and evil. In this sense, then, attacks such as those on the World Trade Centre and the United Nations headquarters in Baghdad were very religious. They were meant to be catastrophic, acts of biblical proportions.

Though the World Trade Centre and United Nations assaults and many other recent acts of religious terrorism have had no obvious military goal, they are meant to make a powerful impact on the public consciousness. These are shows meant for television. They are a kind of perverse performance of power meant to ennoble the perpetrators' views of the world and to draw us into their notions of cosmic war. In my study of the global rise of religious violence, *Terror in the Mind of God*,[1] I have found a strikingly familiar pattern. In virtually all of the recent cases of religious violence, concepts of cosmic war have been accompanied by strong claims of moral justification and an enduring absolutism that transforms worldly struggles into sacred battles. It is not so much that religion has become politicised, but that politics have

---

[1] Mark Juergensmeyer, *Terror in the Mind of God: The Global Rise of Religious Violence* (3rd edn.), Berkeley: University of California Press, 2003.

become religionised. Worldly struggles have been lifted into the high proscenium of sacred battle.

This is what makes religious warfare so difficult to combat. Its enemies have become satanised—one cannot negotiate with them or easily compromise. The rewards for those who fight for the cause are trans-temporal, and the time lines of their struggles are vast. Most social and political struggles look for conclusions within the lifetimes of their participants, but religious struggles can take generations to succeed.

I once had the occasion to point out the futility—in secular military terms—of the radical Islamic struggle in Palestine to Dr Abdul Aziz Rantisi, the late head of the political wing of the Hamas movement. It seemed to me that Israel's military force was such that a Palestinian military effort could never succeed. Dr Rantisi assured me that that 'Palestine was occupied before, for two hundred years.' He explained that he and his Palestinian comrades 'can wait again—at least that long.' In his calculation, the struggles of God can endure for aeons. Ultimately, however, they knew they would succeed.

Insofar as the U.S. public and its leaders embraced the image of war following the September 11 attacks, America's view of this war was also prone to religionisation. 'God Bless America' became the country's unofficial national anthem. President George W. Bush spoke of the defence of America's 'righteous cause', and the 'absolute evil' of its enemies. Still, the U.S. military engagement in the months following September 11 was primarily a secular commitment to a definable goal and largely restricted to limited objectives in which civil liberties and moral rules of engagement, for the most part, still applied.

In purely religious battles, waged in divine time and with heaven's rewards, there is no need to compromise one's goals. There is no need, also, to contend with society's laws and limitations when one is obeying a higher authority. In spiritualising violence, therefore, religion gives the resources of violence a remarkable power.

Ironically, the reverse is also true: terrorism can give religion power. Although sporadic acts of terrorism do not lead to the establishment of new religious states, they make the political potency of religious ideology impossible to ignore. The first wave of religious activism, from the Islamic revolution in Iran in 1978 to the emergence of Hamas during the Palestinian *intifada* in the early 1990s, was focused on religious nationalism and the vision of individual religious states. Increasingly, religious activism has a more global vision. Such disparate groups as the Christian militia, the Japanese Aum Shinrikyo, and the al-Qaeda network all target what their supporters regard as a repressive and secular form of global culture and control.

Part of the attraction of religious ideologies is that they are so personal. They impart a sense of redemption and dignity to those who embrace them. Those attracted to them are often men who feel marginalised from public life, and in that way, humiliated. One can view their efforts to make satans out of their enemies and to embrace ideas of cosmic war as attempts at ennoblement, empowerment, and de-humiliation. Such efforts would be poignant if they were not so horribly destructive.

Yet they are not just personal acts. These violent efforts of symbolic empowerment have an effect beyond whatever personal satisfaction and feelings of potency they impart to those who support and conduct them. The very act of killing on behalf of a moral code is a political statement. Such acts break the state's monopoly on morally sanctioned killing. By putting the right to take life in their own hands, the perpetrators of religious violence make a daring claim of power on behalf of the powerless, a basis of legitimacy for public order other than that on which the secular state relies.

Why Now?

What makes these acts of religious violence occur now, and in a way different from the various forms of holy warfare and sanctimonious killing that have occurred throughout history, is that they are responses to a contemporary theme in the world's political and social life: globalisation. In an interesting way, the World Trade Centre symbolised Bin Laden's hatred of two aspects of secular government—a certain kind of modernisation and a certain kind of globalisation. I say 'a certain kind', in both cases, since the al-Qaeda network was itself both modern and trans-national in its own way. Its members were often highly sophisticated and technically-skilled professionals, and its organisation was comprised of followers of various nationalities who moved effortlessly from place to place with no obvious nationalist agenda or allegiance. In a sense they were not opposed to modernity and globalisation, as long as it was of their own design. But they loathed the Western-style modernity that they imagined that secular globalisation was forcing upon them.

Some twenty-three years earlier, during the Islamic revolution in Iran, the Ayatollah Khomeini rallied the masses with a similar notion, that

America was forcing its economic exploitation, its political institutions, and its secular culture on an unwitting Islamic society. The Ayatollah accused urban Iranians of having succumbed to 'Westoxification'—an inebriation of Western culture and ideas. The many strident movements of religious nationalism that have erupted around the world in the more than two decades following the Iranian revolution have echoed this cry. This anti-Westernism has at heart an opposition to a certain kind of modernism—its secularism, its individualism, its skepticism. Yet, in a curious way, by accepting the modern notion of the nation-state and by adopting the technology and financial instruments of modern society, many of these movements of religious nationalism have claimed a kind of modernity on their own behalf.[2]

One could regard religious politics as a kind of opportunistic infection that has set in at the present weakened stage of the secular nation-state. Globalisation has crippled the secular nationalism and the nation-state in several ways. It has weakened it economically not only through the global reach of trans-national businesses but also by the trans-national nature of their labour supply, currency, and financial instruments. It has eroded its sense of national identity and unity through the planetary expansion of media and communications technology and popular culture, and through the unchallenged military power of the United States. Some of the most intense movements for ethnic and religious nationalism have arisen in nations where local leaders have felt exploited by the global economy, unable to gain military leverage against what they regard as corrupt leaders promoted by the United States, and invaded by American images of popular culture on television, the internet, and motion pictures.

Another aspect of globalisation—the emergence of multicultural societies through global diasporas of peoples and cultures, and the suggestion that global military and political control might fashion a 'new world order'—has also elicited fear. It is this spectre that has been exploited by Bin Laden and other Islamic activists, and which caused many concerned citizens in the Islamic world to see America's military response to the September 11 attacks as an imperialistic venture and a

---

[2] Benedict Anderson, *Imagined Communities: Reflections on the Origin and Spread of Nationalism*, London: Verso, 1983; Samuel P. Huntington, *The Clash of Civilizations and the Remaking of World Order*, New York: Simon and Schuster, 1996; and Mark Juergensmeyer, *The New Cold War? Religious Nationalism Confronts the Secular State*, Berkeley, CA: University of California Press, 1993.

bully's crusade, rather than the righteous wrath of an injured victim. When U.S. leaders included the invasion and occupation of Iraq as part of its 'war against terror' it was commonly portrayed in the Muslim world as a ploy for the expansion of America's global reach.

This image of America's sinister role in creating a new world order of globalisation is also feared in some quarters of the West. In the United States, for example, the Christian Identity movement and Christian militia organisations have been alarmed over what they imagine to be a massive global conspiracy to control the world, involving liberal American politicians and the United Nations. Timothy McVeigh's favourite book, *The Turner Diaries*,[3] is based on the premise that the United States has already succumbed unwittingly to a conspiracy of global control from which it needs to be liberated through terrorist actions and guerilla bands. In Japan a similar conspiracy theory motivated leaders of the Aum Shinrikyo movement to predict a catastrophic World War III, which their nerve gas assault in the Tokyo subways was meant to demonstrate.

As far-fetched as the idea of a 'new world order' of global control may be, there is some truth to the notion that the integration of societies, communication among disparate peoples, and the globalisation of culture have brought the world closer together. It is also true that U.S. consumers have benefited from economic globalisation, and the military power of the U.S. allows American leaders to get their way in shaping global power even when—as in the case of Iraq—many of their own allies war against their designs.

Even without America's heavy-handed intervention in world affairs, however, the social and cultural effects of globalisation create resentment in parts of the world that have not benefited from the global economy in the way that America has. Moreover, the effect of globalisation on local societies and national identities has been profound. It has undermined the modern idea of the nation-state by providing non-national and trans-national forms of economic, social, and cultural interaction. The global economic and social ties of the inhabitants of contemporary global cities are intertwined in a way that supersedes the idea of a national social contract—the Enlightenment notion that peoples in particular regions are naturally linked together in a specific nation-state.

---

[3] Andrew Macdonald, *The Turner Diaries*, Hillsboro, WV: National Vanguard Books, 1978.

In a global world it is hard to say where particular regions begin and end. For that matter, in multicultural societies it is hard to say how one should define the 'people' of a particular nation.

This is where religion and ethnicity step in to redefine public communities. The fading of the nation-state and the disillusionment with old forms of secular nationalism have produced both the opportunity for new nationalisms and the need for them. The opportunity has arisen because the old orders seem so weak; and the need for national identity persists because no single alternative form of social cohesion and affiliation has yet appeared to dominate public life the way the nation-state did in the twentieth century. In a curious way, traditional forms of social identity have helped to rescue one of Western modernity's central themes: the idea of nationhood. In the increasing absence of any other demarcation of national loyalty and commitment, these old staples—religion, ethnicity and traditional culture—have become resources for national identification.

In the contemporary political climate, therefore, religious and ethnic nationalism have provided a solution to the perceived insufficiencies of Western-style secular politics. As secular ties have begun to unravel in the post-Soviet and post-colonial era, local leaders have searched for new anchors to ground their social identities and political loyalties. What is significant about these ethno-religious movements is their creativity—not just their use of technology and mass media, but also their appropriation of the nation-state and global networks. Although many of the framers of the new nationalisms have reached back in history for ancient images and concepts that will give them credibility, theirs are not simply efforts to resuscitate old ideas from the past. These are contemporary ideologies that meet present-day social and political needs.

In the context of Western modernism this is a revolutionary notion—that indigenous culture can provide the basis for new political institutions, including resuscitated forms of the nation-state. Movements that support ethno-religious nationalism are, therefore, often confrontational and sometimes violent. They reject the intervention of outsiders and their ideologies and, at the risk of being intolerant, pander to their indigenous cultural bases and enforce traditional social boundaries. It is no surprise, then, that they get into trouble with each other and with defenders of the secular state. Yet even such conflicts serve a purpose for the movements: it helps define who they are as a people and who they are not. They are not, for instance, secular modernists.

Understandably, then, these movements of anti-Western modernism are ambivalent about modernity—whether it is necessarily Western and always evil. They are also ambivalent about the most recent stage of modernity (or post-modernity): globalisation. On the one hand these political movements of anti-modernity are reactions to the globalisation of Western culture. They are responses to the insufficiencies of what is often touted as the world's global standard: the elements of secular, Westernised urban society that are found not only in the West but in many parts of the former third world, and which are seen by their detractors as vestiges of colonialism. On the other hand these new ethno-religious identities are alternative modernities with international and super-national aspects of their own. This means that in the future some forms of anti-modernism will be global, some will be virulently anti-global, and yet others will be content with creating their own alternative modernities in ethno-religious nation-states.

Each of these forms of religious anti-modernism contains a paradoxical relationship between certain forms of globalisation and emerging religious and ethnic nationalisms. It is one of history's ironies that the globalism of culture and the emergence of trans-national political and economic institutions enhance the need for local identities. They also create the desire for a more localised form of authority and social accountability.

The crucial problems in an era of globalisation are identity and control. The two are linked, in that a loss of a sense of belonging leads to a feeling of powerlessness. At the same time, what has been perceived as a loss of faith in secular nationalism is experienced as a loss of agency as well as selfhood. For these reasons the assertion of traditional forms of religious identities are linked to attempts to reclaim personal and cultural power. The vicious outbreaks of anti-modernism in the incidents of religious terrorism that have occurred in the first decade of the twenty-first century can be seen as tragic attempts to regain social control through acts of violence. Until there is a surer sense of citizenship in a global order, therefore, religious visions of moral order will continue to appear as attractive though often disruptive solutions to the problems of authority, identity and belonging in a global world.

We return, then, to the central question: why do religion and violence often go together? Violence and war have always been a part of the religious imagination, and images of religious warfare are part of every religious tradition's history and mythology. The idea of war, I believe, is part of the way that religion deals with great issues of good and evil, chaos and order. Ultimately, then, images of war lead to images of ultimate order and harmony. The challenge for our times is to find ways in which cosmic war can return to the spiritual plane, and religion in worldly confrontations can become an agent of order, toleration, and peace.

Religion and Peace

One does not have to search far to find the non-violent role that religion can play in world affairs for there are religious strands of reconciliation in the current trends towards globalisation. Even the religious movements that take a confrontational stance towards modernity are often diverse. This includes those movements that reject globalisation in all of its cultural, economic, and political forms. In India, for example, some Hindu supporters of the Bharatiya Janata Party in India have called for a religious state, a sort of Hindu replication of Shi'ite Iran, yet when the party was in power its national leadership was remarkably moderate. Other forms of religious opposition are even less strident. Prophetic religious voices from Bishop Desmond Tutu in South Africa to Tibet's Dalai Lama have called for moderation, justice, and environmental protection, joining those of other concerned global citizens in speaking out against the unbridled excesses of global capitalism and an indiscriminate popular consumer culture. These religious activists do not blow things up, but when it comes to contemporary globalisation they do demur: they seek a better world than the one of global consumerism. So even when religion is the enemy of globalisation, its opposition is varied, and its voices are diverse.

Religion is not only globalisation's foe. It can also facilitate the understanding and tolerance necessary for globalisation's multicultural communities. And it can offer alternative visions of global values of its own. Whatever globalisation is—whether one conceives it as the homogenising forces of economic globalisation, the diasporas of communities, or the easy mobility of peoples around the world—these trends have led to new cultural patterns and shared values that have affected religion along with everything else. If this global interaction of people and information is leading to something more than just cultural diversity—if there is a new global society emerging—then this emerging syncretic society will have religious sensitivities and moral values as one ingredient.

This means that the religious factor in globalisation is often a puzzling one. Its role—though significant—is frequently contradictory. In some cases it provides the resources for shared values—including a universal sensibility toward spirituality and the elements of a global ethic—that provide the cultural basis for trans-national laws and regulations, agencies of economic and social accountability, and a sense of global citizenship. In some cases it can help to ease the cultural difficulties experienced in multicultural societies by providing the shared values that allow peoples of divergent cultures to live together in harmony. In other cases it sounds a prophetic note by warning against the superficial aspects of a homogenous global culture.

This tension between the parochialism of religion and its potentially global reach is at the heart of religion's ambivalence towards globalisation. In some instances, religion can support movements not only for justice but also for mercy, as in the case of the Christian religious groups' support for relief of international debts. In her study of an Islamic movement in Egypt, Carrie Wickham discovered that religious politics can be transformed into more moderate forms that are compatible with secular democracy through a process of 'political learning', and that sometimes these forms point towards a new understanding of globalisation.[4] Wickham's observations about the possibility of the transformation of Islam, for instance, runs counter to the assumption that Islamic notions of religious politics do not allow for social change, tolerance, and democratic ideals.

This Islamic discussion raises an even larger question: whether it is possible to profile any religion. Do the histories and cultures of religious traditions define religions in predictable ways, or do the diversity of religious strands, the changing interpretations of religious tenets, and the various social settings in which religious communities exist make religions so malleable as to be nigh near unpredictable? Social scientists like to deal with known sets of values, but often religious stances are not so easy to predict.

When religion interacts with the forces of globalisation sometimes the result is explosive. But it can also be more positive, and religion is destined to play a creative role in an emerging global civil society.

---

[4] Carrie Wickham, 'The Islamist alternative to globalization', in Mark Juergensmeyer (ed.), *Religion in Global Civil Society*, New York: Oxford University Press, 2005, pp. 149–70.

When religion is seen primarily in limited organisational terms, and when civil society is viewed primarily as trans-national forms of social service, the two may be on different tracks. In the narrow view of religion, the movements of Jihad may indeed clash with the cultural assertiveness of McWorld. But when religion is conceived in its widest sense, as a stratum of spiritual sensibility and shared moral responsibility, it is congenial with the notion of civil society in its broadest sense—the idea of global citizenship.

In this latter case we might envision not a clash of civilisations[5] but the possibility of a coalescence of civilisations. The world's religious traditions have abundant resources for thinking about tolerance, harmony, and human dignity on a global scale. No one tradition—certainly not contemporary Western consumer-oriented popular culture—has a monopoly on a vision of shared values and the family of humanity. Hence there is every reason to expect that members of all religious traditions are potentially participants in a kind of multicultural world civilisation.

It is a truly prophetic vision that some day the emergence of a global society will lead to new forms of shared morality, spirituality and social values. Perhaps a future generation of global citizens will look back on such widely venerated figures of today as Mohandas Gandhi, Mother Teresa, Archbishop Tutu, and the Dalai Lama and see them as global saints. They may be viewed in the future as the harbingers of a global spirituality. As the world changes, the role of religion in global civil society also evolves, often in innovative and surprising ways. It is not inconceivable, then, that one religious response to globalisation will be new forms of spiritual life, as religion continues to be shaped anew in a global age.

---

[5] See Huntington, *The Clash of Civilizations.*

RELIGIOUS WAR, TERRORISM, AND PEACE
A RESPONSE TO MARK JUERGENSMEYER

Gerrie ter Haar

Introduction

Professor Mark Juergensmeyer has provided us with an insightful address on a topic of the greatest importance. This concerns a field in which he has made an indelible mark already, notably through his book *Terror in the Mind of God*, in which he analyses the contemporary use of violence by religious believers and in different religious traditions.[1] In a similar vein he makes a number of important and interesting points in his keynote address. They are made in the course of addressing two questions that he sets out with great clarity. First, he asks why religion is implicated in violence. And secondly, he wonders why is this happening now.

In this response I will limit my observations to these two central issues. I will particularly comment on certain aspects of the relationship between religion and politics, which is so central to the contemporary debate. I will not dwell much on the question of religion and violence as such, not because this is unimportant, but because most people who have a basic understanding of religion as a social phenomenon are fully aware of the fundamentally ambiguous nature of religion. There are certainly some people in the world who believe that religion is always a force for good, in the same way as there are some who believe that it is invariably a negative element in society. It is easy to demonstrate from history that religion has a recurrent connection to violence. In fact, violence has always been part of the religious imagination, as Mark Juergensmeyer has pointed out. By the same token, religion is morally ambiguous, as it is—unlike what many people may prefer to think, especially in Europe—neither inherently good nor inherently bad, and may serve different interests. In this respect, we may say, religion is like politics. Both religion and politics legitimise the use of

---

[1] Mark Juergensmeyer, *Terror in the Mind of God: The Global Rise of Religious Violence*, Berkeley: Los Angeles: University of California Press, 2003 [3rd ed. revised and updated; originally published in 2000].

violence in particular circumstances with reference to the fact that we are not living in 'normal' circumstances, and that exceptional conditions require exceptional measures.[2] Personally, I would say that the 'global war on terror' is a good example of the latter type of reasoning. Hence, religion and politics may have more in common than may appear at first sight.

Religion and Politics

Nowadays, it is often commented upon how much religion has become politicised, especially with reference to Islam. To a large extent this is an awareness that has grown since the 9/11 attacks in the United States and subsequent events, which mark the dramatic escalation of a political process in which the gap between different civilisations has deepened. In the popular view, this gap is often represented in terms of a religious conflict, adding substance to the idea that religion is often a root cause of the violent conflicts that affect our world today. In other words, there is a widespread belief that religion has become politicised in recent years.

Bearing this in mind, it is striking how Professor Juergensmeyer has reversed this idea. He suggests that it is not so much religion that has become politicised, but politics that have become religionised. This being the case, he argues, worldly conflicts have been turned into sacred battles, and this makes violence perpetrated in the name of religion extraordinarily difficult to counter. This is an interesting perspective that underscores the reality that religion is becoming the political language of the twenty-first century. It also highlights the fact that religion and politics constitute alternative sources of power, located in the material and spiritual spheres respectively.[3] Both sources of power can be drawn upon for political purposes. It is precisely because they are competing powers that religion and politics are always in an uneasy relationship. It is important to realise in this respect that for most people in the world 'religion' refers to a way of viewing the world, rather than to

---

[2] See R. Scott Appleby, 'Religions, human rights and social change', in Gerrie ter Haar and James J. Busuttil (eds.), *The Freedom to Do God's Will: Religious Fundamentalism and Social Change*, London and New York: Routledge, 2003, pp. 197–229, notably at p. 200.

[3] Cf. Stephen Ellis and Gerrie ter Haar, *Worlds of Power: Religious Thought and Political Practice in Africa*, London: Hurst & Co./New York: Oxford University Press, 2004.

some organised system of belief that they follow. In a Tylorian man-ner,[4] they believe in the existence of an invisible world, that is distinct but not separate from the visible one; a world which they believe to be the dwelling place of spirit(ual) beings, to which they ascribe effective powers over their daily lives. The invisible world is one with which they can interact and communicate regularly for their own benefit, both materially and spiritually. For them, this is a world that contains power, namely spiritual power, a type of power in which they can fully share, and in that sense rather unlike political power, which often tends to be more exclusive. Spiritual empowerment, therefore, is an effective strategy from a believer's perspective, since it opens up alternative avenues to achieve what is often referred to as the 'good life'. Although not one and the same thing, spiritual empowerment resembles somewhat the concept of 'symbolic empowerment' as used by Mark Juergensmeyer. However, for those who believe in it, the power they derive from religion, in whatever way defined, is not symbolic but real. Spiritual power as *real* power is a concept that most secularists find difficult to grasp, and therefore have a problem in finding appropriate responses.

Religion, thus, is simultaneously a way of understanding the world and of relating to other people. These are important ways in which it is allied to politics. As alternative sources of power, religion and politics can be used—and often are, in fact—to strengthen one another. Many authors, for example, have pointed out the extent to which politics in the age of nationalism took on many of the characteristics of religion. Today, the underlying idea that connects religion and politics—that is, the concept of power—has not really changed; all that has changed are its specific expressions. For example, in modern Africa, the continent I know best through my own work, the esoteric character tradition-ally ascribed to power impels many politicians, including heads of states, to resort to religion—in this case the spirit world—in order to enhance their political power. Obviously—and I will return to that point later—the distinction between religion and politics can be made only by those who believe that these constitute fundamentally different spheres. Whether we like it or not, this is not the case in most parts of the world where, as in Africa, the concept of power brings the two together. In that sense, and for reasons that I will explain below, what

---

[4] The 19th-century anthropologist E. B. Tylor defined religion as 'the belief in spiritual beings'.

we see today is the non-Western world, especially, reconnecting with its own past.[5]

There is no doubt that the connection—or rather: *re*connection—between religion and politics is one of the burning issues of our time. Talk of the relationship between religion and politics assumes that the two can be not only distinguished, but also separated, both intellectually and institutionally. This is precisely what is being challenged in many parts of the world today, notably by Islamists, but also by people in other major religious traditions. Thinking about religion and politics as two separate spheres has probably occurred at some stage in most parts of the world, but it has its most obvious historical origins in Europe. The intellectual and institutional separation of the two spheres in its contemporary form has undeniably emerged from the history of Europe. This separation was notably related to the unique role of the Catholic Church in the history of medieval Europe, the Reformation, and the religious wars of the sixteenth and seventeenth centuries. Europeans brought this experience and this tradition with them when they settled in other parts of the world, including in North America. They also transferred their own historical experiences to parts of the world that they colonised, by imposing the separation of church and state, or religion and politics. In many such places, religion—in its different manifestations—had traditionally played a role in governance, with greater or lesser success, but that is not really the point I wish to argue here. The point I *do* wish to make is that if we want to understand the new interactions between religion and politics, we have to take into account specific histories as they have unfolded in various parts of the world. At the time when so many former colonies of Europe became independent—Latin America in the nineteenth and Asia and Africa in the twentieth century—the belief in separating the spheres of religion and politics in order to live a successful life remained persuasive, also to the new nationalist governments. But what the world is witnessing today—perhaps since the 1970s, with the Iranian revolution as a watershed—is a fundamental rethinking of this assumption and of the institutional arrangements that accompany it. The modernist vision of politics has not brought to all societies in the world the welfare and prosperity they had expected at the time of independence. Nor has the Western vision of development, that subsequently came into fashion.

---

[5] See Ellis and Ter Haar, *Worlds of Power*, notably pp. 182–7.

Hence, many people in the non-Western world are now reconnecting with their own history and relying on their own traditional resources by seeking ways of giving religion a new place in governance. Although they may continue intellectually and practically to *distinguish* between the spheres of religion on the one hand and politics on the other, they may no longer wish to *separate* them on grounds that find their historical justification in the specific circumstances of the West.

Considering the relation between religion and politics and church and state in the history of Europe is a rewarding line of reflection. Part of this process was that politics—and eventually (nation) states—took over the ideas of perfection that had previously been related to the spiritual sphere. The totalitarian regimes of the twentieth century can be understood in light of this history, as others have pointed out. Zbigniew Brzezinski—a former National Security Advisor to the U.S. government as well as an academic—has coined the expression 'coercive utopias' to describe such systems, namely totalitarian governments and ideologies that aspire to create a model society, if necessary by force.[6] To some extent, we may argue, this is also the case with the current ambition of the West to bring democracy to the Arab world, which has become the ultimate justification for the war in Iraq. Such utopias are the secular pendant of the idea of a new world order of global control that Professor Juergensmeyer refers to with regard to religious extremists. In other words, religious and political extremists may actually differ less, both in their thinking and in their choice of means, than may seem to be the case at first sight. The power of ideology is such that what we conventionally think of as religion on the one hand and politics on the other, becomes obscure and makes the distinction between the two an analytical rather than a substantive one. While most Western countries appear to opt for a political ideology to achieve their aspirations, many non-Western countries try and do the same with the help of religious ideology.

One may take the logic of this argument further, and point to a great variety of political projects of the nineteenth and twentieth centuries that have inherited the instruments of both government and politics, and the ideology and techniques of religion. Today this is nowhere more striking than in the project of 'development', which we may summarise

---

⁶ Zbigniew Brzezinski, *Out of Control: Global Turmoil on the Eve of the Twenty-first Century*, New York: Scribner's Sons, 1993.

as the idea that humankind is bound to progress on a way to a better world. 'Development' may be considered among the coercive utopias (and totalising strategies) that have emerged from the history that I have alluded to above. In short, we may argue, the idea of development has a genealogy in Western-Christian religion and can be seen as the secular translation of a millenarian belief, whereby the kingdom of God is no longer projected in heaven but can be created on earth. What binds both types of thought, whether it concerns a religious or a secular utopia, is the aspiration to eliminate evil from the earth in all its forms, including by the appropriate use of force if necessary.

Religion and Violence

This brings me back to the question raised by Mark Juergensmeyer. What is it that makes acts of religious violence happen now, and in ways different from the type of religious violence that we know from history? Professor Juergensmeyer points quite rightly to the social and cultural effects of globalisation, dubbed 'Westoxification' by Ayatollah Khomeini. But the question is whether today's type of globalisation is indeed so fundamentally different from previous phenomena as to ascribe to it the explanatory power it often receives in academia. Here, too, it may be interesting to have a closer look at history and consider if things were so different in the past.

Many historians consider that the contemporary style or phase of globalisation is not fundamentally different from the proto-globalisation of the past—of the seventeenth century, for example, when navigators sailed round the globe, and traders had established intercontinental systems of production and commerce using the silver of South America and transported or coerced labour. Perhaps the only really innovative aspect of contemporary globalisation is the power of the media, as Professor Juergensmeyer affirms. This gives the political activists of today (including religious extremists, since politics has become religionised) an unprecedented mobilising power, via direct diffusion through television especially. Increasingly the internet too plays this role. As a result, we see ideological communities emerging that are not bound to any specific territory or even to any specific national or ethnic culture. These are virtual communities, whose global networks are creating a new type of boundary, based on ideological adherence, whether religion or politics. Such communities can also be mobilised by virtual communication.

Why religion and violence should be combining in such ominous ways now is not, in my view, primarily because of globalisation. Globalisation does, however, provide a unique medium for these new formations to express themselves and mobilise followers. Hence, I tend to disagree with Professor Juergensmeyer on considering contemporary globalisation as a cause of the religious violence that we experience today and that appears to be related to the proposed 'religionisation' of politics. I would rather suggest that the religionisation of politics, sometimes in violent mode, is primarily due to the failure of the modernist project in society and politics in many parts of the world. This applies particularly to what we used to call the third world, but also to some strata in the United States, for example. Even in Western Europe, probably the most secular part of the world, the aftermath of modernisation has produced violent reactions, primarily directed at the presence of immigrants, often of Muslim faith. In keeping with Europe's secular character, the response to this particular manifestation of globalisation is expressed less often, or at least less explicitly, in religious terms than in other forms. But all have in common the factors that Jurgensmeyer has identified, including fear of loss of power and loss of control of the world we live in.

If this line of argument is followed, it implies that the best means of restoring some degree of peace and order to our world is not primarily to find ways in which cosmic war can return to the spiritual plane, and for religion in worldly confrontations to become an agent of order, toleration and peace, as Juergensmeyer proposes. This seems to me a strategy that can work only in a framework that clearly separates the spiritual from the material, which is precisely not the case in most societies. It would presuppose a world where everyone aspires to keep religion and politics separate. This is not very realistic. It is unlikely to happen since, as I have argued, in the world as a whole the intellectual and institutional separation of religion and politics has been a rather brief interlude in a much longer history of associating the two.

I believe that it would be more helpful to aspire to put in place new checks and balances that will prevent violence, whether primarily religious or political in nature, from bursting beyond the bounds assigned to it. This implies our acceptance that violence is indeed inherent to religion as it is to politics. Adapting our visions for peace to the realities of the day may actually do more to prevent the imposition of coercive utopias that are bound to produce violence.

Yet, there is merit in what Mark Juergensmeyer has referred to as 'spiritualising violence'. Research by some Latin American scholars suggests that religion may play a useful role by creating space for *symbolic* confrontations that contest the social and political order without resorting to physical violence. One pertinent example is the devil mythology described in the work of Michael Taussig.[7] Another is the spiritual warfare theologies that are popular in the numerous neo-pentecostal and charismatic churches that are blossoming in many parts of the non-Western world[8] but are equally present in other religions. These are popular religious strategies to keep conflict within certain boundaries by allowing for a symbolic condemnation of others. Symbolic violence may thus have a use as a way of avoiding the type of open conflict that easily leads to physical violence and the indiscriminate killing of 'others'. Rather than dismissing current warfare theologies, we may wish to consider them in this light.

Religious ideas can play an important role in either legitimising or discouraging violence. Today, these ideas are applied in the context of a struggle between the perceived hegemonic powers of secularism on the one hand and forms of spiritual totalitarianism on the other. In his *Terror in the Mind of God* Mark Juergensmeyer has provided us with numerous examples of theological justifications of the use of violence from all major religious traditions. They are evidence of the way in which the religious imagination can become a source of a 'transcendent moralism' that leads to death and destruction. Yet, as he also points out, there is no inevitable link between religion and violence, as many others who have written on the subject testify. The ominous combination of the two depends on the combination of several factors at a particular time in history that provides a suitable context, as appears to be the case today. If there is no automatic connection between religion and violence, the challenge becomes to mobilise the religious potential to resolve and prevent violent conflicts. This may be done by scrutinising religious or spiritual resources for that particular purpose,[9]

---

[7] Michael Taussig, *The Devil and Commodity Fetishism in South America*, Chapel Hill: University of North Carolina Press, 1980.

[8] Daniel Miguez, 'From open violence to symbolic confrontation: anthropological observations of Latin America's southern cone', in Gerrie ter Haar and James J. Busuttil (eds.), *Bridge or Barrier: Religion, Violence and Visions for Peace*, Leiden and Boston: Brill, pp. 81–118.

[9] Cf. Gerrie ter Haar, 'Religion: source of conflict or resource for peace?', in Ter Haar and Busuttil, *Bridge or Barrier*, pp. 3–34.

as is happening today in a great variety of circles, increasingly with religious and secular believers working together from different angles. It shows how spiritual resources can actually be used for the common good, if they are systematically explored.

Clearly, these are matters that concern religious believers in the first instance. But scholars of religion, too, may want a say in the matter. Through their scholarly work, for example, they may provide the building blocks for others to work towards strategies for peace. In my opinion, the study of religion is one of the disciplines most needed today. Its practitioners possess the tools to make a significant contribution to the political debate in the contemporary world and to help steer its course. They should not be shy of doing so.

RELIGIOUS VIOLENCE AMID LOVE, COMPASSION, AND HATE: A RESPONSE TO PROF. MARK JUERGENSMEYER

Manabu Watanabe

Introduction

It is my great pleasure and honour to respond to Professor Mark Juergensmeyer's paper.

I have admired Professor Juergensmeyer's work, especially *Terror in the Mind of God*,[1] which is the result of extensive interviews he had with people involved in terrorist acts around the globe. Having myself experience with interviewing former members of Aum Shinrikyo and other religious organisations, I believe I can understand the difficulties associated with this. Since it is now more than ten years after the Sarin gas incident in the Tokyo subway (20 March 1995), it is appropriate to reflect on this matter later in my response. In the following, I will first give my own reflections, based on my experiences in Japan, before providing a more detailed response to Professor Juergensmeyer's paper.

Since the Aum Shinrikyo incident of 1995, and especially following the '9/11' tragedy of 2001, we have witnessed a drastic shift in the atmosphere surrounding the academic field of religious studies. During this decade, religion emphatically entered the political arena as a social and global problem, not just as the subject of academic research. For example, we can no longer discuss Aum Shinrikyo or al-Qaeda without considering the political implications of their actions. In this contemporary situation, we are forced to ask ourselves whether there is any necessary connection between religion and violence.

As scholars of religion, we cannot help but commit ourselves to studying religions with such connotations. Suppose our field of specialisation is Middle Eastern literature, and the focus of our research, *The Arabian Nights*.[2] We may well find ourselves being asked whether

---

[1] Mark Juergensmeyer, *Terror in the Mind of God: The Global Rise of Religious Violence*, Berkeley: University of California Press, 2000.

[2] *Arabian Nights*, collected and edited by Andrew Lang and illustrated by Vera Bock, with a foreword by Mary Gould Davis, London: Longmans, Green, 1951.

there is any inherent violence in Islam, or how we can justify studying a not-so-relevant theme such as literature. There is no safe ground from which we can evade such questions, especially those put forward by people who do not appreciate the value of research in and of itself. Currently we have become not only observers, but also participants in contemporary religious events. Some of us have become almost like news reporters in a battlefield. From time to time we have been, and will be, hit by the bullet of heavy criticism from either side, that is, the side of our audience or of the subject of our research, or from both sides at the same time.

I would like to share some personal experiences with you. I have had several opportunities to speak about problematical religions such as Aum Shinrikyo to audiences with an anti-cult interest. On one such occasion, after the audience had listened to my academic analyses, a lawyer stood up and started to criticise me, saying that I had failed to cast blame on the cult members. I was taken aback by his reaction, since I do not think that this is an essential task for a scholar of religion. Similarly, there have been reports about colleagues who have tried to investigate new religious movements without prejudice, and who were subsequently sued by them. Clearly we find ourselves in a difficult position, that may be unsatisfactory to both camps.

Having said this, it seems to me that scholars of religion may be experiencing this difficult position in different ways. There is, for example, a marked contrast between American scholars' experience with the Branch Davidians and Japanese scholars' experience with Aum Shinrikyo. While the former strengthened their credibility with the public and the government by discussing new religious movements in a proper way, Japanese scholars not only lost face but one of them even lost his university position after severe criticism from the mass media.[3] This event in Japan was followed by an embarrassing silence in Japanese academia. It seems to me that in Japan there is a tendency for both secular scholars and fundamentalist religionists to be anti-cultist, while liberal religionists simply remain silent. I must admit that I myself belong to the group of rather silent religionists, at least in Japan. The Aum Shinrikyo affair was a rather traumatic experience for the general public,

---

[3] Manabu Watanabe, 'Opposition to Aum and the rise of the "anti-cult" movement in Japan', in Robert J. Kisala and Mark R. Mullins (eds.), *Religion and Social Crisis in Japan: Understanding Japanese Society through the Aum Affair*, Basingstoke and New York: Palgrave, 2001, pp. 99ff.

but also for Japanese scholars of religion aiming to foster a 'sympathetic understanding' and a 'hermeneutics of reconstruction' for all religions. However, unfortunately it is no longer politically correct for Japanese scholars to understand Aum Shinrikyo in a sympathetic way, or to give any indication that they affirm the group or its activities.

Some Thoughts on the Contemporary Religious Situation

It is no exaggeration to say that religions have today reached a turning-point or crisis. From the late nineteenth to the twentieth century, when scientific naturalism and scientism made their appearance, there were attempts to reinforce the position of religious faith in the forms of revivalism and spiritualism, as well as attempts to combine science and religion. However, this did not prevent scientific naturalism from becoming widespread and accepted as a form of conventional wisdom by most people.

As humankind entered the 1970s, global opposition arose to the worldwide destruction of the environment and the depletion of natural resources. This may be a reflection of the science and technology of the past, which were solely committed to the pursuit of capitalist interests. The Club of Rome's Report *The Limits to Growth* (1972) provided an important momentum for raising an alarm against these urgent problems.[4] In Japan, the general awareness shifted from pollution problems to environmental ones. This could be observed in the establishment of the Environmental Agency in 1971 (in 2001, it was upgraded to the Ministry of Environment). In Europe and the United States, government environmental agencies were established around the same time, and in in 1972 a United Nations Conference on the Human Environment was held in Stockholm. In this way, an awareness of global issues concerning the survival of the human race, such as those related to the environment, energy resources, food, population, and so on, was fostered.

What type of factors must be considered in relation to the shift from the end of the twentieth century into the twenty-first century? Since the end of the cold war in 1989, globalisation has spread rapidly

---

[4] Donella H. Meadows et al., *The Limits to Growth: A Report for the Club of Rome's Project on the Predicament of Mankind*, New York: Universe Books, 1972.

throughout the world.[5] Amid these conditions, a global culture was created, while at the same time some religions moved in an opposite direction, becoming identified with one particular culture. In this way, the position of religion underwent a great change.

This kind of change expressed itself in the form of marginalisation and secularisation of religion on the one hand, and in the rise of fundamentalism—which can be considered a phenomenon challenging these tendencies—on the other. Here, I would like to discuss the situation in Japan as a specific example of the marginalisation and secularisation of religion, while discussing fundamentalism from a global perspective.

Marginalisation and Secularisation of Religion in Contemporary Japan

It is no exaggeration to state that in Japan religion is today marginalised more than ever in before. There may be several reasons for this, but we could start with the following two. First, traditionally in Japan, religion was practised particularly in connection with annual festivals and religious rituals, which did not develop into a self-conscious, subjective faith. Secondly, since the Aum Shinrikyo incidents in 1995, a new tendency is notable that links religions with so-called cults and also with a form of terrorism that is connected to religious faith. This way, religion has become associated with fanatical belief and violence. These conditions cannot be ignored when we discuss religions today.

Since the grave acts committed by Aum Shinrikyo members became known, there has been a continuous stream of information about fraud and questionable affairs related to religious groups. These include the sale of fraudulent spiritual charms, a practice that has existed for some time; claims by a leader of a certain religious group and its members that they possessed a mummified body that was alive; and the stealing of money from members of a new religious group by its own leaders, after promising to make them millionaires. The rejection of blood transfusions has also continually been based on extreme religious beliefs, and in one hard-to-believe decision, a court recognised the claim made

---

[5] For example, the following definition for globalisation can be found: 'In general, globalization means to deepen economic relationships in the world through activating transactions of capital and work forces across national borders and expanding overseas investment or transfer of goods and services via trade'. 'No growth without reformation IV', in *Annual Economic Report* (report by the Economic and Fiscal Policy Minister), Japan Cabinet Office, 2004.

by the patient's family against a doctor who saved one of its members through a blood transfusion. The list of such affairs never ends.

Committing oneself to a particular religious group, whether or not it is one of the new religions, can be a meaningful way for people to expand their personal network and their connections with other people. However, it also implies various kinds of strictures, such as participation in meetings and monetary contributions. Therefore, people who 'dislike religious groups but love mystery' usually avoid joining a religious group but are attracted to other religious expressions, such as mysticism, spirituality, and healing.

In summary, in Japanese society, religion is clearly marginalised. Religion in Japan has become just a form of social activity, an event to enjoy, and it may have nothing to do with religious faith. Furthermore, Japanese people do not like someone else's faith in a particular religion, even if it is their individual choice to believe in that religion. Prohibitions are usually linked with religious teachings, but these prohibitions are not taught by ethics classes or even in schools anymore, as ethics has not figured on the curriculum for the last thirty years. Instead, a desire for efficiency and profitability (materialistic interests) is preferred to ethics.

Fundamentalism in the World Today

When we survey the current condition of religions, politics and society in the world, it appears that the power of fundamentalism has great impact, and in a way that is different from mainstream Japanese religious consciousness. Fundamentalism refers to a type of faith in which the followers of a particular religion ascribe literal truth to their sacred book. It is often characterised by conflict with other religions and with secular society, which religious fundamentalists believe to be against them.[6] For fundamentalists, secular society is essentially corrupt and so, in their minds, if they were to hold to mainstream beliefs that were in harmony with secular society, this would mean committing the very same sins as secular society. Therefore, adopting a fundamentalist type of religious belief can imply becoming confrontational with the majority or with secular society. Such characteristics are typical of any sect that

---

[6] Cf. Martin E. Marty and R. Scott Appleby (eds.), *Fundamentalisms Observed*, University of Chicago Press, 1994.

breaks off from a majority religion, and fundamentalist sects all tend to show these significant features.

From the perspective of the evolution of a religious group, when it enters into its second and third generation, the sense of cohesion loses intensity and the institutional aspect is strengthened instead. This occurs even when a certain sect consciously emphasises religious devotion. The majority of churches in the United States are denominations of such sects, which have developed their own structure. However, they have lost their radical momentum.[7] One thing we should not lose sight of in this respect is the fact that denominations that represent institutionalised sects are acceptable to secular society because they are able to adapt themselves flexibly to it. By contrast, such denominations are seen as having been corrupted when considered from the viewpoint of the internal logic of the sects. Revivalism of sects means breaking away from this 'corruption.' At the same time, we have to pay attention to the fact that this also indicates a deepening of the tendency towards fundamentalism.

All this brings me to my next point, which is that we should not forget that new religions such as Aum Shinrikyo, which have committed terrorist acts, have an aspect of fundamentalism. In order to gain authority, Aum Shinrikyo not only used the history of Buddhism, which goes back more than two thousand years, but it also returned to the origin of Buddhism in India and Tibet. In Aum Shinrikyo's case, the basic works of Buddhism were re-translated and used as teachings. This can be understood as an effort by Aum Shinrikyo to construct its own validity, independent of traditional Buddhism.[8]

It is essential to realise that, while these acts of self-validation by certain religions serve to strengthen strained relationships with other religions and with secular society, they can also foster confrontations with them. This is a problem in the modern world, where people of diverse values have to co-exist.

---

[7] H. Richard Niebuhr, *The Social Sources of Denominationalism*, New York: Meridian Books, 1960.

[8] Susumu Shimazono, *Gendai Shukyo no Kanosei* (The Potential of Contemporary Religions), Tokyo: Iwanami Shoten, 1997.

Why is Religion Involved in Violence?

I will now respond to Professor Juergensmeyer's paper more specifically. The structure of Prof. Juergensmeyer's presentation is very clear
and distinct. After his introductory remarks Professor Juergensmeyer
first asks: 'Why is religion involved in violence?' and then: 'Why is this
happening now?'

It is the authority of religion that gives the terrorists the moral legitimacy of employing violence. That is, it is their religion that makes the
terrorist acts legitimate in their view. They become 'acts of God,' that
is, they take on inevitability. In that sense, they are ultimately righteous
in the mind of terrorists. Therein lies the real danger and the helpless-
ness of the victims of these incidents. It is a clash between good and
evil, or a 'cosmic war,' if we use Professor Juergensmeyer's term. And
there seems no way out of these tragic events. A religious belief that
lets people become actively involved in terrorism places them on the
side of justice, allowing them to imagine that they are following God's
will. Terrorism, in their mindset, almost seems to be a necessary sacrifice
for the divinity that seeks justice.

Surprisingly, this line of reasoning is not only contemporary, but
also ancient. If we take this point of view, we can read the Old Testament from a new angle. The Book of Joshua records how the ancient
Israelites conquered the land of Canaan. There is the famous story
of the fall of Jericho in Joshua 6. The relevant point here is not how
the wall fell, but rather how and why the Israelites attacked Jericho
at that particular time. It is written that 'the city and all that is in it
shall be devoted to the Lord for destruction' (Joshua 6:17), and that
the Israelites slaughtered 'all in the city, both men and women, young
and old, oxen, sheep, and donkeys' (6:23). They had no remorse in
pursuing what the Lord had asked them to do. It was a testimony to
their strong faith.[9]

In the case of Aum Shinrikyo, although the Sarin attack in the
Tokyo subway system had a secular purpose—namely, to prevent the

---

[9] I am grateful to Professor Tsai Yen-zen (National Chengchi University, Taipei,
Taiwan) for his presentation entitled, 'Ritual violence and communal sanity: the case
of Hērem in Biblical Judaism' in the panel 'Conflict and Communalism: Taiwanese
Perspectives on Violence in World Religions' at the IAHR Congress in Tokyo on 26
March 2005. I was given an opportunity to respond to his paper and others' on that
occasion.

imminent police raid on its facilities—it was justified from a doctrinal position. Asahara ordered his disciples who participated in the attack to recite the following phrase ten thousand times after they came back to the Aum headquarters: 'It was nice to be blessed by the guru, Shiva, and those who have attained the Supreme Truth'. Asahara developed and falsified the Tibetan Buddhist notion of *poa*, that is, transference of the soul, and he claimed that the murders he ordered his disciples to commit were '*poa*' and that it meant salvation for the victims. Therefore, there was a good reason for Aum members to support the terrorist act. Several Aum members have claimed that if they had known beforehand that Aum Shinrikyo was planning the attack in the Tokyo subway, they would have wanted their heretical parents to be on the train so that they could be been saved by the guru's *poa*, even though the victims were not Aum believers. Following this logic, it was an act of compassion and salvation for Aum members to carry out this terrorist attack.[10]

I had an opportunity to interview an ex-Aum member who became involved in the killing of one of Asahara's unwilling disciples as a result of an order from the guru himself. He said that he had committed the crime believing that it was *poa*, a salvational murder. However, after he quit Aum, he could not help trembling with fear, realising that what he had done was murder, plain and simple, and nothing else. However, it is also a relief for us, because he dared not to go back to Aum Shinrikyo in order to clear his bad conscience.

It may also be pointed out that traditional Buddhism provides a textual background that supports this way of thinking. The *Upāyakauśalya Sūtra* (The Skill in Means Sūtra) narrates that the Buddha in the last of his previous lives, when he was the captain of a ship, killed a thief in order to save the lives of five hundred merchants.[11] The story has a happy ending. The Buddha proudly reports: 'Son of the family: For me, *samsara* was curtailed for one hundred thousand eons because of that skill in means and great compassion. And the robber died to be reborn in a world of paradise. The five hundred merchants on board

---

[10] Manabu Watanabe, 'Religion and violence in Japan today: a chronological and doctrinal analysis of Aum Shinrikyo', *Terrorism and Political Violence*, vol. 10, no. 4, 1998, pp. 80–100.

[11] *The Skill in Means (Upāyakauśalya) Sūtra*, Delhi: Motilal Banarsidass, 1994, pp. 73–4. Cf. Damien Keown, 'Paternalism in the Lotus Sūtra', *Journal of Buddhist Ethics*, vol. 5, 1998, pp. 203ff.

are the five hundred future Buddhas of the auspicious eon.'[12] Therefore, a murder can be justified if the cause is right, even in the Buddhist context. There is an old saying in Japan that a lie is also a skillful means (*uso mo hoben*). However nobody would have dared to say that a murder could function in this way.

During World War II, a famous Japanese Buddhist monk claimed that it would be impossible for the Japanese army to commit an atrocity in the battlefield, because it was acting in accordance with the principle of Buddhist compassion. 'All things, including friend and foe, are my children... Given this, it is just to punish those who disturb the public order. Whether one kills or does not kill, the [Buddhist] precept forbidding killing [is preserved]. It is the precept forbidding killing that wields the sword. It is this precept that throws the bomb.'[13] As Robert Lifton points out in his book on Aum Shinrikyo, *Destroying the World to Save It* (1999),[14] we can see a similar logic at play in the Aum Shinrikyo event. Within their so-called acts of 'compassion', we find a lack of respect for otherness, or respect for the individuality present in others.

We dare not say that, when it comes to such notions, Christianity is immaculate. In the Christian context, the so-called situational ethics based on love has a similar logical structure. There are pro-life activists who have assaulted clinics in order to save unborn babies from abortion and who have killed doctors and nurses as result. For example, on 30 December 1994 the former hairdresser John Salvi III assaulted two clinics in Brookline, Massachusetts. He fired and killed the receptionists and wounded five others.[15] During his trial, there was a picket in front of the court house. One of the pro-life activists' banners said: 'John Salvi saved lives', meaning that he prevented abortion at those clinics. There is a real and serious paradox in claiming that certain types of killing are equal to the saving of lives.

However, in thinking about the nature of both Buddhist compassion and its Christian counterpart in the examples above, we cannot

---

[12] *The Skill in Means (Upāyakauśalya) Sūtra*, p. 73.

[13] Robert Jay Lifton, *Destroying the World to Save It: Aum Shinrikyo, Apocalyptic Violence, and the New Global Terrorism*, New York: Henry Holt, 1999, p. 251. Cf. Brian Victoria, *Zen at War*, New York and Tokyo: Weatherhill, 1997.

[14] See note 13.

[15] Anne Fowler, Nicki Nichols Gamble, Frances X. Hogan, Melissa Kogut, Madeline McCommish, Barbara Thorp, 'Talking with the enemy', http://www.publicconversations.org/pcp/resources/resource_detail.asp?ref_id=102 accessed on 4 August 2005. Published in *The Boston Globe*, Sunday, 28 January 2001, Focus section.

help but notice that there is an essential difference between the two. On the one hand, in the Buddhist context, the person who is killed by compassion is the one who is saved; while on the other hand, in the Christian context, the person who is killed is not the one to be saved but the one deemed to be evil, and somebody else is saved from this evil person.

In early 2005 there was a widespread dispute in the United States over the life of Terri Schiavo, a woman who had collapsed in February 1990 when she was 26 years old and had incurred severe brain damage. While her parents wanted her to continue living, her husband believed his wife did not wish to live in that way, and he filed a petition to remove her feeding tube as early as 1998. However, the Florida lower house passed 'Terri's Law', allowing the governor to order doctors to feed her. In September 2004 the Florida Supreme Court rejected the law, and in March 2005 the Florida court allowed the doctors to remove the tube. After that, there were severe disputes involving the higher courts, politicians (including the President), and the mass media. On 31 March 2005 Terri Schiavo eventually passed away.[16] Clearly, acts of love can conflict with one another.

In this example, a beautiful case of love and compassion can, ironically, result in the destruction of life. Here we find ourselves asking questions for which there are no easy answers: How can we avoid destroying others by loving them? How can we avoid this kind of 'extreme love'?

Why is This Happening Now?

Professor Juergensmeyer clearly shows the reason why acts of religious violence, such as the Sarin attack in the Tokyo subway or the '9/11' attacks are happening in the contemporary world. As he explains, they are responses to globalisation and to what is regarded as 'Westoxication'. They are also related to what is thought of as the 'ploy for the expansion of America's global reach'. I totally agree with Professor Juergensmeyer in this respect.

In addition, Prof. Juergensmeyer points out that 'often the evil forces are imagined to be Westernisation, or globalisation, or specifically

---

[16] See Justin Webb, 'Schiavo case tests America', http://news.bbc.co.uk/1/hi/programmes/from_our_own_correspondent/4400865.stm, accessed on August 4, 2005. See also Part Two of the present volume.

George Bush and the U.S. government'.[17] The way in which he makes this point suggests that this applies only to the mindset of terrorists. However, as we all know, it is not only terrorists, but also half of the American population, as well as major European countries like France and Germany, that did not agree with the Bush administration's decision to initiate war against Iraq in 2003. What is the reason there was so much opposition to the war? The answer might seem obvious, but I would find it very valuable if Professor Juergensmeyer could provide us with some insights into the motivations behind this opposition in a religio-political context.

This question leads me to another one. I noticed that Professor Juergensmeyer does not use the term 'fundamentalism' in his paper. I wonder what his definition is of this term and why he refrains from using it? It is a simple question, but I am sure that many of us would be interested to hear his answer.

Lastly, I would like to ask Professor Juergensmeyer about the moral commitment of scholars of religion with regard to the problem of war and peace. Facing, as we do, conflict and terrorism that is often bloody and monstrous, we cannot help but feel powerless in our inability to influence others. What can and should we do to help foster peace in this troubled world?

There are many questions to be answered, but Professor Juergensmeyer's presentation provides us with a clear picture of contemporary religious violence and its connection to globalisation.

---

[17] See p. 7.

PART TWO

TECHNOLOGY, LIFE AND DEATH

TECHNOLOGY, LIFE AND DEATH
INTRODUCTION

Eiko Hanaoka(-Kawamura)

Human beings have toiled with the idea of controlling nature with technology ever since Francis Bacon (1561–1626), who used the power of science and technology to objectify and abstract nature. 'Knowledge is power' was one of his epigrams. As a result of controlling nature with technology, human beings have gradually lost touch with their humanity, and have continued to destroy the environment of the planet Earth. Moreover, since the last half of the twentieth century, technology has progressed particularly in the field of medical science, as in-vitro fertilisation, surrogate motherhood, and birth through cloning have become realities. We now know that internal organs can be cured by the use of embryonic stem cells taken from human beings, and that brain cells from an aborted embryo can be transplanted to patients suffering from Alzheimer's disease, with a good prospect for a cure.

Via modern media technology, experiments in which seemingly 'dead' material is transformed into a living organism may be directly transmitted to us. For example, in August 2005, Japanese press and television reported that African wild cats which were originally cloned had bred naturally and produced offspring in a research institute in New Orleans. This shows that even cloned animals can breed naturally, promising preservation for species that are in danger of becoming extinct.

However, while the development of technology has contributed to world peace and to the improvement of human life, it has also led gradually to a loss of humanity itself, and to the despoliation of the earth's environment, resulting in a crisis of our very existence on this planet. Furthermore, each part of the human body is in danger of being separated from the whole and commercialised. Then, the human being is eventually deprived of the dignity of the personality. In order to put a religious constraint on these dangers, we must reflect on what bioethics is. At the level of the individual, we need a religious ethics that is based on religious experience. Secondly, we need a political ethics that builds on a conjunction of politics and religion at the level of the state, or of the nation, or of institutions. Thirdly, we must have a universal ethics of dialogue, a responsibility grounded in love for one's neighbour, and the solidarity necessary to live in a form of international cooperation, as the United Nations was originally intended to achieve.

In order to overcome the loss of humanity and the destruction of the environment by the abuse of technology, and to avoid the nihilism that is a natural result of such loss and destruction, every religion has the ability to reinforce ethics at the level of the individual, of which self-awareness is the core. Such ethics can be found in the works of, amongst others, Buber, Suzuki, the early Heidegger, Nishitani, Nishida, and Merton.[1] However, implicit in all religious ethics is the existence of an authoritarian principle that is invariably represented by a person, as in 'Omu Shinrikyo' (the Aum sect).

At the collective level—comparable to the species in a biological system of classification—a religious ethics might serve to overcome the destruction and nihilism that result from the abuse of technology. This could conceivably take the form of a national religion or even of a world religion in which politics and religion are united. Nevertheless, a collective religious ethics carries a risk of crises between nations and religions. This can of course take the form of war and persecution, but may also occur as a result of a transition from a democratic to an imperialist state, involving struggles over the control of technologies in various fields. In such a crisis, a world religion could provide a measure of control.

Thirdly, a religious ethics at a higher level corresponding to the biological classification of a genus, in other words an ethics with a universal dimension, could overcome the various difficult problems caused by the misuse of technology. Such a dimension may be found in the works of the thinkers mentioned above and in others to be referred to shortly, such as the concept of *Gestell* in Heidegger's view of technology. One example is in regard to the ethics of Heidegger's *Spiegel-spiel* ('being mutually mirrored'), an interaction between sky, earth, mortal and divine. This is an ethics in which life is represented almost as a game. A second example of this universal dimension is the concept of loyalty in the work of Whitehead, in which each individual, state, or nation, and all humankind, has responsibility to itself inasmuch as each is a subject and possesses its own unique 'feeling'. As a third example, we may refer to the ethics of loyalty contained in Nishida's concept of religion,

---

[1] For details, see the bibliographical references at the end of this volume.

grounded in the idea of compassion,[2] as well as the ethics of responsibility in Hans Jonas's work, such as in his *Das Prinzip Verantwortung (The Principle of Responsibility)*.[3] Nevertheless, the universal level of ethics also carries a hidden danger, that of 'demoniac' and 'intellectual violence', or of utopian violence, as Nishida, Heidegger and Jonas demonstrate. However, because an ethics grounded in religious experience, such as proposed by Whitehead and Jonas, is based on feeling or will, and not on human intellect only, such an ethics is much more appropriate for overcoming the difficult problems caused by modern technology than types of ethics that are based solely on reason.

In conclusion, we may see that an ethics grounded in religious experience at the individual level holds more promise than an ethics at the collective and universal levels, because at those levels the tendency to collective violence always lies hidden. The ethics at the individual dimension can be found not only in the works of Whitehead, Jonas, Picht, and early Heidegger, but also in those of Nishida, Suzuki, Nishitani, and Merton (1915–1968) and others, based on Buddhism or Dogen-Zen. Dogen understands life and death from the standpoint of original life. The core of the ethics of all these thinkers is to be aware of the true self. Finally, we must pay attention to the fact that an ethics grounded in individual religious experience should in future be able to be integrated at every dimension: individual, collective and universal.

---

[2] See Kitaro Nishida's *Complete Works*, Vol. 11, p. 445.
[3] Hans Jonas, *Das Prinzip Verantwortung (The Principle of Responsibility)*.

NEUROPOLITICS AND THE BODY

Ebrahim Moosa

Introduction

In recent years Muslim scholars, especially those who deliberate the
questions of law and ethics, have had to confront a number of challenging questions that inflect the concepts of technology, life and death.

One question that ethicists of all traditions have to encounter in
radically altered conditions of technology is: when is a person dead?
Not that the religious traditions of old did not provide us with tests to
determine death. To the contrary, they did indeed provide very helpful
indicators for death. Nevertheless, these criteria have been subverted
and surpassed by the technologies of modernity and the new gaze we
have of the body. Hence, in late modernity a body supported by a
respirator can pulsate with visible signs of life without performing any
of the functions of a living human being. The case in point is that of
the Florida woman, Terri Schiavo, who was on life-support measures
for fifteen years, while her physicians had declared that she was in a
persistent vegetative state.[1] As a result of the intervention of modern
bio-technology our inherited notions of life and death are subverted.
Machines now keep the seriously damaged body nourished intrave-
nously and provide it with some of the external symptoms of life as
we know it.

Contemporary Muslim jurists of a broadly traditional bent are confronted with the question whether a patient diagnosed to have suffered
irreparable brain-stem damage can be categorised as dead, even though
the body exhibited the traditional features of a living human being such
as breathing with the aid of a machine. The question becomes even
more complicated since the body is kept functional in order to harvest
organs for transplantation purposes. In most cases, the withdrawal of
the life-support machine would inevitably result in the patient loosing the power to breathe and exhibit all the signs whereby we would

---

[1] Joan Didion, 'The Case of Theresa Schiavo', *The New York Review of Books*, June 9
2005; see also ibid., 'After Life', *The New York Times Magazine*, September 25, 2005.

say a person is dead. One of the paradoxes that modern technology introduces is that we can point to a patient who exhibits all the signs of a living body, but we are no longer sure whether this same body is also a living person. It raises a fundamental if not most troubling of all questions: what is a person?

Like all good ethicists and jurist-theologians, Muslim scholars disagree with each other. Most Muslim jurists in the Arabic-speaking world, through their regional and national political and ethical associations, accept the fact that irreparable brain-stem damage is the new criterion of death. This is the view endorsed by the Islamic Fiqh Academy, a committee of the Organization of Islamic Conference (OIC), on which a number of prominent traditional scholars serve who have widespread credibility and popularity in their local and national contexts. A minority viewpoint opposes the new definition of death.

In another issue related to brain death, there is also wide disagreement between different traditional Muslim ethical communities on the question of organ transplantation. While most traditionalist constituencies in the Arab Middle East, such as al-Azhar and the OIC's Islamic Fiqh Academy, have approved of transplantation surgery, the predominant consensus among traditional Muslim authorities in the Indo-Pakistan subcontinent do not permit organ transplantation.[2] For this group the question of brain-stem death does not even arise. What is of interest to us here is to explore how both sides to this ethical conundrum filter modern bio-technology on life and death issues in their discursive treatments of Muslim ethics.

Embodied Ethics

The pro-brain death argument, made by two experts in Muslim ethics, Muhammad Na'im Yasin and Sulayman al-Ashqar, creates a discursive and epistemological link between Muslim juridical ethics and medical technology.[3] Their working assumption is that Muslim juridical ethics

---

[2] Muhammad Shafi'i, *Tanshit al-Adhhan fi 'l-Tarqi' bi A'da al-Insan: Ya'ni Insani A'da ki Paywankari* (Urdu) [Exercising the Mind in Matters [related] to the Joining of Human Organs: In Other Words, Combining Organs], Karachi: Dar al-Isha'at, 1972 (2nd edn).

[3] Muhammad Na'im Yasin, 'Nihaya-t al-Hayat al-Insaniyya fi daw Ijtihadat al-'Ulama' al-Muslimin wa al-Mu'tayat al-Tibbiyya' ['The end of human life in the light

is a science, *'ilm*, like positivist medical science and its accompanying technology. This relationship of equivalence is critical to their ethical enterprise. All the remaining arguments become secondary. Since there are no revealed norms for determining the end of life, they argue, the issue of brain death is in the realm of human discretion and subject to human intellectual and discursive effort (*ijtihad*). The absence of any revealed norms offers the Muslim ethicist considerable leeway to entertain alternative criteria of death. They conclude that the underlying logic is that the criteria of death are constructed by human conventions.

Yasin and Ashqar can then create a dialogical relationship between ethics and medical science, where the latter informs the former. Yasin points out that death must be determined by expert knowledge, in this case by the physicians. While religious experts and ethicists can collaborate with medical experts, it is quite evident that expert knowledge in this instance would trump the authority of the religious experts who now have to set aside their conventional criteria that determine death by means of cardio-pulmonary indicators. In the forums of the OIC Islamic law panel, medical experts are summoned in order to share their expertise with the Islamic law and ethics experts.

In Yasin's analysis the brain is the seat of volition. This analysis on his part is a crucial component of his argument, since volition determines whether a patient enjoys the status of a person or is rendered to be merely a biological entity. In the case of brain death, he argued, brain activity determined by the extent of a patient's volition and other clinical neurological tests were all critical in determining whether a person was dead. Both Yasin and Ashqar move away from a perspicuous test for death, which renders some amount of certainty, especially when you can see that a patient has ceased to breathe. Instead, they argue that the verificatory clinical test to determine the death of a patient must reach a certain quantum of conclusiveness.

---

of Muslim scholarly research and the given realities of medicine'], *Majalla-t Majma' al-Fiqh al-Islam*, hereafter referred to as *MMFI*, vol. 3, no. 2, 1987, pp. 635–60; Muhammad Sulayman al-Ashqar, 'Nihaya-t al-Hayat', ['The end of life'], *MMFI*, vol. 3, no. 2, 1987, pp. 661–71; see also Ebrahim Moosa 'Languages of change in Islamic law: redefining death in modernity', *Islamic Studies*, vol. 38, no. 3, 1999, pp. 305–42 for detailed discussions of the various opinions on brain death among scholars of religion in Muslim circles; and ibid., 'Brain death and organ transplantation—an Islamic opinion', *South African Medical Journal*, vol. 83, nr. 3, 1993.

Arguing against brain death is Tawfiq al-Waʿi,[4] who does not try to link the language of Muslim ethics with the language of bio-technology. Waʿi is opposed to criteria that reduce the integrity of a human being to brain function. In his view, a human being is the combination of body and soul. Therefore, the integrity of the body, with or without the soul or a functioning mind, is still something worth preserving. He argues that mental capacity and cognitive sense-perception are insufficient criteria for a test that intends to make a comprehensive determination of life. Surprisingly, in Waʿi's view, it is obligatory to keep a patient on a ventilator and take care of the body.

Clearly, Yasin and Ashqar, if they were asked to give an opinion on the case of Terri Schiavo, would both side with the Florida courts and the late Schiavo's husband who had argued that she had lost substantive brain function. While Schiavo might have exhibited signs of biological life, by all accounts she suffered serious clinical impairment to function as full human being. Waʿi and other jurists, such as Muhammad Mukhtar al-Salami, would argue that biological life was an indicator of personhood. In fact, Waʿi would hold a physician liable for homicide if he or she disconnected a ventilating apparatus or suspended the feeding of a patient.

If we turn to the arguments related to the permissibility or prohibition of organ transplantation, then again the critical ethical issues centre on the question of integrity and dignity of the body. Those who favour transplantation argue that it is precisely in order to preserve human dignity that transplantation is necessary. They would cite scriptural passages and invoke common sense to support their case while rebutting other arguments that would in their view undermine their warrant against transplantation. A report attributed to the Prophet Muhammad warning that breaking the bones of the dead is as offensive as breaking the bones of the living, is an often cited proof offered by those who oppose transplantation. Scholars in support of transplantation in turn, provide an interpretation of that report. The statement was made, some contemporary Egyptian jurists explain, when a grave-digger gratuitously battered a body to bury it in a narrow grave. Witnessing this indignity to the body prompted the Prophet Muhammad to resoundingly repudiate

---

[4] Tawfiq al-Waʿi, 'Haqqat al-Mawt wa al-Hayat fi al-Qurʾan wa al-Ahkam al-Sharʿiyya' ['The meaning of death and life in the Qurʾan and the rules of the Shariʾa], *MMFI*, vol. 3, no. 2, 1987, pp. 695–718.

such treatment. Those who oppose transplantation surgery deem the very act of dismembering one body for the purposes of healing another person to constitute a supreme act of the degradation of humanity. The consensus held by the Indo-Pakistan traditionalist scholars is that organ transplantation subverts the notions of the inviolability and dignity of the body, and therefore it is prohibited. However, some authorities on the subcontinent have made some concessions and do allow the use of prosthetic devices permanently joined to the body, instead of cadaver or live body transplantations. And they also permit chimera, the grafting of specific animal organs into the human body, on the strict proviso that it provides relief to life-threatening conditions.

Another instance are the *fatwas* related to abortion. Muslim jurisprudence has historically viewed the foetus to be in varying degrees of sanctity from conception to birth. There were also commensurate sanctions, with increasing gravity attached to violation of such sanctity. However, it was generally accepted, for instance, that a foetus under 120 days from the time of conception could be terminated if such pregnancy impeded the lactation of a nursing infant and when the family could not afford a nurse or milk supplements, or in the event of the unavailability of both.[5] The underlying reasoning according to the eighteenth-century Hanafi jurist Ibn Abidin, was that a foetus is not yet a human being and that ensoulment of the foetus occurs after 120 days. Indeed, pre-modern expressions of personhood, especially in relation to foetuses but also other issues related to the body, were often approximated along bio-cultural lines. In other words, biology informed cultural practices and *vice versa* in manifestly interdependent relationships.

For instance some scholars at al-Azhar's Department of Juristic Responsa, the Dar al-Ifta, have amended their earlier ruling of permitting termination within 120 days in the light of new medical technology, such as sonograms and scanning equipment that suggest evidence of brain waves in foetuses in early stages of pregnancy. Technology now offers observers a new gaze of foetal life a fact that influences their perception of what is 'ethical'. Hence, there has been increasing resistance on the part of some of the scholars associated with al-Azhar to

---

[5] See Marion Holmes Katz, 'The problem of abortion in classical Sunni fiqh', in Jonathan E. Brockopp (ed.), *Islamic Ethics of Life: Abortion, War and Euthanasia*, Columbia, SC: University of South Carolina Press, 2003, pp. 25–50.

sanction abortions for the purposes of contraception within 120 days
or terminate foetuses produced as a result of rape. A good example is
the opinion offered by some ethicists that even victims of rape during
the Iraqi invasion of Kuwait and the Serbian invasion of Bosnia-Her-
zegovina should not terminate their foetuses.

Reproducing the various discursive traditions of Islamic law and
ethics in the form of casuistic reasoning or synthetic arguments is less
interesting. And exploring the rationales behind rulings such as the
ones schematically cited above makes little sense unless we explore
how Muslim ethics and law inflect the ideologies and discursive narratives related to technology. It would not be incorrect to argue that the
various ideologies of technology actually interpellate and colonise the
inherited discourses of Muslim ethics and deploy these in an instru-
mentalist fashion.

Ethics in the Grasp of Technology

Neil Postman in his very readable book *Technopoly: The Surrender of Culture
to Technology* tells us that technology is our friend for two reasons.[6] First,
it makes life easier, cleaner and longer. Second, due to the intense and
inevitable relationship of technology to culture, technology invariably
does not invite a close examination of its consequences. However, the
lack of self-reflexivity about technology also results in the uncontrolled
growth of technology that in turn, destroys the vital sources of our
humanity.

To illuminate our case, he points out that cultures may be classified into three types. The first type of culture are tool-using cultures,
whose main characteristic was to do two things: a) to solve specific
and urgent problems of physical life, such as in the use of waterpower,
windmills and the heavy-wheeled plough; b) to serve the symbolic
world of art, politics, myth, ritual and religion, as in the construction
of castles and cathedrals.[7] One of the distinctive features of tool-using
cultures, even in the case of military technology, is that spiritual ideas
and social customs acted as controlling forces. 'We may say, further,
that all tool-using cultures—from the technologically most primitive to

---

[6] Neil Postman, *Technopoly: The Surrender of Culture to Technology*, New York: Vintage,
1993, p. xii.
[7] Ibid., p. 23.

the most sophisticated—are theocratic or, if not that', says Postman, then they are 'unified by some metaphysical theory. Such a theology or metaphysics provides ordering and meaning to existence, making it almost impossible for technics to subordinate people to its own needs'.[8] However, Postman also cautions that it is an over-simplification to say that tool-using cultures never had their customs and symbolic life re-oriented by technology.

The second type of culture is what Postman identifies as technocracies, where 'tools play a central role in the thought-world of the culture. Everything must give way, in some degree, to their development. The social and symbolic worlds become increasingly subject to the requirements of that development. Tools are not integrated into the culture. They attack the culture.'[9] The first significant step towards a technocracy was taken in the West, by Kepler, who separated theology and philosophy, authority and reason. A technocracy is defined by its essential 'separation of moral and intellectual values, a separation that is one of the pillars of a technocracy.'[10] Francis Bacon was the first man of technocracy. '... [P]eople came to believe that knowledge is power, that humanity is capable of progressing, that poverty is a great evil, and that the life of the average person is as meaningful as any other.'[11]

The third type of culture is the rise of the technopolis in Postman's schema. Before the rise of the technopolis, it was eminently possible for two opposing worldviews—the technological and the traditional—to coexist in an uneasy tension. But with the rise of technopolies, one of the thought-worlds disappears, namely the traditional one. Technopolies eliminate alternatives to themselves in precisely the way Aldous Huxley outlined in *Brave New World*. 'Technopoly, in other words, is totalitarian technocracy,' notes Postman.[12] According to one of the major figures of scientific management, Frederick W. Taylor, society is best served when human beings are placed at the disposal of their techniques and technology. This leads Postman to reach the grim conclusion that in the technopolis human beings are worth less than their machinery.[13] Technocracy, and its successor the technopolis, were both fuelled by

---

[8] Ibid., p. 26.
[9] Ibid., p. 38.
[10] Ibid., p. 31.
[11] Ibid., p. 28.
[12] Ibid., p. 48.
[13] Ibid., p. 52.

information about the structure of nature and the structure of the human soul. The end-point is the emphasis on speed and information. 'This is the elevation of information to a metaphysical status,' notes Postman, where information is viewed 'as both the means and end of human creativity.'[14]

Talking of speed and the obsession with efficiency is what brings me to some of the insights of William Connolly, whose book *Neuropolitics: Thinking, Culture, Speed* was the provocation behind some of the thoughts and explorations in this article.[15] Connolly eloquently makes his case by alerting thinkers of contemporary Western political and cultural thought to a dimension that was long ignored but carefully nurtured in some non-Western contexts, namely, the link between nature and culture; affect and thought; feeling and thinking. Connolly makes the point that technique is part of culture and that thinking is neuro-cultural. He helps us to explore how thinking itself can sometimes modify the micro-composition of the body/brain processes, as a new pattern of thinking becomes infused into the body/brain processes. Neurons that fire together, wire together, he approvingly cites two leading neuroscientists.

He also introduces us to the idea of what he calls 'immanent naturalism'. Immanent naturalism 'does not repudiate the transcendental,' says Connolly. 'Rather, it is translated into an immanent field that mixes nature and culture. To immanent naturalism, consciousness emerges as a layer of thinking, feeling, and judgment bound to complex crunching operations that enable and exceed it. The immanent field is efficacious and inscrutable (to an uncertain degree), but not immaterial. It is, you might say, infra-sensible rather than super-sensible... That is, as the practices of Buddhists, Epicureans, and several monotheistic religions have presumed for centuries, human power of cultural inscription and experimental intervention into the inscrutable domain, while limited, nonetheless *exceed* those of direct conscious control and scientific explanation.'[16]

Connolly's emphasis is on compositional thinking, rather than representational notions of thought. He continues:[17]

---

[14] Ibid., p. 61.
[15] William E. Connolly, *Neuropolitics: Thinking, Culture, Speed,* Minneapolis: University of Minnesota Press, 2002.
[16] Ibid., p. 86.
[17] Ibid., p. 104.

Thinking is not merely involved in knowing, explaining, representing, evaluating, and judging. Subsisting within these activities are the inventive and compositional dimensions of thinking. To think is to move something. And to modify a pattern of body/brain connections helps to draw a habit, a disposition to judgment, or a capacity of action into being. Thinking not only expresses our identities; it participates in composing, strengthening, and modifying them. The cognitive—that is, the representational and explanatory—dimension of thinking coexists with its expressive, creative, and compositional functions...For the idioms of ordinary speech may remain too fettered to the logic of recognition, knowledge, and representation while philosophical reflection, brain research, cinema practice, and the accelerated speed of everyday life coalesce to call the *sufficiency* of that logic into question.

Paul Virilio warns of scenarios already commonplace in our decade of political deliberation that will only be exacerbated by the increasing growth of technology in our lives, combined with the effects of representational modes of thinking. There will be a greater emphasis on the speed of transporting bombs, and how bombs, whether nuclear or other kinds, become political instruments and the ultimate weapons of political surveillance. Furthermore, social conflicts arise over rivalries between those who occupy an eco-system, and in defence of such interests will be prepared to make any sacrifice, including sudden death which would regrettably be viewed as deserving. 'Sudden death is preferable to the slow death,' Virilio warns, 'of the man deprived of a specific place and thus of his identity'.[18] Not only does the increase in speed rapidly diminish our freedoms, but it also accelerates the contraction of time and the disappearance of territorial space. What we have is the 'Extreme Makeover' version of time: before and after, which designates past and future. In the polarities of these extremes the 'present' disappears into the instantaneousness of the decision.

Lewis Mumford some time ago already forewarned against the impending technological power complex, that he called the 'megamachine.'[19] Mumford defined the technological power complex as an authoritarian form of monotechnics, one compatible with a mechanical conception of nature and a mechanical mode of existence, culminating in plastic surgery and the megastar singer, Michael Jackson. Thanks to

---

[18] Paul Virilio, *Speed and Politics: An Essay on Dromology*, New York: Semiotext(e), 1986, pp. 140–1.

[19] See Gregory Morgan Swer, 'The road to Necropolis: technics and death in the philosophy of Lewis Mumford', *History of the Human Sciences*, vol. 16, no. 4, 2003, p. 42.

mechanisation, humanity becomes detached from its cultural history, which invariably leads to destructive behaviour, observed Mumford. For in his view the human organism requires very different conditions for its full development. It is the pursuit of mechanical perfection, now further accentuated by speed, we should add, that has led to the creation of a deathly state that is inimical to life. The myth of the machine is profoundly connected with the manifestation of the death instinct in contemporary society, perhaps not only in Western society. 'It is the pursuit and worship of the machine,' writes Gregory Swer in his commentary of Mumford's ideas, 'that has caused these drives for self-annihilation and destruction to appear and it is simultaneously the machine that will satisfy these urges and realize this death wish.'[20]

In the view of the Italian thinker Giorgio Agamben, drawing on the work of the French thinker Michel Foucault, the stakes are even higher.[21] For Agamben it is not the machine *per se*, but the machine-like nature of the political, bio-politics, that is most odious, culminating in the death camps of twentieth-century Europe. But one should not forget the genocidal practices of colonisation and the imperial conduct of Europe in Africa, South America and Asia that in many ways foreshadowed Europe's death camps. Agamben draws on the semantic difference between two Greek terms used to describe 'life': *zoe*, which expresses the simple fact of living common to all living beings (animals, men, or gods) and *bios*, which indicates a form or way of living proper to an individual or group.[22] It is the politicisation of bare life, *zoe*, as such, that in Agamben's view constitutes the 'decisive event of modernity' that also signals the radical transformation of the political-philosophical categories of classical thought.[23] In relation to state power and governance, human beings as living beings no longer present themselves as objects but as the subjects of political power.

Here the difficult question arises: Where is sovereignty located in the late-modern period, and what is the expression of sovereignty? Foucault told us that an analysis of sovereignty in the modern state is misplaced in juridico-institutional models. Rather, power penetrates the bodies and forms of life of political subjects. Through political techniques, the state claims to integrate the care of the natural life of individuals

---

[20] Ibid., p. 45.

[21] Giorgio Agamben, *Homo Sacer: Sovereign Power and Bare Life*, Stanford University Press, 1998.

[22] Ibid., p. 1.

[23] Ibid., p. 4.

into its very function, from social security to policing functions. In addition, it also deploys technologies of the self, by which the individual becomes tied to his or her identity and consciousness, but at the same time also binds them to an external power. Often that external power is the ideology of the state, that can even include certain theistic and transcendental dimensions.

But the technopolis or technocracy, I would argue, is more invidious: it interpellates and embraces governance by means of technology. Here I invoke the term technology in its Heideggerian sense of meaning both a 'means to an end' and as a 'human activity'.[24] But Heidegger, in the end, views technology in its essence to be a form of revealing, which is, at its base, connected to causality. Hence, technology ceases to be a 'means' but as a form of revealing becomes coterminous with the 'truth'. In this sense, technology as *techne*, is not only the skills of the craftsman but also the arts of the mind. *Techne* belongs to bringing-forth, it belongs to *poiesis*, it belongs to something poetic: where the truth happens. Technology is dependent on modern physics, which is not experimental physics, but pure theory. Modern physics applies an apparatus to the questioning of nature. As pure theory, physics, and by inference technology, is a way of ordering nature: it is enframing, in Heidegger's terms, and during his time there was still some debate about the essence of technology and its impact as well as mobility.[25]

Sovereignty, then in my view, is gradually shifting to technology; the expression of sovereignty, drawing on Agamben and others, is to a large degree the power and capacity to decide, stipulate, regulate and actualise who may live and who may die. Politics is increasingly the work of deciding who will live and who will die. It could occur in domestic politics in activities as mundane as deciding on medical questions as to whether a feeding tube should be removed or kept in place in a radically diminished human body, or in manipulating international institutions to decide when and how wars will be declared followed by unleashing technologies of destruction on bodies as part of collateral damage, or where force will be withheld in order that massacres and genocides may take place, such as in Rwanda and Sudan in most recent times.

---

[24] Martin Heidegger, *The Question Concerning Technology and Other Essays*, New York: Harper, 1977, p. 252.

[25] See Hubert L. Dreyfus, 'Between techne and technology: the ambiguous place of technology in *Being and Time*', *Tulane Studies in Philosophy*, vol. 32, 1984, pp. 23–35.

Achille Mbembe, in his instructive essay entitled *Necropolitics*, shows that modern wars have resorted to the nomadic practices of hit-and-run rather than the conquer-and-annex type of territorial wars to which we have been accustomed.[26] It is the age of B-2 stealth bombers, weapons that silently wreck their destruction on civilian populations, and of the figure of the suicide bomber. Two types of bodies: fuselage and torso; metal and flesh. In the one, height and distance from the target is the tactic of ambush; in the other, it is the intimacy and proximity, if not the anonymity of the candidate for suicide, which becomes the tactic of ambush.

Conclusion

Let me in return to my examples from discussions in Muslim ethics to illustrate how technology inscribes itself into the practices and subjectivities of Muslim communities and how technology is resisted. For those jurists who subscribe to organ transplantation and accept notions of brain death, there is an organic link between *techne* and *episteme*. Both are terms for knowing in the broadest sense. Hence, the two modes of knowing pertinent to the practices under discussion, the knowledge practices of morality and ethics and the knowledge practices or informatics of technology, are in an a-symmetrical relationship. This model, and its accompanying practices of transplantation and related health care practices effectively format the moral discourse into a technology of healing.

Those jurists who refuse to accept the writ of technology deploy their *episteme* against *techne* and retain the strict difference between the two forms of knowing. In fact, technology is 'used' to the extent that another mediating narrative, namely the narrative of Islamic law and ethics, permits such use. In Neil Postman's words, they are 'suspicious of the idea of progress, and…do not confuse information with understanding.' They 'admire technological ingenuity but do not think it represents the highest possible form of human achievement' and they 'do not believe that science is the only system of thought capable of producing truth.'[27]

---

[26] Achille Mbembe, 'Necropolitics', *Public Culture*, vol. 15, no. 1, 2003, p. 31.
[27] Postman, *Technopoly*, p. 184.

Both the suicide bomber and the jurist who tries to create a seamless epistemological link between ethics and technology with the goal of creating epistemic coherence do not differentiate between the sovereign subject and the tool. The tool interpellates the body and its ethics. There is a desire to join art and science together. As two aspects of poetics, art and science serve different kinds of orders. To conflate them is to render both immanent and possibly also signal the abandonment of transcendence.

In the thirteenth century Ibn al-Jazari advanced some description about the relationship between the human subject and technology. In his *Book of the Knowledges of Ingenious Mechanical Devices (al-Jami' Bayn al-'Ilm wa al-'Amal al-Nafi')*, al-Jazari reminisced about his experience in the court of his patron, Nasir al-Din Abu 'l-Fath Mahmud bin Muhammad bin Artuq, the king of Diyar Bakr:[28]

> I was in his presence one day and had brought him something which he had ordered me to make. He looked at me and he looked at what I had made and thought about it, without my noticing. He guessed what I had been thinking about, and unveiled unerringly what I had concealed. He said: 'you have made peerless devices, and through strength have brought them forth as works; so do not lose what you have wearied yourself with and plainly constructed. I wish you to compose for me a book which assembles what you have created separately, and brings together a selection of individual items and pictures'.

Ibn al-Jazari brings forth devices as works, as a craftsman who made products. In the Heideggerian sense, the subject brings forth a 'human activity' that naturalises the order of doing.

---

[28] Ibn al-Razzaz al-Jazari, *The Book of Ingenious Mechanical Devices*, Islamabad/ Dordrecht, The Netherlands: Pakistan Hijra Council, 1409/1989.

'NATURALLY' CONFOUNDED AND CONFUSED BIOETHICS, TECHNOLOGY, AND RELIGION

William R. LaFleur

Terri Schiavo in a Procrustean Bed

Discussions of bioethics and religion had a significant role in the IAHR World Congress in 2005. And very often when some of us as participants, retired to our hotel rooms in Tokyo in late March we were, by switching our attention to CNN, hit in the face by America's bizarre bioethical melodrama involving the life-or-death tug-of-war over the body of Terri Schiavo. Our televisions would show old footage of a woman in bed, appearing to be neither fully alive nor fully dead. And outside her bedroom the crowds of protesters were shown angrily supporting either her husband, who wanted Terri's artificial life-support system removed or, far more vociferously, her parents, who felt that their Catholic beliefs required them to demand that she be kept alive in the hope that she might recover completely someday.

What could have been a valuable discussion of the pros and cons of the removal of life-support systems in certain cases, had been turned into a politicised struggle. What was especially unseemly in the Schiavo case was the manner in which politicians in Washington rushed into the affair, hoping to score election points with an American public that they—wrongly it seems—thought would want to see them help 'Terri' live on!

During this rather embarrassing spectacle (at least to Americans), I remembered having read in a work by the Japanese bioethicist, Yonezo Nakagawa (1926–1997), that in our debates about bioethics we sometimes put real people, suffering people, into the post-modern equivalent of the infamous bed of Procrustes, a bandit in Attica who, at least in Greek legend, captured travellers and then *forced them to fit* into an iron bed. If they were too short he stretched their bodies, and if they were too tall he cut off as much of their legs as was needed to get them down to the right size.[1]

---

[1] Yonezo Nakagawa, *Igaku no Fukakujitsusei* (The Uncertainty of Medical Science), Tokyo: Nihon Hyoronsya, 1996, pp. 176–84. It is important to note that the books and articles written by Nakagawa show he was very knowledgeable about not only

The reason for making this comparison is that our inflexible concepts often do not allow for those bodies that do not fit them. Our present tendency is to take bodies that are not clearly either fully dead or fully alive and *force them* into either one category or the other. What is in-between makes us uncomfortable. Although in the Florida case I believe that Terri Schiavo's husband had the stronger basis for the position he took, it is important to recognise that it is our own technological 'advances' that now give us more and more bodies that do not fit easily into the categories of 'living or dead' or those of 'person or non-person'. But ethically we cannot easily tolerate the many newly 'unfittable' bodies that our technology gives us. So, like Procrustes, we *force a fit*. The merely 'brain dead' get legally defined as 'dead enough.'[2] And bodies with minds that will never recover consciousness and eyes that are, in fact, blind, are treated—as by Schiavo's parents—as if able to see, to interact, and potentially even to regain fully conscious life. And, perhaps most egregiously in the United States, politics and politicians add pressure to such situations.

Therefore, even as Professor Ebrahim Moosa was presenting his fascinating paper, 'Neuropolitics and the Body' to us in Tokyo, an internationally televised 'episode' in the ongoing public drama of bio-ethics was underscoring the point made by him about the accelerated conjunction of politics, bodies, and technology in our world. That conjunction has certainly been sped up. But it also has sped up the rate at which new forms of 'in-between' bodies are presented to us—along with the unprecedented ethical dilemmas they pose.

Seduced by Technocracy

Professor Moosa asks us to take a step beyond Foucault. It is no longer sufficient, he asserts, to recognise the degree to which the power of the state 'penetrates the bodies and forms of life of political subjects.' Moosa writes: 'But the technopolis or technocracy, I would argue, is more invidi-ous: it interpellates and embraces governance by means of technology.' And, further, 'sovereignty is gradually shifting to technology.'

North America's debates about medical ethics, but also concerns about sky-rocketing health costs, etc.

[2] This problem is captured even in the title of an excellent study of the German discussions of brain death. See Werner Schneider, *'So tot wie nötig—so lebendig wie möglich!' Sterben und Tod in der fortgeschrittenen Moderne*, Münster: LIT Verlag, 1999.

I agree. The irony within this, however, may be most salient to historians of religion. This is because, given what we know about how in the past religious institutions such as the Catholic Church resisted certain new forms of technology because they seemed to violate what was deemed 'natural', today within what Professor Moosa refers to as the technopolis we will find virtual inversions of that—namely, persons and groups merging a faith in biotechnology with what they themselves take to be a stance they assume to be that of their traditional religion.

The Terri Schiavo case is an example of this. Her parents, standing next to their clergy and insisting on their rights as practising Catholics, maintained that the machinery in their daughter's hospital room was capable of keeping her 'alive' and might even be able to return her to full consciousness at some future point. Having gone public about being religious, they embraced the hope offered within technocracy. Terri's husband, by contrast, made no appeal to 'religion' and was widely perceived as having taken a stance that is 'secular', maybe even hostile to religion. Yet it was he, not the parents, who invoked the category of 'the natural' when simply stating that Terri's wish was to be allowed to die *naturally*. To some degree, at least, he was far less inured to the invidious pressures of the technocracy.

Many of us will more readily assent to the position taken by him—that his wife be allowed to die in as natural and technologically unencumbered a way as possible. But if we do so, we need to recognise that we are privately invoking a category—namely, *the natural*—that, at least within the public intellectual ambit we usually inhabit, we shun. The fact is that among those of us who usually self-identify with a liberal perspective, the 'natural' is not a comfortable term. It invokes what is called the 'naturalistic fallacy'. We are very aware that in the past it was used, often by religionists, to justify a variety of illiberal, even totally objectionable, ideas and practices: a 'natural' inequality of the races, the condemnation of certain sexual acts as 'un-natural', the subservience of wives to their husbands, and the like. The category of 'the natural' has often been the language of paternalism of many kinds. In fact, for most non-Catholics and even for many Catholics, the Church's invocation of the traditional notion of 'natural law' is seen as a residual and objectionable basis for approving some behaviours and censuring others. Therefore, for some time now, 'natural' is a word we who deem ourselves to be intellectually and socially liberal dare not use.

But..., in fact, we sometimes use it!

Theory Contradicted by 'Gut' Reaction

And when we do so, I suggest, this viewpoint will most likely have shown up spontaneously as a 'gut' reaction to a specific way in which the accretive and aggressive technocracy of our time is violating or destroying something we prize. It is, for instance, a reaction we will likely feel concerning the growing use of new pharmaceuticals, such as Modafinil, to sustain the activity of neurotransmitters known as orexins, a chemical intervention that makes it possible for humans to feel no need for sleep for multiple days and nights. The Pentagon's inordinate interest in, and financial support for, such research makes it especially worrisome since the stated goal is to eliminate the need for sleep and create an advantage in force deployment, long-range bombing, and the fighting of wars.[3] In this, I suggest, techno-politics subverts the very sleep rhythms that we humans have since the beginning of time regarded as somehow 'natural'.

And, of course, even in societies that have legalised brain death and routinely perform cadaveric organ transplantation, there is retained in the minds of not a few the impression that something 'natural' has been violated—both in terms of waiting for a cessation of *all* bodily functions and in terms of how sacrosanctly the neo-mort is to be treated.

But, as suggested, in Europe and especially in North America we often become tongue-tied when trying to state our concern. Having pointed out that natural law theology has far too often given ideological support to illiberal and even repressive social practices, we do not currently know how to build a *positive* concern for 'the natural' into our bioethics.

Having engaged in a sharp and sustained critique of 'the natural', we are in conflict because we have a 'gut' response to a range of technological innovations that strike us a un-natural and ultimately harmful to human flourishing. And the ironic result is that we have deprived ourselves of a potential theoretical base for resistance to the very technopolies that Professor Moosa, making skillful use of recent studies by Neil Postman and William Connolly, depicts so well.

From the materials presented in 'Neuropolitics and the Body' I do

---

[3] William R. LaFleur, 2004, 'Adjusting the body-clock: archaic aspirations and contemporary chemicals', in Walter Schweidler (ed.), *Zeit: Anfang und Ende*, Sankt Augustin: Academia Verlag: 417–30.

not, however, gain a clear sense that persons doing studies and evaluations of medical ethics in the Muslim world have reached the point of being able to show us a way out of the dilemma I here sketch. Professor Moosa writes of two varieties of Muslim jurists—on the one hand, those who 'subscribe to organ transplantation and accept notions of brain death, [seeing] an organic link between *techne* and *episteme*' and, on the other, those who 'refuse to accept the writ of technology [and] deploy their episteme against *techne*...'. This, if I understand it correctly, is not substantively different from the kind of bifurcation we have in most of Europe and North America. I would be eager to know if the Islamic sources can provide any direct insight into how a *positive* concept of 'the natural'—a socially loaded term, I assume, in the Islamic world as well—can be used in order to raise the level of resistance to the technopoly and its invasive power within our lives.

My impression, based on my readings in Japanese bioethics, is that the category of 'the natural' has been somewhat more effectively deployed there in a positive way. Perhaps this is because Japan, by the exigencies of history, did not have an established notion of 'natural law' based on theology. Social practices describable as 'paternalistic' certainly did not fail to find a place in Japan and some scholars, especially in the West, have been endeavouring to monitor and disallow Japanese usage of the concept of 'the natural'.[4] Yet my impression is that this concept has, for better or for worse, retained a certain viability and importance in Japanese discussions, especially of technology and bioethics. In other words, Japanese who write on these subjects, in comparison to their counterparts in North America, appear to be not so deeply split between a theory that disallows 'the natural' on the one hand, and 'gut' responses that, on the other, show up rather spontaneously and move on to express skittishness about what seems 'unnatural' in biotechnology.[5]

---

[4] See, as an example, Julia Adeny Thomas, *Reconfiguring Modernity: Concepts of Nature in Japanese Political Ideology*, Berkeley: University of California Press, 2001. See also a critical review of that book in William Lafleur, Review of Julia Adeny Thomas 'Reconfiguring Modernity' in *Philosophy East and West*, vol. 56, no. 1, 2006, pp. 172–8.

[5] Professor Shimazono, I think, has adroitly taken advantage of this 'openness' and created a new sub-discipline, *shiseigaku*, a field of inquiry which widens the scope of 'bioethics' by allowing much more room for attention not only to how death too can be valorised and enculturated in religious ritual, but also to the 'affect' dimension in these things. (Susumu Shimazono, *Toward the Construction of Death and Life Studies* [Bulletin of Death and Life Studies, Vol. 1], University of Tokyo, Death and Life Studies, 2005, pp. 7–10).

Jonas, Technology, and a Way Forward

I conclude here with what I think might be instructive in that regard. Professor Moosa brings Heidegger's post-war essays, collated in English as *The Question Concerning Technology and Other Essays*, into his discussion.[6] But, in truth, I do not see Moosa finding much of an *answer* to the 'technocracy' problem in or by way of Heidegger. Neither do I.

By contrast, I wish to offer, close attention to what Hans Jonas (1904–94), one of Heidegger's students, wrote about dealing with technology can be much more instructive, even perhaps having the capacity to pull us out of the dilemma sketched above. Jonas's 1979 work, *Das Prinzip Verantwortung: Versuch einer Ethik für die technologische Zivilisation*, translated and published in 1984 as *The Imperative of Responsibility: In Search of an Ethics for the Technological Age*,[7] is, while alert to how appeals to 'the natural' can be ideologically used by those wishing to do so, not willing to abandon concern for either 'nature' or 'the natural.'[8] Jonas did not hesitate to state that human beings have responsibilities that are *natural*, the paradigmatic instance of which is the responsibility that a parent has for its children. 'In the parental example…we have a case of responsibility instituted by nature, which is independent of prior assent or choice, irrevocable, and not given to alteration of its terms by the participants….'[9] Jonas held that both the natural world (which we too easily regard merely as our 'environment') and what can only be called 'human nature' as it has always been are not only inextricably connected but also now in grave jeopardy.

Jonas emphasised that he was not opposed to technology *per se* or someone who could be charged with 'anti-scientism'. This notwithstanding, he pointed out that technology is scarcely in need of advocates

---

[6] Martin Heidegger, *The Question Concerning Technology and Other Essays*, New York: Harper and Row, 1977.

[7] Hans Jonas, *The Imperative of Responsibility: In Search of an Ethics for the Technological Age*, University of Chicago Press, 1984.

[8] Although Jonas fled Germany to escape the Holocaust, during the last few decades of his life he was regarded as one of the principal inspirations for Germany's ecological movement.

[9] Jonas, *The Imperative of Responsibility*, pp. 94–5. This is not to deny that, as shown in Scheper-Hughes 1993, women in abject poverty, denied all access to contraception, and subjected to far too many pregnancies and childbirths, may develop an *enculturated* aversion to some of their own children and lose the sense of parental responsibility which otherwise would have been theirs. (Nancy Scheper-Hughes, *Death Without Weeping: The Violence of Everyday Life in Brazil*, Berkeley: University of California Press, 1993.)

today: 'As things are with us, the technological drive takes care of itself—no less through the pressure of its self-created necessities than through the lure of its promises, the short-term rewards of each step, and not the least through its feedback-coupling with the progress of science.'[10] My sense is that this fits the viewpoint adopted by Professor Moosa.

I admit that, given the degree to which it has been under attack, the concept of 'the natural' will not be one whose *positive* dimension and uses we will recognise easily or without debate. But my contention is that by relegating this concept to the ideational trash-bin, we humanists have inadvertently opened ourselves to becoming patsies within the far more powerful—and dangerous—ideology of the technopolis.

My view is that we have scarcely begun to mine Jonas for what within his writings is the potential for critical address to the problem posed by the encroaching technocracies. I would be curious to know whether or not Jonas has readers and commentators within the Islamic world. I know he has, unfortunately, very few within North America, where he spent the last decades of his life and where his viewpoint has been virtually ignored by professional bioethicists. Happily, what he had to say personally and in his writings has had a more positive response in Germany. And in Japan, especially since the appearance of a translation of *Das Prinzip Verantwortung* into Japanese in 2000, Jonas's influence upon ethics and bioethics has been growing steadily.[11] It is worth noting that even at this meeting of the IAHR World Congress there is an entire panel devoted to Japanese scholars' papers evaluating the importance of Hans Jonas. I am, frankly, envious. I wish we had a similar level of interest in Jonas in North America.

---

[10] Jonas, *The Imperative of Responsibility*, p. 203.

[11] Even prior to the appearance of that translation we see the importance of Jonas discussed in Hisatake Kato, Bioethics *to wa Nani Ka* (What is Bioethics?), Tokyo: Mirai-sha, 1986, pp. 63–6 and 94–7, as well as in Seishi Ishii, 1995, *Iyashi no Genri:* Homo Curans *no Tetsugaku* (The Principle of Healing: The Philosophy of *Homo Curans*), Kyoto: Jinbunshoin, 1995, pp. 58–76. Kato and Ishii had access to the German originals.

TECHNOLOGY, LIFE AND DEATH FROM A FEMINIST PERSPECTIVE

Haruko K. Okano

A view from Japan

The heated discussion about the issue of death with dignity in the case of the Florida woman who was on life-support for fifteen years, has recently also become the object of public attention in Japan. For many Japanese, the family traditionally plays an important role regarding the question of life and death of a family member, determining ultimately in the case of brain death whether this is true death or not. Does one regard such a role of the family as indispensable in order to decide on this question, and on whether the organs of the deceased ought to be donated?

Let me cite some instances of these conflicts in Japan. In October 1997, the law for organ transplantation came into force, according to which brain death is defined as the death of a human being, and removal of organs is permitted by the state, on condition that the person concerned has left a 'living will'. However, the law requires in addition the assent of the family, which is an essential distinctive feature from European countries. Most Japanese people are not used to the new definition of death. Hence, the family has the right to determine which death is true, heart death or brain death. The brain-dead person is breathing with the help of a respirator, has circulation and can under certain circumstances give birth to a baby. Such a person is, according to Japanese feeling, not yet dead. The idea of the materialisation or socialisation of braindead bodies as common resources for society is a strange concept for the Japanese. The body of the braindead person belongs rather to the intimate sphere of the family, and this person should be sublimated into an ancestor spirit in complete bodiliness.

The following statistics show us how firmly such a traditional view of life and death is ingrained in the minds of the Japanese. Within nine years after the approval of the law, we had only thirty-six cases of transplantation from a dead body, as opposed to roughly two thousand cases in the United States within one year. But in reality a great number of Japanese patients are waiting for the donation of organs. In order to satisfy these needs, organ donations (such as kidney or liver) from live bodies far outnumber those from cadavers, and these are mostly from a circle of close relatives. In emergency cases concerning a family member the Japanese usually donate organs for transplantation, based on the Confucian commandment of filial piety, which has been internalised in Japanese ethics for several centuries. But there are enough objections against this tendency in contemporary Japan, partly because this traditional commandment can work as an obligation or pressure.

In any case Japanese generally set a high value on the complete bodiliness (of the deceased), on the unity of body and spirit, and on the intimate solidarity of a family as an ontological unity with its ancestors. Advanced medical technology contributes indeed a great deal to people's welfare, but regarding life and death in each concrete situation in daily life we cannot simply ignore traditional views of bodiliness, and regard family and ethos as being old-fashioned, for we are all living in a network of relations, in which each person interacts constantly with others within a system of power. Hence, with regard to this problem, we must rather pay attention to the question by whom, for whom, for which purpose, and to what end a certain technology is applied. As Professor Moosa rightly remarks, with reference to Michel Foucault, we should consider what the result would be in each case, and that the person in power is the one who can deploy the technologies of life and death. By trial and error we are moving carefully towards a new universal ethical norm that does not exclude the particular, as the traditional Japanese norm-ethics has done. The new norm is namely not only attained as a result of ideal abstraction, but by full consideration of problems in concrete situations. Each person concerned should be individually perceived in the context of his or her age, gender, personal history and personal conditions.

The Japanese are at present caught in a vicious circle of conflict between medical technologies, a desire for a high quality of life, and the traditional views of the bodiliness unified with the spirit and of the integration of family members. The key concept for this complex problem is without doubt neither the capitalistic nor the utilitarian interest contained in the slogan 'The greatest happiness of the greatest number', nor the honour and power required among medical men, but the dignity of human beings, by which they can realise themselves through self-determination.

The Need for a Feminist Perspective

In Professor Moosa's highly informative paper, I only missed the integration of a gender studies-based approach, as this might provide an alternative perspective on the matter. In the following, I therefore would like to comment on the subject from a feminist perspective.

The waves of political and economical globalisation have neither produced any harmony nor a peaceful federation of the world, but on the contrary, a consciousness of crisis, feelings of nationalism and localism have been further incited, since the existing economic imbalance is becoming more and more visible. Criticising such a type of globalisation that is based on universal capitalism, feminist theology proposes a global sisterhood, in and by which women are ready to mutually help suffering women all over the world. Meanwhile, feminists and womanists have faced the North-South problem in their own way. Maria Mies, in my view, has made an epoch-making contribution to this feminist thought stream with her book *Patriarchy and Accumulation on a World Scale.*[1]

Post-modern feminism, which reflects on the shortcomings of earlier feminism, namely those of white women in Western societies, recognises and respects differences between women in all parts of the globe. I would like to enrich the debate raised by Professor Moosa with this particular feminist perspective that criticises the naive worship of scientism, utilitarianism and rationalism, which all have their origin in capitalist interests.

First of all, we have to remember that the ideas of objectivity, neutral value, and the universality of science have already all been questioned since Thomas Kuhn.[2] Therefore, nowadays, we cannot welcome any kind of science or technology uncritically.[3] In the theory of science and in the application of technology, a particular view of the world and the human being is reflected, which is in most cases androcentric. Modern science has attained a certain power: to define the world's reality, based

---

[1] Maria Mies, *Patriarchy and Accumulation on a World Scale*, London: Zed Books, 1986.

[2] Thomas Kuhn, *The Structure of Scientific Revolutions*, University of Chicago Press, 1962.

[3] See e.g. Alexandra Manzei, *Körper-Technik-Grenzen: Kritische Anthropologie am Beispiel der Transplantationsmedizin*, Münster: LIT Verlag, 2003.

on its own authority due to technology and economic efficiency. So did the androcentric worldview come about, for modern scientists are principally male.[4] While science functions as a yardstick for rationality and efficiency and is increasingly valued, the idea of nature as mother, on the other hand (represented in the metaphor of the female), which nurtures human beings and all other creatures, tends to be rated low. We have to re-examine critically how, in which historical context, and against which social-economic background modern science is promoted in order to solve today's problems.

As the well-known controversy between the American psychologists Lawrence Kohlberg and Carol Gilligan suggests,[5] discourses on traditional ethical terms such as 'truth', 'justice' and 'god' are formed and constructed in particular social and cultural contexts. These values of human relations are defined from a male perspective (usually white men in good health), so that they are often not available for women, for the sick and the weak, and for people from foreign cultures in a society.

I will come back to the delicate problem of modern technology, political power and a capital market, citing an example of the assisted reproductive technology which guarantees a healthy and 'normal' baby. Modern technology seems to be a boon especially for women. However, regardless of the cultural environment in which this technology is utilised, it can also lead to situations in which human dignity and happiness are violated. Reproductive technology no doubt brings a benefit for many people, but the good and bad sides weigh each other out, so that one should pay more attention in considering this technology. Reproductive technology is not an abstract act, but is applied to concrete persons with an irreplaceable individuality and their own personal history. It is worth to reconfirm in a fundamental way whether sterility means misery for the person concerned at all times, or only for those who actually want a child. Feminists are further critically re-examining other problems, such as the fact that only rich people are able to benefit from this modern technology. Once again we have to ask under what circumstances human life may be produced on a commercial basis, and whether a child can be possessed by the parents, an issue that concerns

---

[4] See Evelyn Fox Keller, *Reflections on Gender and Science*, Chicago: Yale University Press, 1986.

[5] Carol Gilligan, *In a Different Voice*, Cambridge, MA: Harvard University Press, 1982.

the Roman Catholic Church too. In any case the concrete otherness of a child, born or unborn (foetus), must be considered too.

With regard to the complex subject of 'Technology, Life and Death', I wish to propose an alternative suggestion from the viewpoint of feminist theology, which aims to deconstruct androcentric ethics. The intention of this feminist ethics can be summarised in the following keywords: 'autonomy', 'mutual relations', 'care', and 'justice'.

A Feminist Ethics[6]

In bioethics, 'autonomy' is a delicate term, which must be used with care with regard to women. On the one hand, 'autonomy' refers to the liberation of women, creating the opportunity for self-determination as best represented in the idea of reproductive rights and reproductive health. On the other hand, at the same time we have to question the worth of this 'self-determination', as in the case of abortion. Likewise, self-determination, which is inconceivable without a network of relations and which always has certain social effects, can lead to the problematic issue of eugenics, as seen in choices made based on prenatal or pre-implantation diagnoses. If a majority in a society is in favour of abortion of foetuses or embryo's with potential disabilities, this will result in discrimination against people with disabilities and against women who do not have the luxury to choose whether to have the child or not. It is nearly impossible to make decisions of this kind without any influence from one's family, community, or society. The tension that is present in the coexistence of self-determination and social relations is a problem to be solved without any paternalistic force.

In this context I would like to propose here a kind of blue-print for an alternative society that may overcome the complex problem of women being forced to abort a defective foetus. In such a society, mothers (and fathers) are the ones to take the decision about whether or not to give birth to a child. Such a society creates a system that supports mothers with handicapped children, and handicapped people are not discriminated against or subjected to prejudice. With or without handicaps,

---

[6] Some relevant works on feminist ethics are included in the bibliography at the end of this book, including by Hille Haker, Haruko Okano, Annemarie Pieper and Ina Praetorius.

every person will be treated as precious. There is enough information available for raising handicapped children with the help of various social support systems. This will be a society where every person will have a fundamental peace of mind in developing human relationships, for he or she is unconditionally accepted as a member of it.

The second important feminist concept, 'relationship' or 'mutual relations', which is highly esteemed in feminist theology today, is indispensable to a woman's or man's realisation of self-determination. Life in itself becomes empowered through a relationship with the divine and with other human beings. The American theologian Rosemary Radford Ruether sees the concept of mutual relations justified in religious experiences of an original harmony, which she regards as a symbol for feminist spirituality. Binary concepts like 'male and female', 'mind and body', 'nature and humans', 'the divine and nature', are all part of a dichotomous patriarchal thought pattern. Within the concept of original harmony, all beings belong together and are components of the original harmony. What has traditionally been called 'sin' is for Ruether the breaking up of this state of original harmony of being. In her view, the broken relations between original dualities such as human beings and god, and human beings and nature, have not only resulted in changed ways of thinking and perceiving, but also in obscuring where responsibility for evil lies. The unilateral thought of men and patriarchal domination are considered the reason for this type of sin. Through the recovery of the state of original harmony, human beings rediscover their wholeness and their state of being in unison with the universe.[7]

The third feminist key-concept, 'care', is to be understood not only as the responsibility of women, but also as that of men. According to Paul Ricoeur, to care means to admit that one makes efforts based on a sense of responsibility, aiming for the well-being of others.[8] In the sphere of bioethics, care in this sense is important as a complementary factor to the idea of self-determination that plays emphasis on the individual.

---

[7] Rosemary Radford Ruether, *Feminist Theology and Spirituality in Christian Feminism: Visions of a New Humanity*, New York: Harper & Row, 1984. Cf. also Carter Heyward, *The Redemption of God: A Theology of Mutual Relations*, Washington, DC: University Press of America, 1982.

[8] Paul Ricoeur, *Das Selbst als ein Anderer*, München: W. Fink, 1996.

The fourth feminist keyword, 'justice', clarifies the problem of power relations. The feminist understanding of this concept, which has been frequently invoked, is based on a passage in the Bible: 'And the king will answer them, "Truly, I say to you, as you did it to one of the least of these my brethren, you did it to me"'.[9] Biblical justice holds that the life of the lowest in a society should be appreciated and improved. In this way, a person of power will be obliged to convey human dignity and human rights to the weakest human beings to grant them the opportunity for self-determination without oppression. In this context, I would like to quote the following words of Jesus as his innovative calling on the Emperor (the person of power) to ensure justice: 'Then render to Caesar the things that are Caesar's, and to God the things that are God's'.[10]

In connection with this biblical and feminist understanding of justice, we should remain watchful that the disabled are not discriminated against. As is widely known, the fact of disability alone does not necessarily lead to unhappiness. The disabled can live fruitful lives as long as there is a positive social and human environment. Further, we have to be aware of the inherent mechanisms of standardisation or normalisation in social systems and in the institutions of nation-state: are they using the body of women as instruments, and are they marginalising certain groups because of the existence of certain genes? If this is the case, the logic of the powerful will define what is normal or abnormal. In that respect it would be interesting to hear from Professor Moosa what his ideas are on the ideal society in Islam, in which everyone can live a good life and die a natural death, regardless of whether he or she is handicapped.

---

[9] Matthew 25, vs. 40.

[10] Luke 20, vs. 25. Feminist theology interprets this verse not as a proclamation of the separation of church and state, but as a demand to the person in power to ensure justice in this world.

PART THREE

GLOBAL RELIGIONS AND LOCAL CULTURES

GLOBAL RELIGIONS AND LOCAL CULTURES
INTRODUCTION

P. Pratap Kumar

Sociologists, such as Steve Bruce, in recent times have argued that religion as a social phenomenon will eventually disappear as our modern life makes it difficult for the transmission of religious ideas and rituals through conventional modes, such as temples, churches, family structures and so on, as they become less relevant or attractive to modern societies.[1] Nevertheless, there is a certain resurgence of religion in various modern spheres of life, such as politics and society. Whether or not religious practice in its conventional sense will continue in modern society might be a moot point. There is, nonetheless, a visible social phenomenon that might be identified as 'religious revival'. This modern phenomenon is very different from, for instance, a religious revival through devotional surge in medieval India. This new phenomenon is one that is used for political and social control in many societies. We hear about ethnic cleansing in the name of religion in the former Soviet states of Georgia and Ukraine, or 'religious persecution' in Bangladesh by Muslims against religious minority groups (Hindus and Christians), or Hindu attacks on Muslims in Godhra in the state of Gujarat as a reaction to the Ayodhya events in India. We also have seen events as they unfolded in Afghanistan and Iraq in the aftermath of 9/11 and the consequent Islamic response not only in those regions but as far afield as Indonesia, Egypt, Nigeria and other places.

Whether religious practice will be overtaken by a modern life-style or not, as an ideology religious worldviews still seem to persist, and often provide a challenge to modern forms of democracy around the world. It is here that the assumption that modern democracy is based on a secularist worldview is beginning to be challenged by world events. The polarisation of the religious and the secular seems to be increasingly problematic as modern politicians resort to placating the sentiments of

---

[1] Steve Bruce, *Religion in the Modern World: From Cathedrals to Cults*, Oxford: Oxford University Press, 1996; Ibid., *God is Dead: Secularization in the West*, Malden, MA: Blackwell, 2002.

religiously-based communities, as happened, for instance, in the 2004 elections in the United States.

The plenary session at the IAHR World Congress in Tokyo on 'Global Religions and Local Cultures' has addressed these issues. Professor Talal Asad takes up the Egyptian case and examines it with a view to providing a meaningful explanation to religious revival in the context of Egypt. He argues that Islamic revival in Egypt cannot be explained by economic developments. Instead, he locates the Islamic revival in Egypt within the older Islamic tradition of renewal (*tajdid*). Speaking on behalf of ordinary Muslims, as it were, he argues that it is misleading to interpret Islamic revival in terms of cultural identity, or fundamentalism as a desire for 'impregnable certainty' in the face of modernity. He therefore questions the privileging of secular discourse by some sociologists, and asks if secularism is well suited to deal with modernity's problem of social disruption and economic failure. He argues that the so-called world-wide revival of religion, which is not a homogenous phenomenon, is an outcome of the 'scepticism about the old discourse of secular progress'.

Responding to Professor Asad from a South American context, Pablo Wright agrees with Talal Asad's implied criticism that the key concepts used in a Christian-liberal point of view, such as morality, ethics and religion, are indeed not independent of their socio-cultural context in the West. He is, therefore, deeply appreciative of Asad's attempt to deal with religious revival within a specific socio-historical context, namely Egypt. Drawing upon his own Latin American context, where 'pre-modern, modern and postmodern elements coexist simultaneously', Wright points to the possibility of what Stanley Tambiah and others have called 'multiple modernities', or modernity moving in multiple directions.[2] The global revival of religion can, therefore, have multiple causes.

In contrast, Vasudha Narayanan, in her response to Asad, is uncomfortable about discounting economic reasons for religious revival, albeit that the media have overplayed these. She is also sceptical about the idea of the 'construction of an Islamic society', as this might be problematic in countries such as India. Hence, she asks whether it is real-

---

[2] Stanley Tambiah, 'Vignets of present-day diaspora', in Eliezer Ben-Rafael with Yitzhak Sternberg (eds.), *Identity, Culture and Globalization*, Leiden: Brill, 2002, pp. 327–36.

istic to expect non-Muslims in a Muslim country to abide by Islamic principles. In general, Narayanan is unconvinced that a global religious revival is indeed taking place. She suggests that what the media portray as religious revival is, in fact, attributable to factors such as an increase in population and a reassertion of nation-states.

Whether or not a revival or resurgence of religion is taking place in our world today, and whether or not one accepts Professor Asad's explanation that the causes for such religious revival are beyond mere economic factors and that one needs to look at the specific social and cultural aspects of given societies, what seems to be clear is the accentuation of the political role that religion is playing globally. Public policy in many countries is now focused on how to understand the reasons as to why politicians, bureaucrats and criminal elements alike everywhere seem to deploy religion, often in disruptive social forms. In the light of this instrumental role of religion, one perhaps needs to ask the questions: Is religion, or are the religious and the sacred, any more than other forms of social life? Can religion continue to claim the custodianship of morality and ethics? In the context of conflicting truth-claims of religious worldviews, can the universality of moral and ethical values rest on religious truths? Or, are moral and ethical values in themselves universal, notwithstanding the diverse religious foundations on which they might be based? These and many more issues could indeed be raised in our ongoing discussions on the topic of this keynote address.

EXPLAINING THE GLOBAL RELIGIOUS REVIVAL
THE EGYPTIAN CASE

Talal Asad

It is a truism that global forces have greatly heightened social instability, economic distress, and cultural uncertainty in the contemporary world. The widespread phenomenon of religious revival is said to be part of the picture. How should one explain the resurgence of religion across the world—as a cry of misery, an assertion of identity, a revolt against the uncertainties produced by modernisation? It is evident that how we try to explain it will determine our expectation of its promise and its threat. But there is also the question of exactly *what* we are required to explain, of how we are to identify a world-wide phenomenon called the religious revival. Is there an essence here that connects it to what our historians and anthropologists have called the past of religion? In what sense was the BJP (Bharatiya Janata Party) government in India rooted in historical Hinduism? What connects the Christian Right alliance with the American administration to the Islamist opposition groups in Egypt? Should we see al-Qaeda as an integral part of the Islamic revival? Is the growth in everyday piety in numerous countries integral to 'fundamentalism'? Should we regard the increasing interest by philosophers, anthropologists, and historians in theological languages as part of the same 'religious revival'—even though very many of them are non-believers—or simply as scholars for whom the language of theology is suggestive of new ways of thinking about some problems in the modern world?

In statistical terms Christianity is, of course, globally pre-eminent: scattered across the world, Christians now constitute one third of its population—and a third of them live in what were once Euro-American colonies. It has been pointed out that although Christianity was brought to these countries by European missionaries, it is now an integral part of the ethnic identity of the populations who profess it. Christian movements in one ex-colonial country even proselytise energetically in another. All of this is part of the global religious revival. In contrast, the spread of Islam over the last two centuries has been globally much less dramatic. A mere fifth of the world's population, the presence of

Muslims in Europe and North America, is due to their migration from Africa and Asia rather than to conversion; African-American converts to Islam are the only significant exception to this generalisation. In purely statistical terms the relative strength of Muslims in the world is unremarkable. And yes, there are acts of violence carried out by small groups of Muslim militants around the world, but these can scarcely be compared in scale with the recent destruction wrought by Christian American and (to a lesser extent) Jewish Israeli armies. So what are we trying to explain?

I want to begin by focusing on some explanations of the so-called world-wide revival, but with special reference to the world of Islam, and within it to the part I happen to know best. I shall concentrate on the Arab countries, and particularly on Egypt. I hope, nevertheless, that testing explanations of the religious revival in one country will throw some light on how we might view such explanations in general. Because an important aspect of this so-called 'revival' is that however trans-national such movements may be, they are all placed within the context of particular nation-states, and part of their strength comes from their ability to address that context.

The common assumption that the Islamic revival in all its forms needs to be explained by reference to the acute economic and sociological problems of those countries is reflected in media reactions to the 2002 UNDP report on Arab countries. Thus, *The New York Times* article on the report by Barbara Crossette quoted extensively from it, focusing on the many negative features in the socio-economic picture of 'Arab culture', and concluded: 'Then came the attacks on the United States, giving the report unexpected new relevance as explanations for Arab anger against the West are being sought.'[1] The clear implication of this remark, as well as of others in which supposedly authoritative commentators on the Middle East are cited in support, is that the violence connected to political Islam—and perhaps the Islamic revival itself—is generated by the economic uncertainties, political failures, and social instability of something called Arab culture. Thomas Friedman was even more explicit. 'If you want to understand the milieu that produced Bin Ladenism, and will reproduce it if nothing changes, then read this

---

[1] Barbara Crossette, 'Study warns of stagnation in Arab societies', *The New York Times*, 2 July 2002.

report.'[2] For Friedman and others, the frustrations of uncontrolled change in the Middle East are being directed, through the religious revival, at the innocent West.[3]

So I begin by looking at the 'economic distress' explanation. The social composition of each Arab country, and its unique history during and after colonialism, have contributed to considerable variation in the overall picture. But several of them have a political-economic feature in common: after the collapse of the attempt to establish welfare states based on attempts at autonomous industrialisation (IS), financial bankruptcy following rapid economic liberalisation compelled post-colonial governments to resort to foreign loans, a move that led to the structural adjustment (SA) programmes being imposed by the IMF (International Monetary Fund) and the World Bank[4]—a phase that coincided with some loosening of state control over public life, including the ending of two decades of fierce state repression against Islamic movements. The economic disruption of life in these countries is not the result of 'Arab culture' or of 'Islam' but of other factors.[5] The main point I want to endorse here is one made by several acute analysts of the Middle East: that economic and social distress does not explain the

---

[2] Thomas Friedman, 'Editorial Desk' section, *The New York Times*, 3 July 2002.

[3] And yet some years previously Friedman had noted with great satisfaction that 'In the globalization system, the United States is now the sole and dominant superpower and all other nations are subordinate to it to one degree or another' (Thomas L. Friedman, *The Lexus and the Olive Tree*, New York: Farrar, Strauss and Giroux, 1999, p. 11). If this relationship has any meaning it signifies a continuous intervention in the conditions of life of subordinate nations—by economic, cultural, and military means. Clearly the hostilities expressed in those nations towards North America are not unrelated to its status as 'the sole and dominant superpower.' But then clarity of thought has never been one of Friedman's great virtues.

[4] For the Egyptian situation in the 1970s and 1980s, see Heba Handoussa, 'Crisis and challenge: prospects for the 1990s', in *Employment and Structural Adjustment: Egypt in the 1990s*, edited by H. Handoussa and G. Potter, Cairo: AUC Press, 1991, pp. 3–21. See also the empirically useful—but theoretically often questionable—comparative study by Clement Henry and Robert Springborg, *Globalization and the Politics of Development in the Middle East*, Cambridge University Press, 2001.

[5] It has been claimed, incidentally, that such economic improvements as there have been recently in Egypt can be attributed to the large amount of aid received from the United States. But in reply it has been pointed out that although U.S. aid was useful in improving Egyptian infrastructure, most of the aid money has gone back to the States because it was tied to American goods (including military hardware) and American consultants. Perhaps the most significant consequence of the aid on Egypt's political economy has been the emergence of local businessmen loyal to U.S. interests. Thus the way this aid has been given and used has re-enforced class privileges in Egypt and the spread of American consumer culture.

existence of Islamic political movements, if only because the main cadres of these movements are generally among the more privileged sectors of society.

These comments apply particularly to the most important Arab country, Egypt, on which I will now concentrate my remarks. It is from Egypt, with its history of modern disappointments, that the lead authors of the UNDP report come.[6] And it was in Egypt that the most influential Islamist movement—the Muslim Brotherhood—began. The movement was proscribed by Nasser in the early 1950s, its cadres imprisoned, tortured, and exiled because of the threat they posed to his one-party government.[7] The lifting of the ban against the Brotherhood by Nasser's successor Sadat was part of a strategy of loosening the hold of Nasserites and Marxists on state power. This is why the left often claims that the Islamic revival in Egypt owes its prominence today to the political manipulations of Sadat's right-wing regime. Sadat's 'opening-up' (*infitāh*) of Egypt's political economy certainly provided a public space that allowed Islamist discourses (and others as well) to be expressed. But in my view the increasing political *influence* of Islamists—including, most importantly, of the Muslim Brothers—was a consequence of their appeal to the Egyptian masses and not of Sadat's efforts.[8] There is an old tradition of reform as renewal (*tajdīd*) in Islam, and this has been drawn on again and again in the modern period. There is also the tradition of authoritarianism inherited, it is said, from the past—although I think it is more useful to focus on the emergence of the modern nation-state and the trans-national market so that one can distinguish pre-colonial, colonial, and post-colonial forms of authoritarianism.

In Egypt (as in other Muslim countries) Islamic tradition has always been central to the life of most of its inhabitants—albeit in different

---

[6] The Egyptian political economist Galal Amin has written an incisive critique of the report's methodology, entitled '*al-Taghrib wa-l-ightirab fi taqrir al-tanmiya al-insaniyya al-'arabiyya*', in *Wajhat Nazar*, vol. 4, no. 46, November 2002. Among other things he argues that the indices chosen by the report reflect not merely 'deficits' in Arab society—as explicitly intended by its authors—but political economic pressures from a co-opting world power: the USA.

[7] Gilles Kepel was one of the first to describe this repression in his *The Prophet and the Pharaoh*, London: Saqi Books, 1985.

[8] A classic study of the movement is Richard Mitchell, *The Society of the Muslim Brothers*, Oxford University Press, 1969; a useful study of the militants who broke away from the mainstream Muslim Brothers in an extremist direction, is Gilles Kepel, *The Prophet and the Pharaoh*.

ways in different classes. In that sense the term 'revival' may not be appropriate here. The state has sought to use Islamic piety for its own purposes, and different oppositional groups have reinterpreted it for theirs. The discursive tradition has enabled various responses to changing perceptions of threat and reassurance both within the nation-state and beyond. As circumstances that are the objects of these perceptions have changed, so too has the tradition, and with it the aspirations and sensibilities of its followers. Thus there is now a strong sense of world-wide connection among Muslims, built on circuits of communication and sympathy. The *umma* so conceived is indeed 'an imagined community', as Olivier Roy has recently proposed.[9] But unlike him I would emphasise that the world Muslims share with non-Muslims is the scene of complicated interactions between political, economic, and ideological forces, internal and external. This imagined community is not isolated, as Roy appears to suggest, and so it cannot be understood on its own. The *umma* is locked into a larger world of powerful interventions and seepages. The economic consequences of these processes have been well analysed, but there is less understanding of their religious consequences. The Muslim communities in Western countries are an interesting example of this condition—at once residents of numerous liberal democracies that are dominated by non-Muslims, as well as part of the trans-national *umma*.[10] But non-Muslim powers are also intimately present in the life of Muslim-majority countries. So the *umma* is not simply an imagined community, it is a moral space within which there is a struggle for right doctrine (orthodoxy). But even this struggle is not simply confined to Muslims as members of the *umma*. They are constantly subject to pressures to incorporate Western liberal traditions (economic as well as cultural) as signs of the modern.

All of this is certainly an important part of the context in which the Islamic revival is located. But when it is suggested that the revival is best understood as a religious mask for political-economic discontent led by ideologues—whether opportunistic or simple-minded—I remain unconvinced.[11] Of course there are opportunists and fanatics

---

[9] See Olivier Roy, *Globalized Islam: The Search for a New Ummah*, New York: Columbia University Press, 2004.

[10] The European Council for Fatwa and Research attempts to deal with this dual belonging at the level of 'the jurisprudence of Muslim minorities' *fiqh al-aqalliyāt*. See its website www.ecfr.org.

[11] This is the view of specialists on contemporary Islam such as Gilles Keppel.

in contemporary Egypt as there are everywhere else. Certainly there is corruption in public life, increasing economic inequality in the country, continuous political repression by the Mubarak regime. But the suggestion of people like Thomas Friedman that Egypt's difficulties (in which the U.S. is of course never seen as having any part) create a general state of pathological despair that then leads to 'Islamism' is surely disingenuous. The violence of Islamic 'fundamentalists' is not the only violence there is—as the indiscriminate brutality of state security forces (including the widespread use of torture) testifies.[12] And although the U.S. is not directly responsible for the political-economic problems encountered in Egypt, its intervention does have something to do with them—and therefore with the ways Egyptians construct their religion.

However, my main argument so far is that the personal experience of social and economic difficulties is neither a sufficient nor a necessary cause of political Islam in Egypt—or for that matter elsewhere in the region. My suggestion therefore is that instead of seeing deteriorating social conditions in society as the cause of discontent that is then exploited by Islamists, we should first consider these conditions as the objects of a diverse and evolving religious discourse that engages with these conditions and gives them political force.

*   *   *

It is because explanations of the so-called Islamic revival in terms of economic distress are seen as wanting that an alternative account (which still focuses on the search for security) is gaining popularity. The revival, it is said, is really all about cultural *identity*: in a rapidly changing modern world individuals (both rich and poor) are seeking a sense of certainty. But I find this explanation equally unpersuasive.[13] True, people who are part of the so-called 'Islamic revival' are moved by various interests—and their commitments vary in intensity and seriousness over time. And of course there *are* people for whom 'the rhetoric of Islam' is merely a tactic, merely a means for achieving a variety of objectives. But then that is also true of people who employ the rhetoric of 'freedom and democracy', and yet generally we distinguish (in my

---

[12] The destruction of human lives and property carried out by U.S. occupying forces in Iraq is as striking, in its own way, as the murder and mayhem perpetrated by the insurgents.

[13] See, for example, the work of Gema Martin-Munoz who makes a strong case for explaining the Islamic revival in terms of cultural identity.

view rightly) the moral potentialities of that rhetoric from the designs of politicians who use it. Islamic discourse, even the militant forms that advocate a new concept and a radical practice of *jihad*, is about justice in this world—not, of course, for its own sake, but for the sake of a divine dispensation.

A case can be made for saying that some aspects of thinking that arose in the state socialist era have been incorporated into political Islam, including the mainstream non-violent form. Perhaps the most important of these is the notion that society has a moral obligation to the underprivileged, so that the idea of justice (*'adl*) is considered to be more important than the notion of freedom (*hurriya*)—although in practice even Islamists know that the two are not easily separated. The idea of justice finds expression not only among small groups of Islamic militants, but also in the emergence of new social spaces for the exercise of commitments to the deprived. The old Islamic notion of *da'wa*—of calling one's fellows to become better Muslims—is being reformulated from its previous primary preoccupation with ritual practice and religious doctrine to include material welfare: the provision of cheap medicines, loans, youth clubs, emergency shelters, etc., in a state that is increasingly unable or unwilling to provide any of these things. Rules pertaining to religious devotion remain important, but there is now a new opportunity for a discourse of responsibility towards others in society. Charity to the poor has always been a major religious value in Islam (it is one of the five pillars) but many Islamists now say that one cannot be a good Muslim unless one has the material means to ensure health and security in life, that it is therefore a *religious* requirement, one that entails a duty on the Muslim community as a whole to provide these things to all Muslims. Hence it is not the same as individual charity (*sadaqa*), nor the same as the work performed by secular welfare institutions (*mu'asasat khayria*). The difference consists in the fact that *da'wa* requires an appropriate moral attitude in the giver, and seeks a developing moral response in the taker. (This is not only an intellectual viewpoint; the poor are adopting it too.) The point I want to stress is that the concern here is not with poverty in the abstract, nor simply with it as an occasion for virtuous giving, but with the material deprivation that disables people from living 'a virtuous Islamic life'. This is usually accompanied by the assumption that a single conception of the virtuous life can and should be imposed on all Muslims, and that a major purpose of the state is to ensure the conditions for its attainment, including the elimination of poverty.

Basic to the discourse and practice of *da'wa* (so I am reminded by many Egyptian friends) is the notion of 'thanking the benefactor' (*shukr al-mun'im*)—that is, of thanking the divine giver for his bounty to humankind which the Qur'an repeatedly speaks of as his wondrous signs (*ayāt*).[14] One may detect an invitation to enchantment in this idea, although the word *sihr*, which is the usual rendering of 'enchantment', is never used by Muslims in this context. I refer to it here partly to problematise its use in the standard Weberian account by suggesting that it relates to something rarely noted by social theorists:[15] an encounter with wondrous things and events in the world, a world that, for the Muslim believer, has been made by the Creator.[16] Regarded in this way, 'enchantment' is not simply an obstacle to reason, something that has to be shed when modernity is achieved. It becomes the ground for engaging with the world in a particular way. Enchantment 'charms' one out of a habitual state of indifference into a state of wonder made possible by alerted senses. Of course, enchantment may deceive (the sources of deception are man), but the loss of enchantment is more than simply the removal of a source of delusion. It constitutes a particular loss.

---

[14] The classical Arabic word for 'to give' is the same as the word for 'to guide'—*hada*—and it occurs with great frequency throughout the Qur'an. It is central to the opening chapter of the Qur'an, the *fātiha*, recited in every prayer, and is the object of subsequent writing, both pietistic and theological. Gratitude is continually expressed for God's gifts (*ni'māt*) in everyday formulas (e.g. *al-hamdu lillah*). Another verb used in the Qur'an for giving is *a'tā*, having the general sense of giving a thing—and sometimes of endowing it with an attribute. God gives life to things and gives them their nature. If God's guidance is a gift to the faithful Muslim, it addresses him or her uniquely, describing the way to follow their nature. Gifts are, however, ambiguous: although they are given gratuitously and received freely they must not be rejected and—as the anthropologist Marcel Mauss first pointed out—they have the power to draw a return. Because gifts have this power they may (like all powerful things) be dangerous. But the gifts that God bestows on mankind cannot be reciprocated in kind: humans cannot give God any*thing* because he lacks no*thing*. Humans can, nevertheless, give thanks (*shukr*) for his bounty and an acknowledgment of obligation—which in relation to God means willing obedience.

[15] I borrow this idea of enchantment from Jane Bennett's book *The Enchantment of Modern Life* (Princeton University Press, 2001). Bennett points out that enchantment as a mode of being in the world is present in a positive way in secular modernity.

[16] The Qur'an refers many times to God's 'signs' (*ayāt*) in the world, and commentators usually regard this as its attempt to persuade by reference to evidence. Since all the 'signs' referred to in the Qur'an were familiar to early listeners, and since most later Muslim listeners needed no convincing of its divine status, I think more is involved here than an exercise in forensics. Many Muslim readers of the Qur'an regard the reference to these signs as an invitation to listeners to participate in 'wondrous encounters' through an alert use of their senses.

I am proposing in effect that to deepen our understanding of the so-called religious revival we need to enquire not only into how Muslim intellectuals see 'the West' and the political solutions they offer, but into what ordinary Muslims themselves say and do in their daily lives, what demands they typically make of their sensations, how they try to discipline themselves to live *as Muslims*—what, in short, becomes 'natural' to them, taken-for-granted. I am not, incidentally, making a plea here for 'listening to the Other', about which one hears so much nowadays.[17] My proposal has to do with recognising the complexity of the notion of 'religious agency',' and with the need for analysing the subtle and dynamic ways that intention, action, and ownership of the action are brought together in 'religious life'. (It is a common prejudice to think that for every action there corresponds a determinate human actor; the agent may be either less or more than the individual.) Such enquiries have rarely been done adequately partly because most sociologists dealing with the Muslim world tend to have too impoverished a conception of agency and subjectivity.

At any rate, my own view is that the public Islamic discourse is not simply a response to the anxious question: 'How can I be true to what I *really* am?' There *are* such concerns, but its proponents are usually Westernised secularists[18] (when Islamists express that concern it takes a more complicated form). What is assumed in such identity discourse is that one has an authentic essence reflected in one's feeling, something

---

[17] See, for example, the religious scholar Amy Hollywood, 'Gender, agency, and the divine in religious historiography', *Journal of Religion* (vol. 84, no. 4, 2004), who wrestles with the old question 'how seriously should one take the beliefs of religious subjects?' through the social science binary between describing (including mistaken beliefs) and explaining (scientifically valid accounts). She turns to the distinction between History 1 (the history of capital, and of progressive liberation, based on homogeneous time) and History 2 (the history of pre-capitalism, based on beliefs about the supernatural, and on non-homogeneous time) made by the post-colonial historian Dipesh Chakrabarty, that allows her to make a plea for listening to discourses that are disruptive of rational history but that at the same time don't close off the possibility of criticising obstacles to liberation (Chakrabarty speaks of a dialectic between History 1 and History 2). Hollywood is right to worry about these things but her solution doesn't seem to me satisfactory because it doesn't go beyond an assertive moralism. She needs to consider why she *wants* to write something that is disruptive of 'rational' history and why 'liberation' matters. What are the stakes here?

[18] See, for example, Sayyid Yasin et al. (eds), *al-Turāth wa tahadiyyāt al-'asr fi al-watan al-'arabi aw al-asāla wa al-mu'āsira*, Beirut, 1985. The secularist Yasin engaged in a well-known debate with the moderate Islamist Kamal Abu Magd (founder of the Centre Party, *hizb al-wasat*, which the Egyptian government has refused to register) in the columns of the daily paper *al-Ahram*—May 30, June 8, June 20, 1994.

one has the right to express publicly and have publicly recognised, and that one's primary responsibility is to oneself, to the body, emotion, and mind one owns absolutely. Yet this assumption is by no means part of the language and mode of life of most ordinary Muslims.[19]

So I argue that for most ordinary Muslims the so-called 'Islamic revival' is not a search for cultural identity or authenticity in a time of social instability, that for them other questions are more meaningful: 'Since I am a Muslim, how should I behave in accordance with God's commands? Since I live among Muslims, how should we behave towards one another? To which Islamic authority should I turn to find an answer to these and other similar questions?' While most people do not normally ask themselves such abstract questions, the Islamic discursive tradition—to which people turn with varying commitment—does assume them. (By the Islamic discursive tradition, incidentally, I do not refer to the manipulative intentions of leaders or to the closed world-view of believers but to the space in which verbal, emotional, and bodily resources are made available to Muslims *as Muslims*, to be taught, criticised, defended, and reformulated, in relation to founding texts.) Thus even the material services that the poor are offered, and that the professional syndicates[20] provide, are talked about in a particular religious-moral language—both by activists and recipients. I want to stress: it is not that the language of cultural identity is never to be found in the so-called 'revival'. Indeed it is present, and especially in the discourse of intellectuals. But even where the language of cultural identity *is* used by them, the fact that it is accompanied by a sense of spiritual obligation complicates the subjective and discursive object to be explained. It is therefore different from a straightforward 'search for identity' in a general period of uncertainty. What one seeks is an agency that is at once one's own (one has chosen it) and not one's own (one submits to divine power).

Apart from such complications, it seems to me that explanations in terms of 'identity' generally miss something very important: the fact that the primary form of public discourse about 'identity' is attached to the modern state. Here the question that matters is not 'Who am I?' but 'Who are *you*?' In this context one should not think of the individual's

---

[19] For a well-known discussion of this assumption in modern Western culture, see Lionel Trilling, *Sincerity and Authenticity*, Cambridge: Harvard University Press, 1972.

[20] Various professional syndicates (lawyers, doctors, engineers) are important centres of Islamist opposition.

right to express uniqueness but of the state's power to identify similarity. This concern is with *identification*. Identity in this sense is essential to modern state control and security which continually records and classifies bodily and verbal signs of identification. The question: 'Who are you?' is always put by an officer of the state and typically accompanied by a demand for identity papers (*awrāq al-huwīyya*)—especially when crossing national borders. Here the uncertainty is not existential but administrative and political, and the response is not in terms of religion but of techniques of surveillance as well as of coercion that are at once Western and indigenous. So I want to make two points here: First, political Islam is inconceivable without the formation of the nation-state and its ambitions; second, questions about existential identity are related to the modern state's interest in identifying suspicious foreigners and nationals (criminals, traitors, terrorists). Thus loyalty to the state's normative constitution overrides all others, and sets the limits to the subject's legitimate identity. At the same time state and market (national and global) are intimately connected, and in an increasingly consumerist economy, consumption—for those able to afford it—has become a duty and a need, indispensable for the individual to express his or her modern identity. The opportunities and constraints of the market for individual consumers on the one hand, and on the other hand the powers of the nation-state, at once solicitous and disciplinary towards a national population, are together more important for the question of identity than the ill-defined notion of 'a legacy of authoritarianism' in the Middle East. In fact I would say that it is only when the ambition of the post-colonial state and the destructiveness of the post-colonial market are taken into account that post-colonial authoritarianism can be fully explained.

*　*　*

It is a widely-reported fact that during the last century movements of Islamic reform have encouraged the de-professionalisation of religious interpretation, and that—together with increasing literacy, the widespread use of audio and video tapes, and now also of the internet—this has led in effect to a significant shift of religious authority. This process of de-professionalisation has often been compared to the Protestant Reformation, and some liberals have pinned their hopes on an outcome similar to that which Europe eventually experienced and defined as 'modern'. There are certainly some important comparisons to be made here. Among these is the increasing salience given in the reform literature to tenets (*'aqā'id*, sing: *'aqāda*) primarily as an internal state. But the analogy cannot be pressed too far, because obviously the Christendom of early Protestant sects was profoundly different from the contemporary world inhabited by Islamist movements. The historian Herbert Butterfield once pointed out that sixteenth-century Protestants were *not* struggling to create the world we call modern, and that the sixteenth-century Catholic Church was *not* determined to prevent that world from emerging. They had their own very special preoccupations that were expressed through their notions of salvation.[21]

More attention needs to be paid to the idea that the Reformation was a rebellion against a centralised religious authority which also sought to control the definition of legitimate knowledge, and that even in the Protestant parts of Christendom official concern remained strong to locate, assess, and regulate belief as an internal psychological condition. Islam, as is well known, never had a centralised religious authority. Nevertheless, for two centuries Muslim societies have had to confront the Euro-American claim to a monopoly of knowledge and the criteria that ensure its legitimacy. For many modern Muslims, claims to knowledge are valid simply because they issue from Euro-America—and only because this is the centre of capitalist power. For others, knowledge is 'inauthentic' if it comes from 'outside'. Opponents of 'Islamic fundamentalism' find in this latter position evidence of an 'anti-modern'—because 'anti-scientific'—mind-set, an expression of the desire to cling to religious certainty in place of scientific scepticism. Yet this judgement is questionable, and not simply because many so-called Islamists are themselves professionally active in the sciences or because they use modern gadgets. Philosophers of science have increasingly come to recognise that there is no single 'scientific mind-set'. Practices that are effective for one set of scientific problems are inappropriate for others. This is true for both the natural and the moral sciences. The notion that there are two blocs of knowledge, one dealing with 'nature' the other with 'culture', each internally homogeneous, has long been problematised. There is great diversity in the conditions in which

---

[21] Herbert Butterfield's well-known comment is especially apposite here: 'The issue between Protestants and Catholics in the sixteenth century was an issue of their world and not of our world, and we are definitely being unhistorical, we are forgetting that Protestantism and Catholicism have both had a long history since 1517, if we argue from a rash analogy that the one was fighting for something like our modern world while the other was trying to prevent its coming', in H. Butterfield, *The Whig Interpretation of History*, New York: W. W. Norton, 1965, pp. 36–7.

knowledge is accumulated, in the techniques on which it draws and in the ends to which it is applied. Disagreement (technical and ethical) occurs at numerous levels in the world of scientific endeavour. And contrary to popular understanding, scepticism is by no means a continuous or pervasive attitude of modern scientists towards their work.[22] So when people argue against particular political-economic constructions on what they claim are 'religious' grounds they are not necessarily being 'anti-scientific'. The question that needs to be addressed more systematically than it has been is whether, and if so, in precisely what sense, Islamist criticisms of the way the contemporary world is arranged amount to a rejection of scientific knowledge—bearing in mind that science itself is intertwined with the ways we live, and therefore with the ethics of everyday life.

*   *   *

I return now to the phenomenon of world-wide religious resurgence to which I referred at the beginning. This has been the object of innumerable explanations by scholars and journalists, and common to very many of them is the notion that people need reassurance in a time of rapid change and instability. This is echoed in much that has been written trying to explain the so-called revival in Egypt, and fits quite nicely with the 'search for identity' idea.

'Modernity', writes Peter Berger in a recent article, 'tends to undermine the taken-for-granted certainties by which people lived through most of history. This is an uncomfortable state of affairs, for many an intolerable one, and religious movements that claim to give certainty have great appeal'.[23] Karen Armstrong has taken this state of affairs to be an explanation of the growth of fundamentalism: 'Fundamentalism', she writes, 'speaks to a popular "desire for impregnable certainty" and simplification in the face of the social dislocations and ambiguities of late modernity'.[24] But are the religious movements of which Berger speaks Armstrong's fundamentalist movements understood in some narrow sense? Or does the term fundamentalism apply to all religious commitments because religion by definition offers certainty?

---

[22] The most famous argument along these lines was of course *The Structure of Scientific Revolutions* by Thomas Kuhn.

[23] 'The desecularization of the world: a global overview', in Peter L. Berger (ed.), *The Desecularization of the World*, 1999, p. 11.

[24] Karen Armstrong, 'Spiritual Prozac', *New Statesman and Society*, 21 July 1995.

However plausible Berger and Armstrong may seem, they do not attend sufficiently to the conditions that witnessed the rise of secularism, which (so I have argued elsewhere) is more than a political doctrine. Perhaps this is because for most of us moderns secularism is not in need of explanation—it is simply the self-evident truth of the world in which we now live. The fact remains that explaining the recent 'rise of religion' as the resort to certainty in a time of social upheaval tends to ignore the story of the emergence of secularism in modern life.

From its beginning modernity has apparently undermined taken-for-granted certainties. All the emblematic writers of the nineteenth century recognised the changing character of modern life. Baude-laire, who introduced the word modernity, represented modern life as fleeting, transitory, and arbitrary. His ideas have been central to later discussions about the character of aesthetic sensibilities in modernism. Marx, famously, saw capitalism as a dynamo of change, a kind of permanent revolution in which the relations and forces of production were constantly in process of being transformed—and with them the entire range of social relations. If social and economic historians are agreed on one thing it is the accelerating speed and widening scope of social disruptions in people's lives during the last few centuries. Instability and anxiety have accompanied the humanist promise of universal progress. And yet it is in this period that secularism—not 'religious fundamentalism'—emerged and triumphed in what we now know as the liberal democratic societies of the West. Do we not need to account for this?

There is a familiar old story about the emergence of modernity which is often narrated in this context: From the sixteenth century, the spiritual and political authority of religion began to be progressively undermined by science and materialism. In the eighteenth century the hegemony of faith gave way to the hegemony of reason. Calculation and practical control of the world by enlightened reason replaced magic and mystery. Progress in knowledge and life was clearly being made. This was what Weber famously called the 'disenchantment' of the world, a notion that stands in epistemological contrast to the one I discussed earlier. By the twentieth century it became increasingly evident that although there was clearly improvement in the material conditions of life made possible by scientific discoveries and technologi-cal innovations, there was also another, less happy, development that Weber referred to as 'the iron cage'. Ultimate values were now elusive, and to make matters worse, even science failed to provide certainty in place of religion. This disappointment with science was linked to an ambivalence about the practical accomplishments of capitalism. The result was what has been called 'a crisis of Enlightenment thought', and a consequent resurgence of religion was one of its results.

The second half of the twentieth century—so this narrative goes—witnessed a further erosion of modernity's belief in progress: Science could now be linked to the horrors of Nazi death camps, to the instant destruction of Hiroshima and Nagasaki. Increasingly, technology seemed unable to deal with the costs of the progress it had enabled. Enlightenment reason was itself in crisis. 'The moral crisis of our time is a crisis of Enlightenment thought', writes the Marxist geographer David Harvey, summing up postmodernist thought. 'The affirmations of "self without God" in the end negated itself because reason, a means, was left, in the absence of God's truth, without any spiritual or moral goal'.[25] I am not myself persuaded that there *is* 'a crisis of Enlightenment thought' that has now left the modern world morally aimless and spiritually anxious. In Euro-America, neither the political and intellectual elite nor most ordinary people believe they are living through a crisis of Enlightenment thought, although they are aware of the disruptions of advanced capitalism. There are fears about terrorism and job insecurity, there is a widespread lack of confidence in the political process, and—especially in Europe—a dislike of non-European immigrants. But I do not think that all that amounts to a deep civilisational uncertainty about 'reason, [which is] a means, [being left] without any spiritual or moral goal'.

But even those who believe that there is 'a crisis of Enlightenment thought' know that religion in Western Europe is a weak presence while remaining strong in the third world. Those countries are of course thought of as pre-modern in the narrative of modern progress. Yet America, the most modern country of all, appears to be an anomaly. Some scholars have proposed a complicated account to explain this.

---

[25] David Harvey, *The Condition of Postmodernity*, 1989, p. 41. Harvey's particular reference here is to the Catholic theologian Rocco Buttiglione, whom he regards as an influential spokesman for one stream of 'postmodernism'. Although Harvey is critical of 'postmodernist' thought, he sees it as a *symptom* of something real—a shift in the political economy of late capitalism. He proposes that a great range of disparate developments, styles, attitudes, should be brought together under a single name ('postmodernity'), and that *that* singularity is a symptom of 'a loss of faith' on the part of the New Left who are seduced by it (see e.g. pp. 353–5). In other words, he suggests that there *is* a crisis of Enlightenment thought—a general loss of faith in universal reason and emancipation—but maintains that 'postmodernists' fail to identify its singular (material) cause.

Thus in *The Romantic Ethic and the Spirit of Modern Consumerism*, Colin Campbell has argued that from the outset there were two ideological tendencies within Protestantism. One—of which Weber wrote—emerged as instrumental rationalism, central to capitalist production. But late capitalism needed something else in addition—an ideological force that would drive mass consumption forward. That force, says Campbell, grew out of the Romantic sensibility, also bequeathed to modernity by Puritanism. As Campbell puts it, 'The cultural logic of modernity is not merely that of rationality as expressed in the activities of calculation and experiment; it is also that of passion and the creative dreaming born of longing'.[26] The result is the distinctive tension in modern capitalism between dream and reality, between pleasure and utility. 'In struggling to cope with the necessity of making trade-offs between need and pleasure, whilst seeking to reconcile their Bohemian and bourgeois selves, modern individuals inhabit not just an 'iron cage' of economic necessity, but a castle of romantic dreams, striving through their conduct to turn the one into the other'.[27] Campbell's story allows one to make some sense of the persistence of ideological sources in the world's most dynamic capitalist society that sustain its religiosity.

However, Campbell is still preoccupied with the question of the re-emergence of religion as a consequence of instability, and the longing for lost certainty. If myth and magic have not been entirely eliminated by modernity, so the story goes, this is because the old belief in illusions (paradigmatically, 'religion' itself) has simply been replaced by others generated by consumer capitalism. In a more elaborate way Campbell's explanation responds to the same old question about illusions: it is the gap between popular fantasies created and encouraged by consumer capitalism on the one hand, and on the other hand the crises of production, which religion seeks to bridge by its own style of aggressive politics and its own kind of illusory certainty. This is quite an attractive account but not, I think, in the end fully usable for my purpose. Its main value lies in reminding readers that the materiality of capitalist consumption goods is inextricably tied up with their imaginary character. But it does not explain the strength of 'religion' in countries where consumer capitalism is least developed, nor account for the

---

[26] Colin Campbell, *The Romantic Ethic and the Spirit of Modern Consumerism*, Oxford: Blackwell, 1987, p. 227.
[27] Ibid.

absence of a revitalised religion in countries where it is relatively well developed—especially Western Europe and Japan. More important, the question that interests me here, however, has to do not with the so-called revival of religion but with the emergence of secularism. And the reason for this interest is that the sociological conditions that are often said to explain the rise of fundamentalist religion in our time are very similar to those that gave rise to secular sensibilities in the modern West. I ask: does this indicate an overlap between the two? Perhaps an overlap, but not—so I say—an identity.

Let me elaborate by taking up a suggestion of Walter Benjamin's in *The Origin of German Tragic Drama*.[28] In this study Benjamin argues that the continuous tension displayed in baroque drama between the ideal of restoration and the fear of catastrophe should be interpreted in light of the social instability and political violence of early modern times. The emphasis one finds on this-worldliness in these plays, so he tells us, is to be understood as a consequence of that tension. Sceptical detachment from all contestable beliefs—*ataraxia*—was conducive to self-preservation, as in its own way was the lack of trust in people's motives and actions. The materiality of objects (i.e. the fact that persons and things were to be apprehended and confirmed through the senses) had a kind of guarantee that people's words no longer afforded. The human body could be enjoyed and attacked and defended against as pure physicality. Social life was full of unpredictable change alternating delight with menace. In a striking sentence Benjamin writes that *even* 'The religious man of the baroque era clings so tightly to the world because of the feeling that he is being driven along to a cataract with it'.[29] The suggestion here seems to be that the anxieties generated by the subversion of social and moral certainties in early modernity did direct people to seek reassurance, but that this did not lead them towards the transcendent—it led them to turn to the material world more insistently than ever before. So it may not be the steady accumulation of facts about the so-called 'real' world that underlies secularism but accidental ruptures, shifts in our collective experience, new fears and satisfactions that push us in a particular direction.

In this connection it is worth pondering something else too. Recent

---

²⁸ Walter Benjamin, *The Origin of German Tragic Drama*, London: Verso, 1998.
²⁹ Ibid., p. 66.

historians of eighteenth-century science have suggested that the Enlightenment fear of the distortion of hard-won 'facts' based on sensations led
them to disdain the imagination—which they feared had a tendency to
create fanciful notions, other worlds, 'enchanted worlds'. This scientific
distrust of the unruly imagination easily fed in to a distrust of the sources
of religion.[30] So the material basis of 'facts' generated its own instability
because fear of the imagination required continual disciplining. As Lorraine Daston has recently reminded us, the so-called sceptical attitude
of the scientist towards belief was a moral stance, but also one that was
not (that cannot be) practised strictly and systematically.[31] This particular
emphasis on physicality was also at the root of the early modern state
and of its neo-stoic theorists—who were among the first to argue for
secularism as a means of strengthening the state.[32] Such considerations
complicate our story. Whether Benjamin is completely right or not, we
may legitimately wonder whether the process of looking for certainty
after doubt has set in is as clear a matter as some of our globalisation
theorists and intellectual journalists would have us suppose.

The so-called Islamic revival has many different forms, and it includes
a revival in interest in Sufism (*tasawwuf*) which is not always regarded
as an alternative to 'orthodox Islam' with its emphasis on prescribed
duties, but as a complement to it. The political movements that are
included in this general resurgence harness diverse interests and means.
Yet it is not uncommon to find all of them treated by both scholars
and journalists as 'Islamic fundamentalists'. Taking this view elides
important differences to be found in movements not only as regards

---

[30] In an intriguing article entitled 'Enlightenment fears, fears of Enlightenment',
Lorraine Daston writes: 'In keeping with the opposition of natural facts to human
artifacts, the errors that most terrified Enlightenment savants in theory and practice
were errors of construction, the fear of fashioning a world not reflected in sensation
but made up by the imagination. Sensory infirmities worried Enlightenment epistemolo-
gists relatively little, prejudices and misconceptions instilled by bad education rather
more so, the distortions wrought by strong passions still more, and the unruly creations
of the imagination most of all'. In: K. M. Baker and P. H. Reill (eds.), *What's Left of
Enlightenment?*, Stanford University Press, 2001, pp. 118–9. For Enlightenment episte-
mologists, then, 'religion' (an unruly creation of the imagination) constituted an obstacle
to the sound accumulation of 'facts'.

[31] Lorraine Daston, 'Scientific error and the ethos of belief', *Social Research*, vol. 72,
no. 1, 2005, pp. 1–28.

[32] See Gerhard Oestreich, *Neostoicism and the Early Modern Statem*, Cambridge University
Press, 1982, especially chapter 3, 'The main political work of Lipsius'. For the neosto-
ics, the state's neutrality towards the religious beliefs of its subjects was a second-best
solution for securing stable power: the best was an enforced religious uniformity.

political power and democratic potential, but also in the theological traditions that inform them. The repeated claim that 'fundamentalists' of all kinds can be defined by their 'certainty' obscures critical distinctions within that very notion: for example between those who claim to possess an overpowering intuition that they are subjects of divine illumination, and those for whom a (sacred) text with unquestionable authority is a taken-for-granted object in the social world. These two forms of certainty are not the same, nor do they have the same social, political and theological implications. And they are not subject to the same kind of doubt, nor are they equally available as a solution to existential uncertainty deriving from changes in human experience in the world.

I am, in fact, at a loss as to how I should confirm the proposition that the subversion of 'taken-for-granted beliefs' has led the Egyptians I know to seek reassurance in religion. When taken-for-granted beliefs are undermined one does not restore them by turning in a self-conscious way to a particular ideology; what happens is a re-orientation of one's commitments. But the new commitment has its own problems. For as any serious believer will tell you, far from being a simple guarantee of comfort and security, 'religious conviction' opens up its own kinds of anxieties and uncertainties.

In any case, for a millennium Islamic theological and legal discourse has distinguished certainty (*yaqān*) from doubt (*shakk*) as epistemological states. Jurists have insisted that only revealed texts provide knowledge of which there can be no doubt[33]—that for the rest one must be content with probability as indicated by prevailing opinion (*ghālib al-zann*). Islamic jurisprudence has always made a distinction between ethical norms that bind the conscience of the individual believer and the norms which the judge is required to apply in legal cases. The individual's conscience (*damīr*) deals with his relation to his God, and in doing so he must refer to absolute criteria. But the individual's conscience is not accessible to others and so will always remain a matter of uncertainty for them. The judge, therefore, must confine himself to his understanding of probable facts (behaviour that is visible) and his knowledge of the legal norms. The tension between legal and ethical norms, between

---

[33] But even classical Qur'anic exegetes have recognised that the Qur'an consists of clear passages (*nusūs*) and obscure ones (*mutashābihāt*) that are subject to various interpretation.

the judgement of God and that of the human judge, between the individual conscience and his memory on the one hand and the court's final decision on the other may result in unavoidable conflicts.[34] But it does not—cannot—lead to a demand for certainty in all things. According to the central tradition of Islam, the domain of uncertainty is always present because it is conceptually necessary for defining by contrast the status of revealed knowledge. Hence the ubiquitous phrase expressed by Muslims, *wa allahu a'lam* (but God knows best—i.e. one cannot be sure). The absence of absolute certainty, whether in the religious law (*fiqh*) or in everyday life, has never been a serious problem in Muslim history. And it is also something with which the Islamists with whom I have interacted are quite familiar.

*   *   *

Finally, I return to the question with which I began: How should one explain the world-wide revival of religion? I have been trying to suggest that given the variety of motives, conditions and feelings there is no unitary phenomenon to be explained. 'Religion'—even 'fundamentalist religion'—is not a homogeneous phenomenon. If my argument is acceptable for Egypt, it should be even more acceptable for the world at large. I have proposed elsewhere[35] that the question to ask is not 'What is religion?' (to which one response might be: Look at religion 'as a cultural system') but: 'How does the concept of religion as a universal arise? And why? How is it defined and with what is it contrasted? And by whom? In what social and historical context? What kinds of sensibilities encourage or discourage its articulation? What is doable in its name?' Since the answers to these questions will differ, so too will the explanation.

But one thing seems clear: The profound problems of globalisation in the domain of national and trans-national economies have led to scepticism about the zealous pursuit of progress. The Three Horsemen of the Apocalypse—War, Famine, and Pestilence—are still riding high, and they have been joined by a new and more terrible cavalier:

---

[34] See Baber Johansen for an elaboration of this point in *Contingency in a Sacred Law*, Leiden: Brill, 1999.

[35] See 'Anthropological conceptions of religion: reflections on Geertz', *Man (New Series)*, vol. 18, 1983, pp. 237–59. Also *Genealogies of Religion*, Baltimore: Johns Hopkins University Press, 1993; and 'On re-reading a modern classic: W. C. Smith's *The Meaning and End of Religion*', *History of Religions*, vol. 40, no. 3, 2001, pp. 205–22.

the irretrievable degradation of our planet. None of this constitutes a gap into which religion 're-enters'. All the things that have been called 'religious' relate to a variety of responses to outcomes supported or at least condoned by a self-declared 'secular discourse' committed to the continuous development of national populations.

One common thought seems to be this: If being modern requires that every country become secular, and if secular culture discourages us from imposing our ethical judgements on others, how can one respond adequately to the horrors perpetrated in the political domain? The disparate phenomena that we group together as 'a world-wide religious revival' deal with questions about morality, politics, faith, and spirituality that lead in very different directions. They do not express a single movement, a single sensibility, a single existential orientation. Perhaps they share only this: a rejection of the confident promises of classical secularism to which rationalist progress has been tied. But then many thoughtful 'secularists' would also agree with this, and unlike other secularists, regard temporality as heterogeneous. At any rate, a consequence of these confrontations is that a new world seems to be emerging in which there is a multiplicity of self-styled 'non-secular' traditions. That world is changing fast. Whether this will lead to a greater sense of interdependence and care for others, a greater awareness of the finiteness of human life and its natural environment, or on the contrary to further hostile targeting of women, immigrants, unbelievers, possible terrorists, and so forth, is something one cannot confidently predict. Nor can one be confident that future dangers will all issue from what we now call 'religion'. On the contrary, I think it unlikely that the greatest threats to our common world will come from the poorer, less efficient nation-states, or from the less powerful immigrant populations in the rich world.

EXPLAINING THE GLOBAL RELIGIOUS REVIVAL
A RESPONSE (1)

Vasudha Narayanan

It is a privilege to respond to Professor Asad, whose work has had tremendous influence in the understanding of the crystallisation of the concept of 'religion'. In his plenary address at the IAHR World Congress in Tokyo and the revised paper for this volume, Professor Asad focuses on the issue of religious revival and argues that social deprivation and instability may be simplistic explanations for the situation pertaining to Egypt. His critique of these explanations challenges the assumption of a secularist teleology assumed by many scholarly works. What we have here is an important voice weighing in on the much debated notions of religious revivalism and secularism.

Professor Asad's persuasive arguments are located in specific socio-political contexts in Egypt. It is possible for us, however, to see the relevance of some of these questions in other contexts in those parts of the world where questions of religion, ethics, and meaning are discussed by the media. In his plenary address in Tokyo, Professor Asad reported that among the intellectuals whom he talks with in Egypt, many who have direct understanding of Euro-American societies and their cultures raise questions such as: Can a society be at once modern and free in a densely interconnected and rapidly changing world? If religion is to be redefined in such a world, can the idea of liberty remain unaffected? How far do the individual's moral and political responsibilities extend in today's world? What resources may one, or should one, draw from to address the contradictions between one's values? Even as Professor Asad was presenting his paper at the Congress in Tokyo, halfway around the world, philosophers, ethicists, politicians, and families were discussing these questions in the context of the Terri Schiavo case in Florida.[1] The questions debated by the American media focused on whether the state and judiciary could grant permission and order a family and the hospital not to force-feed someone who was considered to be brain dead.

---

[1] See also Part Two of the present volume.

Echoing some of the concerns that Professor Asad's friends articulated in a very different context, the public discussions in the media in the United States focused on issues of religion, God, freedom, as well as individual and collective moral and political responsibilities. All this in an industrialised nation and a society that has hitherto taken pride as being in the forefront of modernity.

'Islamism', indeed all traditional religion, is frequently portrayed as an obstacle in the path of modernity. Even scholars assume that modernity is—of course—what every tradition wants to be at when it grows up. It is taken for granted that violence and chaos are part of the teething pains, that problems arise from the turbulent and liminal spaces where there is a confluence of modernity and tradition. Liberal Protestantism tends to think of religion as orderly and private and holds individual faith and conscience as central to religion. No doubt political processes in Europe helped this formulation, and as Spinner-Halev succinctly says, 'the rise of Protestantism and the assertion of state power over the church readily helped transform Christianity into a private affair, a matter of individual conscience, as opposed to a public matter'.[2]

Professor Asad rejects the facile assumption made by the media that dire economic reasons and religious restlessness are connected. Disruptions in many of the countries in the Middle East, he claims, are not so much the result of Arab culture or Islam, but of American aid and the sizeable remittances sent by migrant workers. Drawing from his field work, conversations, as well as his sophisticated interpretation of sacred text and law, Professor Asad makes us re-examine the essentialisation of Islamic culture seen in scholarly and public forums. Such representations, he argues, are not nuanced and attribute to both Islamic culture and economic deprivation the causes for the lack of progress in countries such as Egypt.

Professor Asad rejects several commonly held reasons for the increase in religious revivalism in Egypt. He discusses the multiple reasons for this phenomenon and then argues that in the Egyptian case it springs from the context of the Islamic tradition of renewal (*tajdid*). He rejects the idea that this is because of economic reasons that are perceived to be endemic in Arab culture; instead he lays the blame elsewhere. Yes, there is political-economic discontent and certainly, the United States

---

[2] Jeff Spinner-Halev, 'Hinduism, Christianity, and liberal religious toleration', *Political Theory*, vol. 33, no. 1, 2005, p. 29.

has supported repressive regimes, and there have been disruptive policies that have been deployed by several global agencies such as the IMF and the World Bank. But, he says, the personal experience of social and economic difficulties is neither a sufficient nor a necessary cause for religion in Egypt, or elsewhere for that matter.

It is this issue that I would like to discuss first. Can one reject the issue of economic difficulty totally either in this situation or, historically, elsewhere in the world? While one cannot always make direct links between economic difficulty and religious behaviour, it certainly figures as part of the connecting nexus in many studies. Take, for instance, the study done on the village of Oravisalo (eastern Finland) in the 1820s, where religious revivalism is perceived as probably having its roots in the low status and poor expectations of the future of those who got into the revival.[3] From micro-historical studies such as these, to large macro-studies in the contemporary world, there has been a fair amount of scholarly literature connecting religious behaviour and economic conditions. Pippa Norris and Ronald Inglehart, in a seminal work, have shown correlations between secularisation, religious revitalisation and existential insecurities.[4] They have surveyed data from dozens of countries and cultures around the world and reconceptualised the deprivation thesis by arguing how differential rates of secularisation are connected in complex ways with issues of human security. This sense of security is not defined simply in terms of economic development but as access to schools, literacy, nutrition, water, health care, and a host of other factors. Norris and Inglehart argue that high human security indices are connected with high levels of secularisation and that religion is vital among the most vulnerable sectors of the population in many countries.[5] Their 'World Values Survey', implemented in respect of over dozens of communities, cross-generational in scope in more than seventy countries, makes them conclude that:[6]

> people who experience ego-tropic risks during their formative years (posing direct threats to themselves and their families) or socio-tropic risks

---

[3] Anuleena Kimanen, 'Explaining religious revivalism in a Northern Karelian village—A microhistorical approach'. Paper presented at the Sixth European Social Science History Conference, Amsterdam, 22–25 March 2006.

[4] Pippa Norris and Ronald Inglehart, *Sacred and Secular: Religion and Politics Worldwide*, Cambridge University Press, 2004.

[5] The United States is seen as an interesting anomaly and does not seem to conform to this thesis.

[6] Norris and Inglehart, *Sacred and Secular*, p. 5.

(threatening their community) tend to be far more religious than those who grow up under safer, comfortable, and more predictable conditions.

While it is not just economic conditions per se—Norris and Inglehart deal with a host of other strands that contribute to personal welfare, civic amenities, and socio-political security—monetary and economic contexts, nevertheless, are taken seriously in explaining religious behaviour and secularisation.

In Professor Asad's view, the increasing influence of Islamists in Egypt, including the Muslim Brothers, was a consequence of their appeal to the Egyptian masses and not of Sadat's efforts. Although he acknowledges that there are some who do think of it as a quest for cultural identity, Professor Asad is not persuaded by the argument that religious revival is really about trying to fix cultural identity in an uncertain modern world, or a search for 'authenticity' in a time of social instability. For most Muslims, he argues, Islamic revival provides a range of answers to the question: 'Since I am a Muslim, how should I behave in accordance with God's commands?' It is not a narcissistic, obsessive search for an elusive essentialist nature of a 'true Muslim'.

Helping in this task is the shift in religious authority. Reform movements have encouraged the de-professionalisation of religious interpretation. Increasing accessibility of religious material, mass communication, including audio resources, the internet, etc., has led to this shift. Many liberals compare this to the Protestant Reformation and think that this shift will lead to modernity.

One may also ask why there is greater politically connected religious activity in other parts of the world. I am, at this point, not calling it religious revivalism and will come back to this point a little later. One important reason why people may clamour for media attention or to be heard, is if they perceive themselves as being written out of the picture. That, certainly, is one of the reasons for religio-political activism in India, and, it is often argued, also in North America. The perception that religion in general, and Hinduism in particular, has been ignored by governments seeking to enforce a Western form of secularism in a post-colonial era has led to a vociferous claiming of the culture in India.[7]

---

[7] 'Secularism' is used in this context by many Hindus as referring to a specific political and, to a large extent, academic orientation in India reflecting indifference to the Hindu tradition while trying to accommodate the minority traditions. Words

Professor Asad has been scrupulously specific on the socio-political and temporal contexts in discussing the forms of religious revivalism in Egypt, setting the bar for others who would like to make similar explorations in other areas of the world. His discussion sets the stage for us to look in other areas where there has been accelerated religious activity connected with political contexts. If one should probe further, say, about the reasons why there is political activism connected with Hinduism, we can still come up with several contenders. We will then have to examine these more critically before we accept or dismiss them. These will include suspicion of what is perceived by large numbers as foreign domination (politically in history and culturally at present), resentment at conversion activities of missionaries, as well as perceptions of a secularist agenda which is considered by many to be 'pandering' to the religious minorities. When a majority religious culture perceives itself as being ignored or written out of the picture, the sense of victimisation may certainly give rise to heightened religio-political activity. It is argued, for instance, that there has been considerable support by conservative Catholic and evangelical Protestants in America for the display of the Judeo-Christian Ten Commandments in Kentucky and Texas in 2005. 'There's a religious revival going on,' explains Edward Larson of the University of Georgia. 'These people dominated American culture 120 years ago. They lost all of that, but they've regained control in politics since Jimmy Carter was president'.[8]

Professor Asad asserts that several attempts at rethinking Islamic theology has been going on for quite a while, and he lists several prominent thinkers of today. Contrary to what other cultures may feel, he says that these thinkers share an engagement with the Islamic tradition in the effort to reshape it into a new global order. Television and newspapers contribute to 'cosmopolitan' rethinking; websites offer informed religious opinions on issues of correct behaviour—so there is a direct approach to texts, and also a connection with Muslims elsewhere, in terms of both solidarity and a concern for their plight.

---

like 'pseudo-secular' and 'Marxist' are almost used interchangeably by some Hindu nationalist leaders and some members of the Hindu communities in America to refer to certain academic stances in India. The use of the word 'secular' here is different from the context of the word in referring to India as a 'secular' state, an issue I will discuss shortly.

[8] Noel C. Paul, 'How judge's stand resonates in Bible Belt', in *The Christian Science Monitor*, 25 August, 2003. Accessible from http://www.csmonitor.com/2003/0825/p01s04-ussc.html.

Others see the Islamic revivalism as a way in which Muslims can be mobilised to the collective task of constructing an Islamic society. Now, of course this is a society for, by, and of the Muslims, but in countries like India, some people attribute the adrenaline in Hindu religio-political movements to a fear of precisely movements like these, which want to construct Islamic societies in India's backyard. In other words, they do not see the reconstruction of an Islamic society as insular but as threatening other social orders.

Is it realistic to assume that in Muslim countries one can present programmes based on Islamic principles and expect a non-Muslim to accept them, not because they are sacred but because they are reasonable? What if they do not think they are reasonable? Professor Asad does admit that the full implications of this cannot be determined until there is an opportunity to test it out. I would like to move on to the issue of 'religious revival'. Can we assert with confidence that there *is* a religious revival in the world? I am a bit uneasy with this assumption, both with the term 'religious revival' and with the concept. The term 'religious revival' is often connected with specific forms of evangelical phenomena in American history but now generally used to refer to religious activity in many parts of the world. Revival, of course, implies that something may have been comatose or dormant for a while, and this is not, I believe, what we mean here.[9]

Professor Asad rightly poses the question, what precisely is it that we are asked to explain when we are asked to explain religious revival? First, based on media reports of political leadership in selected countries and connecting isolated incidents, we form a pattern—a discordant raga, if you like—and assume there is a religious revival in the world. And then we, or the media, reinforce these phenomena—the building of temples, the getting together of *bhajan* (devotional singing) groups—by interpreting them as fundamentalism, nationalism, or conservatism, and see all of these in binary opposition to modernity. We view these themes as a rejection of peace and an embracing of violence. Several categories lumped together, several binary issues brought—kicking and screaming—into an unfocused field. Obviously, there may be several big jumps here.

---

[9] Professor Asad has problematised this term slightly in the revised paper for the present volume.

Professor Asad quite correctly probes this question, suggesting that we may be drawing lines between random dots. He asks whether we should lump diverse experiences together and call it all religious resurgence. He acknowledges the very diverse phenomena involved, but my question pushes the matter a bit further. I am asking if we should assume the reality of religious resurgence unless we can show by careful historical analyses—of the kind that Professor Asad advocates—that, in fact, there *are* religious revivals, of a sort that has been hitherto unprecedented. Has there always been religious churning, relevant to the space and time and known locally or regionally until the advent of mass media? Professor Asad has shown quite clearly that the use of mass media has led to a shift of authority in the Islamic world and also to a heightened consciousness of a world-wide community. Have the mass media accelerated our consciousness and made us believe there is a religious revival when, in fact, what we are seeing are various forms of religious phenomena that are proportionate to the increased population and in accord with the new developments in our weapons arsenal? Norris and Inglehart acknowledge that there is an increase in numbers of people whom one can think of as 'religious', but assert that this is largely due to increasing population in the poorer countries:[10]

> Our second conclusion is that due to demographic trends in poorer countries, the world as a whole now has more people with traditional views than ever before and they constitute a growing proportion of the world's population.

I would query if we can we be sure that there is a religious revival, or that many of the phenomena that lie below the epidermal layer are now being made visible. That these are tied to nation-states connected with modernity is undeniable, but that is just one form of religious activity.

We have, of course, so far been re-inscribing traditional dichotomies in this response with some privileging of Peter Berger. I would like to call attention to one of the many underlying concepts in our discussions— the 'secularism'of the 'secular state'. Professor Asad suggests that we assume that just because various strands and elements—secularisation, industrialisation, democracy—come together in many Western notions of modernity, they should be present in other forms of modernity in

---

[10] Norris and Inglehart, *Sacred and Secular*, p. 25.

other locations. And when they are not, we pretend not to recognise it. Professor Wright's comment that it is necessary—as Professor Asad does—to question 'the apparently universal character of the Christian-liberal view of law, democracy, freedom, morality, ethics, and religion', is significant. It is in this context that I ask: can we work with more than one idea of secularism? Although there are many modernities, we work primarily with some 'essential' components found in Euro-American usages. In light of this fact, can we both acknowledge the type of secularism understood in these discourses and also see how, in various other forms of understanding of the term secularism, we can see other ways of understanding modernity? There are, of course, many theoretical schools of understanding secularism, but let me refer here to an on-the-ground example in India.

In 1976, the word 'secular' was added unanimously by the Indian Parliament to the Preamble to the Constitution, to emphasise that India was a secular state. While India is a secular democracy, Indians understand this term quite differently than say, most Western nations. The Indian Constitution, as Justice Bhagwati, former Chief Justice of India's Supreme Court, observes, has not 'wholly accepted the doctrine of a wall between religion and the state'.[11] Irfan Omar and several others have argued that it is extremely difficult to imagine such a separation in real life, in spite of its existence in paper.[12] The state-sponsored television station was the site for some of the best blockbusters that Indian programming has ever known: the religious epics *Ramayana* and *Mahabharata*. It is, indeed, quite common to see pictures of Hindu deities in public spaces.

Secularism is interpreted in India not as involving a separation of church and state. Such ignoring of or indifference to religion, it is thought, may turn the relationship between the two into a hostile one and end in a denial of religious freedom. Instead, India is secular in that the state 'should neither sponsor nor favour any particular religion and should treat all religions with tolerance and equality'.[13] This indeed, is the understanding of secularism by most Indians. In February

---

[11] P. N. Bhagwati, 'Religion and secularism under the Indian Constitution', in Robert D. Baird (ed.), *Religion and Law in Independent India*, New Delhi: Manohar, 1993, p. 14.

[12] Irfan A. Omar, 'Secularism and religious activism in India: a Muslim perspective'. Paper presented at the conference on 'The religions of Abraham concerning state and democracy', International Scholars Annual Trialogue (ISAT), Jakarta, Indonesia, 14–19 February 2000.

[13] Bhagwati, 'Religion and secularism', p. 14.

2005, when some fairly savvy 12th-graders in an international school in Bangalore spoke to me about what they understood by secularism, every last one of them spoke about the equality of religions and representation of all religions without the state patronising and privileging any one of them.

Some religious leaders in India are now articulating the importance of the Indian brand of secularism. Omar refers to Rev. Valson Thampu (Christian), Maulana Wahiduddin Khan (Muslim), and Swami Agnivesh (Hindu) as being in the forefront of this issue. Omar's highlighting of Maulana Wahiduddin Khan may be instructive in helping us see how Muslims from a state different from the one Professor Asad describes conceptualise the relationship between religion, state, and individual freedom:[14]

> Wahiduddin Khan is perhaps the first significant voice from among the ranks of the *ulama* (religious scholar-leader) in India to support the idea of secularism, not just as it is implemented in India but universally. He argues that secularism has many beneficial aspects for Muslims, which they did not have in the past. Firstly, it allows freedom of speech and propagation of one's faith to others. This to him is fundamentally significant because Muslims' main task in this world is to do *da'wah*, or to be more precise, *'amr bil ma'rūf, nahi 'an il munkar*, promoting the good and forbidding what is evil (Qur'an 3:104 and 110).

The *da'wah* mentioned here is the same concept described by Professor Asad in his paper as the calling of one's fellows to become better Muslims. In Egypt, it is being reformulated from its primary preoccupation with ritual practice and religious doctrine to include material welfare. It is this *da'wah* which, according to Maulana Wahiduddin Khan, is being promoted by the secular state in India.

Secularism in India also means that there is some constructive engagement of the state with religion on the ground. The Indian Constitution itself accords the state the power to interfere with religious matters to the extent which is necessary for the maintenance of public order, morality, and health, for the protection of the fundamental rights of people or for providing social welfare and reform. Secularism, in Western, post-Enlightenment discourses, has all the primary meanings of separation of church and state that we take for granted in our scholarship. But are we today not in a global position where we should take the understanding of a billion people seriously?

---

[14] Omar, 'Secularism and religious activism'.

Professor Asad's paper has given us much to think about, much to work with as we set about the articulation of state and religion, and individual and collective responsibilities in a post-colonial world. His critique of the stark dichotomies between scholarship and media, as well as the power relationships between industrialised nations and the developing ones, push us to further questioning and to developing more frames and lenses with which we can see and deconstruct modernity, secularism, global economic structures, and religion in the nation-states from which we come.

EXPLAINING THE GLOBAL RELIGIOUS REVIVAL
A RESPONSE (2)

Pablo Wright

I

Professor Asad's presentation is a subtle and creative review of the images of Islam in the international arena and of the conjectures put forward to explain the phenomenon of religious revival in general, and in Egypt in particular. His interpretations of these phenomena introduce a significant number of categories that have historically been treated by anthropology (such as culture, ethnocentrism and identity among others). When systematically applied to specific cases, these categories can help locate in a critical and geopolitically informed position the vices that academic, political and common sense Western perspectives have constructed on Islam and on the role of religion in the Arab world. The other academic trend that has contributed to this standpoint is post-colonial critique. Professor Asad's paper is an excellent combination of both.

II

Professor Asad's investigation makes a welcome contribution to the literature and it reveals a healthy sense of criticism, nourished by extensive knowledge of the Arab world, its language and Islamic religion. As I regard it, this seems to apply not only to the Islamic world, but can be extended to include, among others, Chinese and Japanese traditions or the Latin American world, both of which are perceived through stereotyped forms of Orientalism and Latin Americanism. For those of us who live outside Europe or the United States, these stereotypes can be seen in many aspects, when pieces of culture—placed as if they were a homogeneous whole with an objective existence—are essentialised metonymically. This has serious consequences: the production of supposedly academic and 'objective' analyses generates linear, flat and generalised visions of processes such as modernity, secularisation, nationalisms, contemporary religiosity or international migrations.

The forms of interpreting Islamic religion as expounded by Prof. Asad share in my view what Mexican anthropologist Guillermo Bonfil defined as plural marks.[1] In fact, I find great similarity between the use of the global category of 'Indian' as a European colonial term, which considered a collection of heterogeneous populations in North and South America as basically alike, and that of 'Islam' or 'Arab'. The only thing that all the social subjects who fall into these categories seem to have in common is negative definition: being neither Western nor Christian. Could it be that old colonial eyes might be giving way to neo-colonial eyes that perceive as equal anything that is alien to their way of seeing things?

III

One of the implications of Professor Asad's paper is that it questions the apparently universal character of the Christian-liberal view of law, democracy, freedom, morality, ethics and religion. This criticism is both possible and necessary simply because, from the viewpoint of social sciences, all these key words as commonly used in the Western world are historical artefacts, and, for that very reason, products of the contingent process of transformation of social life, and not evident abstract truths, independent of their socio-cultural contexts of origin.

This is a serious topic when values and forms of action defined by a sacred transcendent quality, as in the case of religion, are at stake. Although matters become complex, Professor Asad maintains a coherent and informed level of argument, based on his own field experience and on specialised literature. True to good anthropological tradition, in his criticism of Western ethnocentrism, he provides detailed analyses from the natives' point of view, who make up the Egyptian national community (Islamic and secular), and who, in Western eyes, seem to be 'exactly the same'. Likewise, he criticises what may be considered an external and superficial analysis of the emergence of religious revivalism in that country, which shares analytical commonplaces developed to study these phenomena in other regions—in other words the indigenous areas of North and South America, or Africa for that matter.

Professor Asad not only introduces us into the world of Egyptian

---

[1] Guillermo Batalla Bonfil, 'El concepto de indio en América: una categoría de la situación colonial', *Anales de Antropología*, vol. 9, 1972, pp. 105–24.

Islam with remarkable cultural sensitivity, but he also successfully attempts to show us what the New Zealand anthropologist and poet Michael Jackson would call 'the way of being in the world' of Islamists and secularists in Egypt.[2] This way of being 'at home in the world' brings out the paradox of understanding quite precisely not only the social, political and theological bases of the perceived religious revival, but also the limitations of Western observers—unable to historicise its values and concepts—in understanding a world in which Islamic law defines so many aspects of people's everyday life. I shall come back to this point later.

Although Professor Asad's paper deals with global religion and the religious question in Egypt, it has an equally powerful dialectical message. In a dialectic spiral it confronts us with the significance of religion in the Western world and the Judeo-Christian values that are deeply naturalised in common sense, politics and the media, as well as in Western social scientists themselves. An academic congress such as the IAHR World Congress, in my view, is the perfect forum in which to discuss these issues, which are usually relegated to footnotes, informal conversations or intellectual left-wing magazines with doubtful influence on the media.

IV

Professor Asad claims that since Egypt is a post-colonial nation-state, as so many other countries in similar situations, it faced, and continues to face, serious socio-economic deterioration, violence and state corruption. The very structure of the state and its economic infrastructure have suffered the financial policies of the IMF and the World Bank, which have led to a series of entropic effects instead of reforms designed to promote the country's 'social and economic modernisation'. And, as happens in other countries, the authorities of those financial organisations, the media, and even social scientists attribute the 'failure of development' to the shortcomings of local 'culture'—Arab culture, in this case. This essentialist and biased analysis of reality has very little in common with the spirit that moved the founders of anthropology in the United States, such as Franz Boas or Edward Sapir. Is it that

---

[2] Michael Jackson, *At Home in the World*, Durham and London: Duke University Press, 1995.

'development' is always supposed to have a clear, universal and obvious goal? Are there no alternative paths? Is there no history and no transformation?

Professor Asad shows us that Arab culture thus essentialised supposes that there are masses of people with no opinion of their own under the sway of fanatics, and that religious phenomena conceal socio-political discontent, and that all this seems to be related to the search to restore a threatened identity. These interpretations are a true exercise of Ricoeur's hermeneutics of suspicion,[3] but with the paradox that the starting point is an a-critical truth that happens to coincide with the economic, political and religious values of modern Western liberal society.

Instead, Professor Asad's research explores the political and social history of Egypt, recalling that the most influential revivalist group is the Muslim Brotherhood—which was bitterly opposed by Nasser's government—and that the suppression of all currents of opinion in political Islam set many youngsters on the path to terrorism. We are talking politics here, without a hint of essences! His research explores the influence of socialist thought on the political profiles of Islam, which demands from society an ethic of obligation towards its less privileged members. This seems to coincide with the Islamic notion of *da'wa*, which once urged brothers to strive to be better Muslims, but has now been redefined by including not only ritual and religious behaviour, but also material well-being. *Da'wa* concerns an issue of a communal idea of charity, as opposed to an individual one, in which politics aims to provide the conditions to improve the quality of life of the poor. It proposes an 'enchanted' relationship with the world, where if one is alert of senses, life in a state of wonder and enjoyment is possible. All these elements in the text, and others, lead us to observe Islam's discursive tradition, which uses religious moral language to deal with social and political issues.

This reminds me of a counterpart in the West, as expressed in the rhetoric of many international NGO's, which in their eagerness to combat the asymmetries and social and economic injustices produced by contemporary capitalist society resort to language influenced by Christian morality. I believe now is the time to wonder whether this religious

---

[3] Paul Ricoeur, *Freud: una interpretación de la cultura*, Madrid: Siglo XXI eds., 1983 [1965].

rhetoric poses a danger, like the perceived danger emanating from Islam and its values. Perhaps religious preaching and linguistic acculturation, as systematically organised in the tropical jungles of South America by the North American Summer Institute of Linguistics, for example, do not actually pose a critical analysis in terms of the cultural rights of the indigenous population. Are not certain cultural and linguistic rights of indigenous groups threatened by a version of Protestantism that passes on values emphasising writing over orality, the biblical axiological horizon over the native one, and ways of economy and society sharing an 'elective affinity' with Euro-North American industrial capitalism? Is it that important to teach illiterate indigenous peoples to read and write, and, from a religious viewpoint, to evangelise 'pagans' or those who are ignorant of the truths of that version of Christianity? What kind of encounter is this? Could it be what remains between modernity and primitivism, or do we need a better trope by which to understand the power relations that govern it?

V

Islam and Arab culture are seen by Professor Asad as open, complex and reflexive historical, political and cultural phenomena. He disagrees with the idea of approaching them from a univocal image of modernity, in which Islam needs to reform itself to become modern, in a society that should be liberal and democratic in the style of the West. Instead of seeing them for what they are not, he proposes to approach these phenomena from what the actual social actors think about themselves. And the vision here is, of course, not homogeneous. It identifies both Islamists and secularists as holding conflicting positions as to how to understand the Islamic religious revival. For Islamists, a collective effort is required to build a modern Islamic society with possibilities of generating a public sphere where citizens are free to decide whether they want to live according to the *shari‘a*, the Islamic law. For secularists, influenced by Western political thought, Islamists' position constitutes 'mere authoritarianism' and a search for cultural identity. There is no visible resolution to this tension between what I see as revelation and tradition—Islam—and what others perceive as suspicion and control, with religion concealing power and reflecting other more potent levels of reality. These two standpoints seem to summarise the inherent unresolved key contradictions of European modernity towards the poetics and politics of symbolic forms. Is further reflection on this necessary, from the viewpoint of the disciplines that have brought us together here?

Professor Asad's paper makes an interesting contribution here. In my opinion, it proposes two important elements in seeking to understand the global religious revival and the Egyptian situation. On the one hand, it suggests what we could call a political economy of existence, where understanding and explaining social facts is only possible if certain factors such as history, power, politics and culture are considered. On the other hand, it presents critiques of the interpretative matrixes produced in the West to help understand these phenomena. Both contributions can be summarised in the existential, but absolutely political, formula concerning the way in which each sector, whether it be religious or secular, builds a sense of inhabiting a world in common. Criticism is required of various rhetorical expressions of liberal democracy, which appear to act as categorical imperatives, such as the rhetorics of freedom, identity, development and morality. We can claim that they are basic lexemes of the contemporary mythical Western horizon, which has in Christianity, capitalism and science its highest sources of authority.

A search for other paths is imperative at this point, and indeed Professor Asad takes them, at times with a strong spirit and at others with suggestions written in forceful footnotes. His thinking feeds on a healthy post-colonial perspective in which different forms of knowledge (in this case Western, scientific and political on the one hand, and Islamic, religious and Arab, on the other) are given the same epistemological status. And it is here that an instance of knowledge that goes beyond the limitations of the alleged universalism of social science is born, searching for a unique universal essence to the phenomenon of religious revival. Instead, he proposes, as I see it, something similar to what Walter Mignolo calls 'pluritopical hermeneutics',[4] a plural space of interpretation from which to understand the cultural productions of diverse social groups, without automatically resorting to reductionism. Professor Asad refuses to see a single cause for this religious phenomenon, suggesting that it may be related both to morality and politics as well as spirituality. This multiplicity does not bother him, nor does he seek to avoid it for the sake of a totalitarian explanation he does not believe.

---

[4] Walter Mignolo, *Local Histories/Global Designs: Coloniality, Subaltern Knowledges, and Border Thinking*, Princeton University Press, 2000.

VI

I go along with Professor Asad's unease at the use of the concept of modernity and post-modernity in academic fields. It helps when introducing a macro-scenario in which historical events and cultural productions acquire a certain degree of sense, but it is a question of narratives that take for granted a globalisation of cultural processes that is not empirically so. Could it be true that the certainties of Enlightenment are now bankrupt? Or that the human person has disappeared in the intricacies of the discourse? Or that so-called traditional cultures are becoming extinct? (Have they ever actually existed?).

To qualify the discussion it seems pertinent to briefly include the opinions of several Latin American thinkers. For example, sociologist José Joaquín Brunner[5] and anthropologist Néstor García Canclini[6] analyse the characteristics of so-called 'peripheral modernity', which is basically found in the third world and has singular features which, in the eyes of David Harvey[7] or Fredric Jameson,[8] could be defined at some point as postmodern (including elements such as pastiche, intertextuality, and hybridization), since in this part of the world a multi-temporal heterogeneity occurs in which pre-modern, modern and postmodern elements coexist simultaneously. This is a product of political and economic history, and can be viewed as a series of concentric circles of dispersion of goods and services which, in their journey throughout the territories of the world, acquire a non-linear temporality and texture.

Brunner states that there is no unique experience of what is modern. He finds it more reasonable to imagine modernity as a trunk from which branches and sub-branches sprout in all directions, guiding modernity (or rather, the practical application of modern ideals of society) along a multiplicity of paths. Meanwhile, philosopher Enrique Dussel speaks of the myth of modernity from a philosophical critique that reminds us of certain ethnocentric statements analysed by Professor Asad.[9] He

---

[5] José Joaquín Brunner, *América Latina: Cultura y Modernidad*, Mexico: Grijalbo, 1992.

[6] Néstor García Canclini, *Culturas Híbridas: Estrategias para Entrar y Salir de la Modernidad*, Buenos Aires: Sudamericana, 1992.

[7] David Harvey, *The Condition of Postmodernity*, Oxford: Basil Blackwell, 1989.

[8] Fredric Jameson, 'Postmodernism, or the cultural logic of late capitalism', *New Left Review*, vol. 146, 1984, pp. 53–92.

[9] Cited in Mignolo, *Local Histories/Global Designs*, pp. 108–9.

claims that modern European civilisation sees itself as the highest civilisation, and the most highly developed one. This sense of superiority makes it an ethical imperative to 'develop' underdeveloped, primitive civilisations. When primitives oppose the civilising process, the praxis of modernity must resort to violence in order to remove any obstacles to modernisation. This violence leads to a range of victims who must be redeemed by the civilised modern hero (e.g. countries, international agencies, NGOs). From such point of view, the primitive is in a state of guilt on account of his opposition to civilisation and allows modernity to appear as the emancipator of the guilt felt by those victims. Given this redeeming character of modernity, the suffering and sacrifice imposed on immature peoples, slaves, races, the 'weaker sex', are unavoidable and indeed necessary. Without renouncing reason, Dussel proposes a critique of the irrational moments of Enlightenment, but all the while acknowledging the reason of the Other. That is to say, identifying reason in places of differential enunciation.

VII

To conclude, I would like to pose some questions and make some comments. First, how can we prevent the spread of the essentialist narratives of culture that suffuses Western public opinion concerning the Arab and Islamic world? Second, which are the myths of the perceived religious revival and their links with the myths of modernity? Third, which aspects of the Egyptian case may be extended to other Islamic countries? Conversely, which ones may be not? Fourth, which might be the scenario of the religious revival in countries in which being Muslim is not necessarily connected with Arab ethnicity? Fifth, how can we better understand what Professor Asad defines as 'the state of alert of senses' in everyday life of Muslim Egyptians? Last but not least, his paper suggests to me the need for a historical and cultural critique of processes described by terms such as secularism, disenchantment, and rationalisation, to cite but a few. Professor Asad's paper provides useful inquiries to enrich our conceptual and empirical frameworks for a critical understanding of the role of religion in society and in history.

PART FOUR

BOUNDARIES AND SEGREGATIONS

BOUNDARIES AND SEGREGATIONS: INTRODUCTION

Noriko Kawahashi

This plenary session addressed various issues of importance, such as women's religious rights and authority, unequal power relationships between women and men within religious institutions, androcentric interpretations of sacred scriptures and their re-reading, and the role of asceticism and female sexuality in religion. All of these centre upon the question of gender issues in religion.

Although gender is without doubt one of the most critical issues of our time, the field of religious studies has remained rather unaffected by the so-called gender-critical turn. Yet as Ursula King, one of the respondents, has repeatedly argued, 'it is no longer possible to accurately describe, analyze or explain any religion' without recourse to the category of gender.[1] Moreover, King emphasises that gender is not a synonym for women, but rather that gender studies must concern men as well as women, for studying gender involves questions of 'their respective identities, representations, individual subjectivities, as well as their mutually interrelated social worlds and the unequal power relations between them.'[2]

Gender studies have generally been considered to involve a degree of political content that has, unfortunately, been viewed unfavourably from the scholarly perspective of the history of religions. For that reason, it was of tremendous significance that gender issues received such a high profile at the IAHR Congress in Tokyo. This was a ground-breaking event, especially in Japan, where gender issues in religion are still under-represented. In line with the general theme of the Congress, 'Religion: Conflict and Peace', or, put differently, 'Religion and Power', the plenary session dealt with questions concerning the nature of religious discourses, which seem to offer epistemological grounds to regulate relations between different categories of human

---

[1] Ursula King, 'General introduction: gender-critical turns in the study of religion', in Ursula King and Tina Beattie (eds.), *Gender, Religion and Diversity*, New York: Continuum, 2004, p. 8.

[2] Ibid., 'Gender and religion: an overview', in Lindsay Jones (ed.), *Encyclopedia of Religion* (2nd edn.), New York: Macmillan Reference USA, 2005, vol. V, 2005, p. 3296.

beings. Religions more often than not function to demarcate 'us' and 'them', inside and outside, authentic and non-authentic, and male and female. Religions, in unfortunate cases, serve to heighten discrimination and oppression by drawing boundaries, instituting segregations, and justifying and sanctioning ontological differences that are deemed to be unchangeable. The true power of religion, however, lies in its potential to help remedy discrimination against less privileged beings, instead of legitimating oppression and aggression. In this sense, religion must advocate the fundamental freedom and worth of all beings as spiritual agents.

It is in this context that Suwanna Satha-Anand's lucid and thought-provoking plenary address becomes significant. Professor Satha-Anand focuses on the absence of female ordination in the modern Buddhist institution in Thailand, taking a close look at the plight of female Buddhist practitioners who have no religious status in the official institution of the *sangha*. She argues that this form of male-female segregation, which in reality is grounded in sexual discrimination, betrays the Buddhist ethics of tolerance, which embrace all beings as part of one continuum. Such segregation thus leads to a violation of women's right to religious practice. She criticises the institutional subordination of Buddhist women and reconstructs Buddhist arguments for sexual tolerance, so as to re-establish the female Buddhist *sangha*, where women are recognised as fully-fledged spiritual agents.

FLUID BOUNDARIES, INSTITUTIONAL SEGREGATION AND SEXUAL TOLERANCE IN THAI BUDDHISM

Suwanna Satha-Anand

Introduction

One of the most interesting developments of Thai Buddhism in the past decade has been the emergence of ultra-rightist Buddhist groups.[1] This development runs parallel to the decreasing space of religious tolerance in Thai society. The three founders of major Buddhist reformist groups in contemporary Thailand, namely Buddhadasa, Bodhiraksa, and Dhammchayo, all faced different charges from the *sangha* establishment and state authorities.[2] The high approval rate of the Thaksin government which consistently resorts to violent means in dealing with the deep south situation cannot fail to bring up the issue of religious tolerance in Thailand. The mainstream *sangha*'s refusal to discuss the possibility of re-establishing the nun order indicates an attitude of sexual intolerance against women. These phenomena are symptomatic of a failure to appreciate the ontology of difference in Buddhism, thus resulting in the lack of religious tolerance on part of the Thai *sangha*, the state, and society.

This paper comprises three parts. Part one explicates the Buddhist conception of identity as based on fluid boundaries, or what I call an 'Ontology of Difference'. This philosophical basis for tolerance will be analysed from three inter-related dimensions, namely, ethics, temporality and ontological truth. Part two offers a re-reading of the Buddha's initial reluctance and final decision to allow female ordination and argues that the Eight Heavy Rules indicate an institutional segregation which serves

---

[1] For a discussion of the situation, see Suwanna Satha-Anand, 'Buddhist pluralism and religious tolerance in democratizing Thailand,' in Philip Cam (ed.), *Philosophy, Democracy and Education*, Seoul: The Korean National Commission for UNESCO, 2003, pp. 193–213.

[2] Buddhadasa was accused of being a 'communist' by some conservative elements in the Thai *sangha*. Bodhiraksa and Dhammachayo both have problems with legal authorities, on charges of lack of preceptor qualification in the former and embezzlement of temple funds in the latter.

as a compromise by the Buddha with his *sangha* and with secular society.
The compromise was instituted in the Eight Heavy Rules in order to
respect women's right to pursue a spiritual path as a nun. Part three
argues that this re-reading indicates the misuse of those Eight Heavy
Rules by the present day *sangha* establishment.

Fluid Boundaries: Ethics, Temporality and Ontological Truth

The Buddhist principle of causation, Dependent Origination, makes
any essentialist conception of identity problematic. The demarcation
lines drawn to make distinctions between self and others, between past
and present, between this life and other lives, are for tentative, com-
municative purposes. Fluidity—not permanent essentialism—serves as
basis of a Buddhist conception of identity. This fluid understanding
of identity serves well to cultivate tolerance. This section explores the
fuller implication of the principle of dependent origination in the fields
of ethics, temporality and ontological truth and argues that they all
provide fertile ground for the cultivation of tolerance. Fluid boundaries
in all dimensions of lives would make intolerance look odd and out of
place with the cosmologies of beings.

Ethics

In Buddhism, the most basic human misgiving is ignorance (*avijja*).
This means that lack of knowledge is the most significant condition
for human suffering. It is neither sin nor evil. Human beings who have
not realised the truth of impermanence tend to develop attachment
to 'happy' and 'pleasant' moments in life. They develop a sense of
possessiveness towards things material, towards a desire for sensual
pleasure, towards rank and reputation. He or she builds up psychological mechanisms, and create socio-political institutions to protect
and to maintain those 'good' things in life. In order to protect and
maintain those things, people come into conflict, hurt and harm each
other, resulting in massive sufferings of the many. This means that in
Buddhism, lack of knowledge indicates a level of immaturity, not an
inherent evil nature. People have yet to realise that existence is suffering, not that suffering is evil.[3] This distinction is very important because

---

[3] Arvind Sharma, *The Philosophy of Religion: A Buddhist Perspective*, Delhi: Oxford
University Press, 1995, pp. 53–4.

the indisputable existence of moral and natural evil in the world has
served as a compelling argument against the belief in the existence of
a benevolent, all-knowing and all powerful God.[4]

Buddhism, in contrast, does not see suffering as indicative of evil.
Existence is simply suffering. From the Buddhist point of view, the
aggressive necessity to 'get rid' of those who are evil sinners is not there.
The famous analogy of the father trying to get his children out of a
burning house in the *Lotus Sutra*[5] serves to indicate a lack of knowledge,
or lack of maturity in people who have not come to appreciate the
Buddhist goal. In this sense Buddhism could be guilty of patronising
people, but not of condemning them. The reason some people are still
in the dark with regard to Buddhist enlightenment is not because they
are sinful, but because of their own karmic past.

Temporality

Buddhism offers several images to attest to the endlessness of time. The
following are some examples:[6]

> I have heard this: once the Blessed One was staying near Savatthi in the
> Jeta Grove, in Anathapindaka's park. He summoned the monks. 'Yes,
> sir', they replied. The Blessed One said, 'Monks, this process of rebirth
> is without beginning or end. You can't make out any start- or end-point
> for beings who hurry on through rebirth, beset by ignorance and tied to
> craving. If someone were to gather together in one pile all the grass, sticks,
> branches and leaves of this land, and take them to make squares with
> sides of one inch, saying (each time) "This is my mother, this my mother's
> mother", the mother of this man's mother would never be exhausted,
> but the grass, sticks, branches and leaves in this land would be. How so?
> Because this process of rebirth is without beginning or end.'...
>
> 'For such a long time have you, monks, been experiencing suffering,
> feeling pain and enduring distress; and the cremation grounds and ce-
> meteries grow. What I have said (should be) enough for you to be weary
> of impermanent things, to lose desire for them, to be free from them.'
>
> ...'What do you think, monks? Which is more? Your shedding and
> crying of tears as you have hurried through this long road of rebirth,

---

[4] For a good introduction to this issue, see John Hick, *Philosophy of Religion*, New
Jersey: Prentice Hall, 1983, Ch. 4.

[5] Another famous analogy is the depiction of the Buddha as a healer. See details in
Leon Hurvitz (trans.), *Scripture of the Lotus Blossom of the Fine Dharma (The Lotus Sutra)*,
New York: Columbia University Press, 1976. Also notice the absence of an image of
a powerful Satan in Buddhism.

[6] Samyutta-nikaya, Nidana-varga (421–61), *The Royal Thai Tripitaka*, vol. 16, Bangkok:
Department of Religious Affairs, Ministry of Education, B.E. 2514 (1971), pp. 197–215.

> shackled to what is unpleasant and separated from what is pleasant, or all the waters in the Four Great Oceans?'
>
> …'What is more? The milk you have drunk from your mothers' breasts as you have hurried through this long road of rebirth, or the waters of the Four Great Oceans?'
>
> …'For such a long time have you, monks, been experiencing suffering, feeling pain and enduring distress, and the cremation grounds and cemeteries grow.'

In contrast to the 'one life, one chance' theory of human life in monotheism, Buddhism puts forth a theory of aeons and aeons of rebirth for each life. In Buddhism, 'time' is not a subject of speculative metaphysics, but a dimension of continuity of life in the cycles of birth and death. Within this temporal framework, the mistakes one makes in this life are seen from the perspective of former lives, and the consequences will continue through to the next life and the next, until one is liberated from this cycle. In this sense, an accepting attitude of moral shortcomings could be more easily cultivated. Patience and endurance are a matter of accepting the temporal dimension of reality. The term tolerance (*khanti*) includes patience. But this sense of patience is not a matter of 'forced' endurance, but an acceptance of the inter-connections of all lives across eons of time.

The cycle of rebirths is also connected with the idea that all beings are related. Anyone could have been anyone's mother, as indicated in the above passage. The Buddhist argument for universal friendliness among all beings is based on this vision of the continuum of life across time. One might speculate that this conception of time would be conducive to the virtue of tolerance, first with oneself, and then with other beings. In monotheistic traditions, however, temporality is conceptualised as indicating an absolute beginning and a terminal ending, which could result in heaven or hell. This intense and limiting pressure of the present, available only in this one life could easily put the virtue of tolerance in doubt. The idea of the 'next life' in monotheistic religions is the disembodied soul of *this* life, not a continuum of this life in another life. The intensity of the present as the only present available makes moral judgements more absolute and final. Tolerance would be more difficult within such temporal conception.

Moreover, the idea in monotheistic traditions that heaven and hell are eternal and therefore permanent abodes of reward and punishment makes morality a matter of great seriousness. As torments in hell are deemed to be eternal, what is morally right and wrong becomes a deadly serious matter. This kind of understanding would make tolerance of those who are or perceived to be wrong look like another major moral mistake. This does not, however, mean that the teaching of love and forgiveness are not important in monotheism.

Ontological Truth

If one understands the Buddhist theory of Dependent Origination[7] as indicating the Buddhist position on ontological truth, one would view the existence of an entity as always composite. A thing is a complex composite, a set of different elements, tentatively held together in some way, and constantly changing. This theory is the most important explanation of the existence of the world. Even a human person is analysed in terms of the five *khankhas*, with no 'unchanging self' at the core.[8] This much-misunderstood doctrine of non-self (*anatta*) does not indicate the no person exists; on the contrary, it indicates that a person, each and everything, exists in an interdependent condition with other things. In this sense, a self is radically interdependent with other selves. The principle of identity in Buddhism indicates a temporal continuity of a process of co-existing composite elements, not a metaphysical essence of a thing. In this framework, differences are a necessary condition of oneself, and of any thing in the world. The demarcation of a self, or of a group, is not conceptualised through the dichotomy of 'in/out' or 'self/other'. Differences are a primary condition of any being.

Given this conception of ontology, it is not beyond a sound imagination to see fertile soil for cultivating tolerance. The very being of existence indicates tolerance. Tolerance is not only about a respect of difference in others, as difference is *within* each and every existence itself.

Regarding other truths, the Buddha has this to say:[9]

> A young Brahmin once asked the Buddha, 'Venerable Gotama, there are the ancient holy scriptures of the Brahmins handed down along the line by unbroken oral tradition of texts. With regard to them, Brahmins come

---

[7] For a scholarly explication of the Buddhist theory of Dependent Origination (*Paticcasmupada*), see David J. Kalupahana, *Causality: The Central Philosophy of Buddhism*, Honolulu: University of Hawaï Press, 1975.

[8] For an explanation of the Buddhist theory of the five *khankhas* as indicating the human personality, see David J. Kalupahana, *A History of Buddhist Philosophy*, Honolulu: University of Hawaï Press, 1992, chapter VI.

[9] Sharma, *The Philosophy of Religion*, p. 150.

to the absolute conclusion: "This alone is Truth, and everything else is false." Now, what does the Venerable Gotama say about this?'

The Buddha inquired: 'Among Brahmins is there any one single Brahmin who claims that he personally knows and sees that "This alone is Truth, and everything else is false?"'

The young man was frank and said 'No'.

'Then, it is like a line of blind men, each holding on to the preceding one, the first one does not see, the middle one also does not see, the last one also does not see. Thus it seems to me that the state of the Brahmins is like that of a line of blind men.'

Then the Buddha gave advice to the group of Brahmins: 'It is not proper for a wise man who maintains truth to come to the conclusion: "This alone is Truth, and everything else is false." A man has a faith. If he says, "This is my faith", so far he maintains truth. But by that he cannot proceed to the absolute conclusion, "This alone is Truth and everything else is false."'

Absence of a claim to the only Truth in Buddhism is not only a caution for the Brahmins who disagree with the Buddha, the same principle of caution against truth claims is also recommended to apply to the Buddha's own teaching as well.[10]

Apart from this philosophical aspect of Buddhism, Thai Buddhist scholar monks have pointed to the 'critical yet compassionate approach' of the Buddha in dealing with other religious masters during his time. A leading scholar monk, Buddhadasa, made the observation that in dealing with competing religious masters, the Buddha's approach clearly indicates a critical disagreement with their teachings and yet he remains tactfully compassionate in dealing with his opponents. For example, there was a case of a major supporter of the Nikrons, who recently became convinced that teachings of the Buddha were superior to those of his old master. This Upali, a man of wealth, who was contemplating to terminate his support of his former master, received the following instruction from the Buddha:[11]

Not yet, not yet, Upali, your family has been a well providing water for the Nikrons for a long, long time. You should consider it important to continue your alms-giving to them.

---

[10] Phra Dhamma-pitaka, *Looking at World Peace Through Histories of Global Civilizations*, Bangkok: Dhammasarn, B.E. 2542 (1999), pp. 5–22.

[11] Quoted in Buddhadasa Bhikkhu, *The Lord Buddha with Other Religions*, Bangkok: Sukhapab-jai Publisher, B.E. 2543 (2000), p. 111.

Upon hearing these words, the wealthy man, Upali, becomes even more respectful of the Buddha and asks the Buddha to rest assured that he will treat his old master and his followers properly. Buddhadasa Bhikkhu, himself a pioneer in inter-religious dialogue in Thai Buddhism, emphasises the point that for the Buddha these former masters are opponents, not enemies.[12] This attitude of treating others as opponents but not enemies, is a crucial sign of religious tolerance on part of the Buddha. This is because opponents are people who differ with you because of some disagreement or as the result of some type of competition. It could be compared to two sides of a debate, or two teams in a competition. Once the debate or the game is over, the two parties do not have to carry on their adversarial positions. There is neither permanence nor animosity in the relationship. Moreover, a healthy competition could even be a sign of deep and meaningful friendship. The word enemy, on the contrary, indicates some sense of animosity between the opposing parties. It also suggests a longer, or more permanent, adversarial relationship between two sides. Animosity, when expressed in such a sensitive domain as religion, tends to lead to more negative reactions, which over time become sedimentary and difficult to diffuse. The Buddha, who was teaching in an atmosphere of religious diversity, seems to have been well aware of this difference, so he extends a gesture of friendly co-existence to the other opposing religious teachers of the time, without perceiving or treating them as enemies. The course of actions of the Buddha in relation with these other masters continues to foster existing religious diversity and indicates a clear attitude of tolerance, both in the immediate present and in the future relationship with these different groups.

This Buddhist position that fosters tolerance of other religions has been well evidenced by the history of the Buddhist tradition itself. About three hundred years after the death of the Buddha, the first great Buddhist king, King Asoka, was known for fostering an attitude of religious tolerance towards other religious practices in his empire.[13]

---

[12] Ibid., p. 7.

[13] For example, Rock Edict 12 of King Asoka says: 'Beloved-of-the-Gods, King Piyadasi, honours both renouncers and the householders of all religions, and he honours them with gifts and honours of various kinds. But Beloved-of-the-Gods, King Piyadasi, does not value gifts and honours as much as he values this—that there should be growth in the essentials of all religions.' Quoted from Nalin Swaris, *Buddhism, Human Rights and Social Renewal*, Hong Kong: Asian Human Rights Commission, 2000, p. 124.

The entire history of Thai Buddhist kings, from King Narai in the Ayudhaya period down to the all the kings in the present Bangkok period, mostly attest to the historical recognition of the importance of tolerance as a great virtue of a Buddhist king.

Institutional Segregation of the Nun and the Monk Orders

Thai rulers and Thai society in general have been recognised to hold good records in terms of religious and sexual tolerance. In comparison with certain periods in Western history, Thai society has been congenial to peoples of different ethnic background, religious differences, and non-conventional sexual orientations. The particular question of sexual tolerance on the part of the *sangha* has not been an issue. This is because historically there was never a female *sangha*. However, in the past decades, with increasing women's participation in education and in other professional fields, the issue of female ordination in Theravada Thailand has surfaced. Thai Theravada Buddhist institution cannot deny the fact that the Buddha allowed the establishment of a nun order (*bhikkhuni sangha*). However, conservative elements within and outside the *sangha* emphasise the reluctance of the Buddha, as he was recorded as refusing his aunt three times before finally agreeing to her wish to be ordained. Even after the permission, the Buddha laid down the Eight Heavy Rules (*Gurudhamma*) to regulate the institutional relationship between the nun and the monk orders. These rules indicate an 'institutional subordination' of the nun to the monk order.[14] These are the rules:[15]

1) A nun who has been ordained (even) for a century must greet respectfully, rise up from her seat, salute with joined palms, do proper homage to a monk ordained only that day.

---

[14] For a more detailed discussion of the decision of the Buddha to allow female ordination, see Suwanna Satha-Anand, 'Truth over convention: feminist interpretations of Buddhism', in Courtney Howland (ed.), *Religious Fundamentalisms and the Human Rights of Women*, New York: St. Martin Press, 1999, pp. 281–91.

[15] It is interesting to note that none of these rules would be an obstacle for women to practise *dhamma* in itself. Rather, they are rules to regulate the institutional relationship between the two Orders. See Chatsumarn Kabilsingh, *A Comparative Study of Bhikkhuni Patimokkha*, Varnasi: Chaukhambha Orientalia, 1984, pp. 22–3. The Pali version is in *Cullavagga 10.1.1–6* (translated in I. B. Horner, trans., *The Book of the Discipline (Vinaya-Pitaka)*, London: Pali Text Society, 1942.

2) A nun must not spend the rainy season in a residence where there is no monk.

3) Every half month a nun should desire two things from the Order of monks: the asking (as to the date) of the Observance day, and the coming for the exhortation.

4) After the rains a nun must appear before both the Orders in respect of three matters: what was seen, what was heard and what was suspected.[16]

5) A nun, offending against an important rule, must undergo *manatta* (discipline) for half a month before both the Orders.

6) When, as a probationer, she has been trained in the six rules for two years, she should seek ordination from both the Orders.

7) A monk must not be abused or reviled in any way by a nun.

8) From today admonition of monks by nuns is forbidden, admonition of nuns by monks is not forbidden.

It is important to note that none of these rules in itself would become an obstacle for women pursuing the spiritual path, their function is to regulate the institutional relationship between the two *sanghas*. It is quite obvious that these rules are ascribing 'gender' roles for those who have renounced the conventional world of the householder. To the extent that these rules lay down a pattern of behaviour with one sex deferring to the other without regard to years in ordination, merit of practice or other individually achievable qualities, we could say that these rules institute a form of institutional segregation among the monks, into male and female. We should not think only that as they are sexually different, namely male and female, therefore there is a need for the Eight Heavy Rules. We should also think that in ascribing gender roles between the two Orders, these rules are defining the Orders along sexual lines. However, paradoxically, this institutional segregation served as a condition for making it possible for women

---

[16] This Heavy Rule was instituted so that the nun *sangha* would be under the supervision of the monk *sangha*. At the beginning of each rain retreat, all monks are required to gather to announce a 'Pavarana', literally meaning 'permission'. This is a permission to give and to receive a warning or admonition to and from fellow monks, on matters of the *vinayas* or rules of conduct for those ordained. There are 227 rules for monks and 311 for nuns. This mutual admonition could be about something that one has seen by oneself, or about something one has heard, or about something one suspects a wrong has been committed. The monks must do this among themselves, while the nuns must do this twice, first among themselves, and then with the male *sangha*.

to be ordained. The possibility of ordination for women was a sign
that social segregation based on sex and caste was subverted. In other
words, the Eight Heavy Rules served as an indication that there was
sexual tolerance among those pursuing the Noble Path, a possibility
that was not available in the 'secular' world of the householder during
the time of the Buddha.

Apart from setting up the Eight Heavy Rules, the Buddha made
several analogies predicting that the life-span of his religion would
become shortened by half, once women were ordained. All these have
been used as 'evidence' by the conservative Thai *sangha* that the Buddha
did not 'really' wish women to be ordained. The accusing interrogation of Ananda in the First Council on the issue of female ordination
indicates the grudges the male *sangha* had against this particular decision of the Buddha.[17]

The Sangha *as a Middle Path, Boundaries-Crossing Alternative*

Buddhist scholars have put forward an observation that the Buddha
organised his followers into a '*sangha*', an ascetic community that is a
'middle path' between the two extremes of self-mortification (way of
ascetic austerities) and self-indulgence (way of secular life of householders). The *sangha* also served as a middle path between the individual
practitioner and the community as a form of collective co-existence.
The first 'Buddhist temples' were also a middle path between the
wilderness and the city.[18] This 'middle path' analysis of the *sangha* can
be seen as indicative of a practical implementation of the Buddhist
ontology of fluid boundaries, which avoids an essentialist conception
of identity, dichotomy and opposing extremes. The Buddhist monks
were different from many other groups of ascetics in their rejection
of self-mortification as a path to ultimate spiritual achievement. They
practised simple moderation in their daily living. They did not discard

---

[17] For a description of both issues, the prediction and the interrogation of Ananda
on female ordination, see Bunnun Charnnarong, 'Female ordination in Thai society',
Journal of Buddhist Studies, vol. 11, no. 2, 2004, pp. 81–96. Dr. Charnnarong also offers
an interesting analysis of both issues.

[18] For an interesting analysis of Buddhism as a civilisational force, see Robert
A. Thurman, 'Monasticism and civilization', in Yoshinori Takeuchi (ed.), *Buddhist
Spirituality: Indian, Southeast Asian, Tibetan, Early Chinese*, New York: Crossroad, 1995,
pp. 120–34.

city life by going to live in the deep forests or caves on a permanent basis. They had a fixed place to stay and yet they were given instructions to travel and spread the Buddhist teachings. They taught people of all castes, consciously disregarding the Hindu social segregation of the time.[19] The Buddhist principle of causation was an alternative explanation of how things, natural and conventional, have come to be. This was a tacit rejection of the Hindu myths of Brahma as the Lord and Creator of the Universe. The Hindu creation myth served to justify a system of social segregation based on caste. The mythical birth of each caste from the cosmic Body of Brahma was critically called into question by the Buddha.[20]

And yet as a form of human institution, the *sangha* as a collective community of religious individuals, needed to set up rules of practice. The Vinaya basket of the Buddhist Tripitaka testifies to the complex development of implementing a systematic 'way to the cessation of suffering.' The first principle of this particular community is to leave the life of a householder. Ordination as a ceremony which has to be performed within a prescribed boundary (*sima*) is indicative of a symbolically demarcated area wherein a 'crossing of life' is to take place. Ordination is the ceremony which expresses the practitioner's willingness and intention to pursue the Noble Path. In this sense, ordination, not birth or social status, was the basis of a new form of community, based on a distinction between the life of the householder and that of the monk. The fact that people from all castes were accepted into the *sangha* indicates the fluidity of social boundaries. The fact that the monks were grouped into a community different from that of the laity, indicated that a new mode of co-existence was taking place. The principle of hierarchy within the *sangha* was simply age, expressed in terms of seniority of ordination, not biological age. In this sense the *sangha* was a 'universal' institution where potentially anyone could be included. This is perhaps one of the greatest contributions of the Buddha in terms of institution building. According to a leading scholar of

---

[19] According to Professor Gombrich, from a research of 'plausible information' on a sample of over 300 monks and nuns, about 40% were Brahmin, 24% *ksatriya*, 32% *vaisya*, 2% *sudra*, 2% outcastes. This information might indicate that the first followers of the Buddha were people from the upper classes, but it also indicates that Buddhism was a religion which cut across social segregation of the time. See Richard Gombrich, *Theravada Buddhism*, London and New York: Routledge, 1988 p. 56.

[20] See Steven Collins, 'The discourse on what is primary (Agganna-sutta)', *Journal of Indian Philosophy*, vol. 21, 1993, pp. 301–93.

Buddhism, 'It [the *sangha*] was the first [transnational] institution to grant access to any sort of education to members of the castes who were outside the 'twice-born' elite of the Vedic religion, and actually formed the majority of the population.'[21]

Although theoretically speaking, anyone from any caste could join the *sangha*, in practice there are disqualification criteria for some people, who are forbidden ordination. Basically there are three categories of people who are not qualified to join the monkhood. First, those who have committed major crimes like murder, those who lack permission from their parents, those who are fugitives from the law, or those who are animals. Second, those who have certain physical deficiencies, such as dwarfs, those missing a limb, the blind, the deaf, those with boils or with leprosy. Third, those whose sexuality is deficient or aberrant. Janet Gyatso argues that in Buddhist monasticism, women were not only distinguished from men, who are their superiors and mentors; they were also differentiated from another class of persons, those who cannot receive ordination under any circumstances. This is included in the third category of persons who are excluded from ordination on the ground of their sex.[22] Although some of these disqualification criteria might provoke debates today, they could probably be reasonably accepted by the convention of the time. It is understandable that the Buddha, who had just founded a new religion, should set up rules of admission into the new community. As the monks had to rely on support from the laity, respect from the laity was a necessity. However, the big question came at some period in the first half decade after the establishment of the male *sangha*, when Mahapajapati, the Buddha's own foster-mother expressed her wish to be ordained.

At this point it is useful to draw a chart of the different demarcation lines in Buddhism in relation to ordination.

---

[21] Thurman, 'Monasticism and civilization', p. 129. The term 'transnational' is taken from the next sentence in the text and put in parenthesis here for brevity.

[22] Janet Gyatso, 'One plus one makes three: Buddhist gender, monasticism and the law of the non-excluded middle', *History of Religions*, vol. 43, no. 2, 2003, pp. 92–3. The author also brings to attention the groups of people who are excluded as a whole from a variety of Buddhist practices, not only from ordination. According to her, 'A variety of other monastic prescriptions also forbid the *pandaka* and related types from acting as preceptors in ordination ceremonies and even disqualify them making donations to begging monks....(They are, for example, heretics, hunters, magicians, dancers and pig farmers' (p. 98).

GROUP A
Ordination of people from all castes (Age and Sex as Principle of Hierarchy)
Ordination of women (Eight Heavy Rules as Intra-Institutional Regulation)

GROUP B
Disqualification for reasons of family, and state (No permission from family, fugitives from the law, not human)
Disqualification for physical reasons (Dwarfs, the blind, the deaf, those with leprosy)

Disqualification for reason of sex (*Pandaka*)
Disqualification for reason of wrong livelihood (Heretics, hunters, magicians, dancers, pig farmers)

It is interesting to note that Buddhist monasticism lays down qualification criteria for those who wish to join the *sangha*. Buddhism does not seem to be saying that the people in Group B cannot be lay Buddhists, but in order to qualify for ordination, an additional level of expectation is in place. It is important to note that most of the disqualifications are not permanent. One can change one's means of livelihood, one can persuade one's family for permission to ordain, one can serve one's term with the law and be free again. What is not clear is whether or not the people who are disqualified on the basis of sex or of physical disadvantage will be barred on a permanent basis.

As far as the fluidity of boundaries is concerned, it seems to be the case that Buddhism offers the best chance for spiritual transformation through ordination to male members from all castes. To women, Buddhism gives the second best chance to pursue the spiritual path and to cross social boundaries, including those of caste segregation. However, internal segregation was put in place within the *sanghas*.

A Re-thinking of the Buddha's Decision

In another paper, I have brought out the philosophical implications of a refusal to allow ordination for women.[23] Here, I would like to highlight the fact that it is of utmost importance to analyse this decision of the Buddha, together with the intra-institutional relationship laid down as a precondition for his permission. A well-rounded understanding of his

---

[23] See Satha-Anand, 'Truth over convention'.

decision is crucial for developing a ground for re-thinking the female ordination issue in any Theravada country.[24] Let us evaluate the arguments put forward by the traditionalists and the feminists. The former group would emphasise the following: the initial thrice refusals, the Eight Heavy Rules, and the prediction of a shortened life-span of the Buddhist religion. The latter group, on the other hand, would highlight the final decision to allow female ordination, the confirmation of women's equal potential to be enlightened, and the fact that the Eight Heavy Rules are not, in themselves, obstacles for women's religious practice.[25] The most difficult question here concerns the Eight Heavy Rules, as they do not only set down rules of deference based on sex, they also set up an institutional relationship of 'unequal' authority between the monk and the nun orders. It is clear that the institutional relationship between the two orders would be one of the monk 'supervising' the nun. This can be seen as establishing a hierarchy within the *sanghas* based on sexual distinction. The rules of the nun's deference to the monk take precedence over the principle of age (in terms of length of ordination), as evident in the first rule. According to Professor Gombrich, 'While the Buddha had a keen eye for what was merely social convention, so that he saw men of all *varnas* (castes) and classes as essentially equal, there were two social hierarchies he never questioned: age and sex. Even here, all were equal in their capacity for Enlightenment.'[26] This point needs to bring into consideration the fact the Buddha defined 'age' in terms of the 'first' who attained enlightenment by himself, and the length of ordination for others.[27] In this sense, 'age' for the Buddha

---

[24] Many of the publications by Venerable Dhammananda (Chatsumarn Kabilsingh) focus on the 'authentic' lineage of the Dhammagupta, which was originally transmitted from a Theravada tradition and therefore her own ordination would be 'legitimate' from within the Theravada tradition. This is very important as far as the ordination lineage is concerned. However, I think that a well-informed and fair-minded analysis of the Buddha's decision, would be crucial for an 'understanding' of this complex situation, even during the time of the Buddha. This understanding could serve as a basis for consideration of this issue in contemporary situation.

[25] For a survey of the arguments put forward by both traditionalists and feminists in Thai Buddhism, see Charnnarong, 'Female Ordination in Thai Society'.

[26] See Gombrich, *Theravada Buddhism*, p. 105.

[27] See the first book of the Vinaya Pitaka, whose opening passages contain an argument between an 'older' Brahmin and the Buddha about 'who' should be paying respect to whom. See also the reasoning put forth in the answer from the Buddha in Suwanna Satha-Anand, *Faith and Wisdom: A Philosophical Dialogue on Religion*, Bangkok: Chulalongkorn University Press, 2002, pp. 17–39.

was not a form of social convention, but implied a sense of proximity to enlightenment. The question of sex is more complicated.

Professor Gombrich explains further:

> A great many nuns have testimony that they attained Enlightenment; and the tradition that no woman could become a Buddha is not in the Canon. But when it came to social relations, even within the *Sangha*, age and male gender had precedence. (There is a slight difference, in that age was reckoned from ordination not birth, so it was really seniority, *whereas gender is of course absolute*.)[28]

It is difficult to decide which of the two terms is more curious: 'of course' or 'absolute'. When they are put together with such confidence, an explanation is in order. These two terms are used in context of explaining a condition of gender relations 'within' the *sanghas*. The question is why there was a need to establish a segregation within the *sanghas* based on sex? Why was there a necessity to introduce the Eight Heavy Rules to regulate relations between these two groups of ascetics? We need to put into consideration the fact that the Buddha was allowing women to 'cross over' the boundary between the realm of the householder and the realm of the ordained. This was an act of 'de-absolutising' social convention of the time, when women's religious role was embedded exclusively within the family. One of the analogies in the Buddha's prediction is the image of a dam withholding overflow of water into the river. This analogy can be seen as indicative of the precaution against too many women wishing to 'cross over' the lay/sacred boundaries. However, once this 'gate' was open, the internal segregation was devised as a gesture of compromise, not only with the male *sangha*, but also with the social world of the householder. It is important to point out here that this gender segregation created an opportunity for women to enter on the path of ordination. In other words, the gender segregation within the *sanghas* was a necessary condition to overcome sexual discrimination against women in the social world. In order to respect women's rights to the ultimate religious practice, namely ordination, it seemed necessary for the Buddha to create an institutional form of gender segregation within the *sanghas*. In this sense, the religious tolerance necessary for women to cross the threshold of ordination must operate in circumstances of gender segregation within the *sanghas*.

---

[28] See Gombrich, *Theravada Buddhism*, p. 105 (italics added).

It is interesting to investigate to what extent the insistence of Mahapajapati was instrumental in the Buddha's decision. According to the *sutta*, Mahapajapati asked for ordination three times during the Buddha's visit to his town of Kapilavatthu. The three requests were denied. She and hundreds of other royal women then shaved their heads, put on the yellow robe, and followed the Buddha to Vesali. Once they had reached the entrance of the place where the Buddha was staying, they stopped. The *sutta* describes their comportment as with swollen feet, dirty and crying. Ananda saw them in such distress and asked for the reasons. He then took on the task of asking the Buddha himself. Ananda posed two questions, one relating to the potential of women to become enlightened if allowed ordination, the other citing the fact that Mahapajapati had nursed him as a child. The Buddha answered in the affirmative to the first question, and he recognised his debt of gratitude to Mahapajapati. A Thai scholar has pointed out that both for *dhammic* reason and for reason of convention, the Buddha allowed female ordination.[29]

The point is not to argue here about the 'real' motive of Mahapajapati, whether she had real faith in the Noble Path or whether she did not wish to be a widow in the world of the householder. I think it is more important to see her series of actions as a process of 'boundaries-crossing'. First, she repeatedly asked for ordination. After having been denied three times, she changed her strategy. She performed the act of ordination on her own, by shaving her head and putting on the yellow robe. Then, together with other royal women, she walked barefoot to another city to seek an audience with the Buddha. Once at the entrance, she stopped and did not proceed further. Mahapajapati had crossed several boundaries. She crossed a boundary in demonstrating her wish not to continue the life of a householder. She symbolically crossed the boundary of ordination by shaving her head and putting on the yellow robe. She crossed the boundary of a court lady by walking

---

[29] See Charnnarong, 'Female ordination', p. 82. In my paper cited in footnote 14, I have argued that the ultimate truth should overrule truth of convention in analysing the decision of the Buddha. In light of Dr. Charnnarong's article, I would like to refine my position by stating that from this particular angle the reason of convention could be meaningful as well. However, I would confirm the general framework of the original analysis. For a more detailed analysis of the events leading to the decision of the Buddha, see Kabilsingh, *A Comparative Study of Bhikkhuni Patimokkha*, pp. 21–37.

barefoot to another city. All these acts of boundaries-crossing would indicate to the Buddha her strong intention to pursue the path of ordination. And yet, she also knew when and where to stop. This does not only show her great intention to proceed to ordination, it also showed her proper judgement of what was the limit. We can imagine what would have happened if she, together with other royal women, had decided to enter the monks' abode. And what would have happened had they been spotted first by other monks, not Ananda? The transgression of the *sangha*'s boundary would be too radical and could prove self-defeating for her purpose. Mahapajapati knew that.

The Eight Heavy Rules and Sexual Tolerance

One hypothetical question could be illuminating here. What if the social world at the time of the Buddha had been matriarchal rather than patriarchal? Would there have been a need for the Eight Heavy Rules? What if the social world had changed and shown greater respect for women's autonomy and freedom to pursuit their highest spiritual goal? How should we take on the Eight Heavy Rules in the twenty-first century, more than 2,500 years after its origin?

Of course, as Buddhists, we cannot just change any rules to serve our purposes at our convenience. And yet, in order to 'transmit' a tradition, and not to 'fossilise' it, how can we learn to respect a tradition while working for its flourishing in the present and into the future? This is a highly complex question, which needs fuller treatment at another occasion. For our purpose here, I propose a reorientation of concerns. In other words, instead of putting the rules above all other considerations, let us first use our 'concerned judgement', create a forum for open discussion, and then adjust the rules to nurture spiritual life in the present environment. Before we go further, I would like to argue that this proposal for a reorientation of concerns is an approach that follows the instruction expressed by the Buddha himself. One of the Buddha's last instructions for his followers was to give the monks permission to abolish the lesser and minor rules and all they entailed, according to their own judgement. After the Buddha's death, some details would be difficult to understand and might be considered petty. As a guarantee that at least the main rules would be followed, the assembly of monks might decree that minor rules would no longer be binding. Whoever wanted, could keep them, but there would be no compulsion any more.[30]

It is interesting to note that in the First Council, convened some three months after the death of the Buddha, one of the major interrogation points put forth by the Council members for Ananda, was whether Ananda had asked the Buddha what the minor rules were. When Ananda said he had not, it looked as if Ananda was at fault for not asking such an important question. However, if we use the principle of concerned judgement, we could pose questions from different angles. Did the question put forward in the First Council express the main concern of the Buddha on how his followers would deal with changing situations after he was gone? I would like to propose that the question put forward in the First Council was actually misdirected. This is because the main concern in the Buddha's last instruction could be that he was delegating the power of judgement to the *sangha*. This suggests that the concerned judgement of the *sangha* as a whole should be the 'refuge' for deciding what to do and what not to do in the future. However, the emphasis of the interrogation in the First Council was placed on the question whether Ananda had asked the Buddha what the minor rules were.[31] Even if Ananda had asked the Buddha what the minor rules were, this would not have solved the problem for the *sangha* in the future, as it is not beyond imagination that, as the religion developed and expanded, unforeseeable circumstances would arise and the 'concerned judgement' of the *sangha* would be needed. In this sense, Ananda was not 'wrong' in not asking what the minor rules were. The crucial issue for a flourishing future of the religion is the cultivation of the concerned judgement of the *sangha*, not a question of what minor rules are to be changed. Given this analysis, I would argue that a principle of using 'concerned judgement' is in line with the Buddha's last instruction to his followers. It is also in line with the reasons given by the Buddha every time a *vinaya* rule was set up, and how and why some of the *vinaya* rules needed to be adjusted.

---

[30] For a succinct summary of the last instructions by the Buddha to his followers through Ananda, see Hellmuth Hecker, *Ananda: The Guardian of the Dhamma* (translated from German by Sister Khema), Kandy, Sri Lanka: Buddhist Publication Society, 1980, p. 64.

[31] For a good discussion of the *bhikkhuni* issue in the First Council, see Charnnarong, 'Female ordination in Thai society', pp. 86–9. See also Department of Religious Affairs, Ministry of Education, *The Tripitaka* (Royal Thai Version), vol. 7, Bangkok: Religious Affairs Publishing, B.E. 2514 (1971).

Our next step is to address how to apply this 'Principle of Concerned Judgement' to the case of re-establishing the female monk order in present-day Theravada Thailand.

First, let us consider the attitude of the secular society regarding women. With the growing number of women in education and in all professional fields, it is important to note that the question of women's equality with men will be a decisive factor for a healthy future of Buddhism in this century. This is highly pertinent because, according to a recent survey, women in Thailand enjoy the highest socio-economic levels, beating women from twelve other Asia-Pacific nations, including Australia and Japan.[32] Thai women have traditionally played a strong supporting role for monks. Now many of the educated women would wish to develop a form of Buddhism that recognises greater roles for their own spiritual potential.

Second, given the above analysis regarding the Buddhist ontology of difference, the institutional reasons for the Eight Heavy Rules, and the principle of concerned judgement as a guiding principle for Buddhist discernment, we can see that the Eight Heavy Rules were not meant to be set in stone; they were instituted to provide an ordination opportunity for women, not to prevent that very possibility for women.[33] The refusal to discuss the possibility would be tantamount to letting historical contingency, namely the dying out of the *bhikkhuni* lineage in Sri Lanka in the eleventh century, overrule the permission of the Buddha.

Third, if we accept the argument that the Eight Heavy Rules are putting the nun order under the supervision of the monks, we could further argue that it could be the male monk order's responsibility to provide a congenial environment for women to practise the spiritual path. If compassion is the most important virtue in Buddhist ethics, why not practise it for the other half of humanity, many of whom wish to enter ordination?

---

[32] See *The Bangkok Post*, Tuesday, 8 March, 2005, front page. The headline reads: 'Thai women do better than others'. However, a column by Sanitsuda Ekachai strikes a note of caution and highlights the vast discrepancies of pay level and representation between men and women in the workforce and in national politics. See Sanitsuda Ekachai, 'Things don't seem all that wonderful', *The Bangkok Post*, 10 March, 2005, p. 11.

[33] For an argument to refuse the possibility, based on the prioritisation of rules over concerned judgement, see Phra Dhammapitaka, *The Buddhist Attitude toward Women and the Bhikkhuni Ordination*, Bangkok: Sukhapabjai Publisher, B.E. 2544 (2001). As Phra Dhammapitaka is the leading scholar monk of Thai society, his position is probably widely accepted by most monks and perhaps many lay people. However, his position might not be readily accepted by the increasing number of educated women in Thailand.

Fourth, if our analysis in terms of the crossing of boundaries is tenable, it means that ordination, as a form of boundary-change, is meant to provide an alternative to existing forms of social segregation based on caste. Once women are ordained, this also provides an alternative to existing forms of social segregation based on sex. In this sense, to deny the re-establishment of female ordination in present-day Thai Buddhism, is to reconfirm existing forms of social convention. Rather, the role of the *sangha* as a Buddhist institution in this regard should be to lead society closer to the Buddhist goal, namely the possibility of ordination for women.

Concluding Remarks

I have argued in this paper that the Eight Heavy Rules must be understood within the framework of seeing ordination as a form of 'boundary setting' to overcome existing forms of boundaries in the Hindu cultural world. However, during the first years of the newly established *sangha*, the Buddha saw the necessity to establish gender segregation between the two *sanghas*, both as a compromise with the social world and also with his own *sangha*. We have seen that the social world in Thailand has changed over the centuries, and it is not unreasonable to see that the necessity to compromise has decreased in most societies, or ceased to exist in others. The major problem seems to lie with the Thai Theravada *sangha*.[34] In order to respect the principle of sexual tolerance, the Thai *sangha* needs to reconsider the issue of female ordination. In that process, it is crucial to rethink the contextual significance of the Eight Heavy Rules. A process of using 'concerned judgement' would be more in line with the philosophy and practice of the Buddha than just adhering to rules for their own sake. What is at stake is not only the issue of female ordination in Buddhism, but also the authoritative credibility of the *sangha* as the 'highest' Buddhist institution in the contemporary world.

---

[34] It is interesting to note that certain elements in the Theravada *sangha* in Sri Lanka have been supportive of female ordination. An ordination ceremony has been held for many aspiring women, including Venerable Dhammananda of Thailand, who was ordained there in 2002. A few monks in Thailand who have voiced support for the women have received severe criticism from the more conservative *sangha* members.

FLUID BOUNDARIES, INSTITUTIONAL SEGREGATION AND BUDDHIST SEXUAL TOLERANCE: A RESPONSE (I)

Ursula King

I greatly appreciate the invitation to respond to Professor Suwanna Satha-Anand from Thailand, which is a great honour.

The 'Boundaries and Segregations' theme was initially introduced by the organisers of the IAHR Congress with the statement that 'Religions offer epistemological schemes to understand, evaluate, and order objects, events, and humans in the world. Drawing clear lines between 'us' and 'others', inner and outer groups, etc. is one important function religion may assume.' Among the examples given is a reference to the universalist claim of human rights, and also a mention of the fact that religions 'have often recognised the importance of particular distinctions among humankind, for example those of men and women, and as a result legitimised certain forms of discrimination'. It is with the latter issues that Professor Satha-Anand's paper is particularly concerned in her discussion of Thai Buddhism, and the differences between the monks and nuns of the Theravada Buddhist *sangha*.

I certainly agree with the words 'Fluid Boundaries' in the title of the paper. Although religious traditions have treated boundaries of religious teachings and practices often as well-established and stable, boundaries have usually been far from static, and have remained open to the possibility of subtle changes. All boundaries originated at some time in the past; they have evolved and developed in different ways, as is clear from the development of Buddhism within the different cultures of Asia, from south to north to east Asia. But once well established, boundaries are often regarded as delineating firm and undisputed territories that cannot be easily changed. This attitude is found among religious practitioners and teachers alike; what is more, this tendency has been further enhanced by scholars of religion who, through modern scholarship, have clearly articulated, highlighted or reinforced and strengthened existing boundaries or even created new ones. This can be shown in many fields of the study of religion, from definitional issues to methodological debates, and it applies to the conceptualisation of entire religious traditions such as Buddhism, Hinduism, Judaism or new religious movements (NRM)—to name just a few examples. The existence of boundaries and the segregating out of different elements is also clearly present in the embedded gender dynamic of different religious traditions, as Professor Satha-Anand has shown for Theravada Buddhism. My response will bear first on particular points of her paper, and then I will comment in a more general way on important issues in the study of religion and gender.

Particular Points Raised by the Paper

Professor Satha-Anand uses the methods of philosophical analysis to show how Buddhist ontology, ethics, and the understanding of temporality provide strong grounds for cultivating tolerance at the theoretical level, but how in practice there exists a lack of religious tolerance among the Thai *sangha*, the state and society. In the second part of her paper the institutional segregation of the Buddhist male and female *sangha* is discussed. To speak of 'the male and female monk orders', as Satha-Anand does, may sound somewhat misleading in English since 'monks' are usually male. I would prefer to say either 'monks and nuns'[1] or to speak of 'male and female ascetic communities'. The *Gurudhamma* of the nuns or the 'Eight Heavy Rules' are cited as markers of difference; these indicate 'institutional subordination' of nuns to monks. However, it is then argued that the institutional segregation, which was required by these Rules, was the very condition for the ordination of women as *bhikkhunis* coming into being, and that sexual tolerance was exercised through this segregation since the social segregation of sex and caste that pertained in Thai society at the time of founding the *sangha* was being subverted. I much valued the detailed discussion of the *sangha* as a middle path of 'boundaries-crossing alternatives' between different alternative forms of living. The 'fluidity of boundaries' within the emerging Buddhist *sangha* is certainly very well demonstrated by the examples given in Professor Satha-Anand's paper.

---

[1] 'Nuns' is used as a general phenomenological category for women ascetics here, as I have explained in my entry on this term in the *Encyclopedia of Religion* (2nd edn. (Lindsay Jones, editor-in-chief), New York/London/Munich: Macmillan Reference USA [Thomson Gale]: 2005, 15 volumes; further citations to this publication will be referenced as *EOR*; see 'Nuns: an overview', *EOR* X: 6756–9. (First edition by Mircea Eliade, 1987).

In the following section of her paper Professor Satha-Anand raises important questions under the title of 'A Re-thinking of the Buddha's Decision' to found a female *sangha* at all. Hermeneutically she argues for a reorientation of concerns about the original instructions expressed by the Buddha himself. Instead of placing the Eight Heavy Rules above all else and consider them the ultimate basis for action, she pleads for the use of what she calls 'concerned judgement', the creation of a forum for open discussion, and recommends then to 'adjust the rules to nurture spiritual life in the present environment'. This seems to me an absolutely decisive move if one is concerned with 'a flourishing future of the religion'. Far from only being applicable to the Buddhist situation, I would argue that this is an issue which concerns all religious traditions, for it relates to their viability and credibility in the contemporary world, but more than that, it articulates the need to nourish spiritual life and provide the most suitable conditions for its development, in this case particularly the development of spiritual life and the dedication to the highest spiritual ideals among women—in this case Thai women who aspire to full ordination.

Thus Professor Satha-Anand argues for the re-establishment of the ordination possibility for Thai women and points out in her conclusion that more is at stake than just female ordination—the issue is much wider than this since it calls into question the 'authoritative credibility of the *sangha* as a 'highest' Buddhist institution in the contemporary world'. I would add that given our belief in equality and human rights, women are called to aim for the highest spiritual and institutional attainments in the same way that men are. This contemporary position is by no means unique to Buddhism but, under different conditions, the same arguments are put forward in other religious traditions for women to have their share in living, teaching, and practising the ideals of their faith. Numerous examples could be given from Hinduism, Judaism, Islam and Christianity—as well as other traditions—to substantiate this point.

Professor Satha-Anand's paper provides excellent evidence of the existing contradictions between the ethical and philosophical framework of fluid boundaries and greatly valued tolerance within the teaching of Buddhism, while at the same time the practical intolerance and the segregation of different groups in society is strictly maintained in spite of these theoretically fluid boundaries. It is in international conferences such as this IAHR Congress that such contradictions can be fully highlighted and critiqued, and that scholars studying different religious traditions can compare the similarity and parallels of contradictory and unjust gender issues in different religions. At a practical level, however, much social and political will for transformative action and a close examination of the existing power imbalances are needed to put egalitarian gender ideals into practice. In practical terms religious institutions around the world often lag considerably behind new gender developments in contemporary society at large.

General Remarks

This brings me to some more general remarks on the importance of analysing gender boundaries and segregations in different religions, whether at the scriptural, doctrinal, ritual or institutional level. To begin with, two important issues need to be made clear. First, 'gender' is not simply a synonym for 'women', as is often thought, but it is a category that applies to both men and women, the nature of their relationship, and their understanding of each other. Second, gender issues are an international, not a merely Western, concern and are now attended to at a global level. Critical and constructive gender analysis is important for three reasons:

1. the articulation of new research questions about gender similarities and differences is new in the history of human consciousness and culture;
2. together with other new developments (such as the study of human rights, for example) critical-analytical gender perspectives represent a significant paradigm shift in the contemporary study of religion;
3. the results of critical gender analysis have strong implications for all religions as studied and practised. This means that in a newly emerging multiform planetary civilisation, which is now evolving on our globe, all religious traditions will be affected by critical gender analysis and will therefore face the task of renegotiating their institutional and any other boundaries in new ways.

It is impossible in this short response to probe these different possibilities by examining all the necessary details; in any case, this would require the concerted effort of numerous scholars who are specialised in the study of different religions while being united in their trans-disciplinary effort of applying innovative critical gender perspectives to their respective data. It is a truly collaborative effort of international dimensions.

Gender studies have arrived rather later in the study of religions than in most other academic disciplines, and there are still many publications which make no reference to it at all.[2] In the present context concerned with Thai Buddhism, a telling example is provided by a study on *The Sociology of Early Buddhism*[3] which makes no reference whatsoever to *bhikkunis* or Buddhist women; only 'the Holy Man' is studied, as if women had never been part of the Buddhist *sangha*. Buddhist nuns and lay women still remain a largely forgotten part of Buddhist history.

It is gratifying, by contrast, to see that the voluminous overview on *New Approaches to the Study of Religion*, edited by Peter Antes, Armin W. Geertz and Randi R. Warne,[4] contain under their section on 'Critical Approaches' in Volume I a perceptive and balanced account on 'Gendering the History of Religions' by the Norwegian woman scholar Lisbeth Mikaelsson.[5] This article begins with the laconic statement, 'The concept of gender points to culturally produced differences between men and women', and helpfully points out that gender has the merit of being 'an open and *unbounded* category, inviting many types of analytical perspectives'(my emphasis).[6]

I am largely in agreement with Mikaelsson's arguments and cannot enter into a discussion here on where I disagree with her approach, but I certainly endorse her conclusion when she writes:[7]

> One can hardly say that feminist perspectives have become a common horizon in the history of religion, but one may safely declare that gender is on its way to being established as a fundamental category of analysis and an integrated topic in many areas of research. If wide-ranging gender analyses still are few in number, it is increasingly being recognized that gender and religion is a field inviting a host of vital questions.

---

[2] See e.g. the large historical study edited by Gerard A. Wiegers in association with Jan G. Platvoet, *Modern Societies and the Science of Religions: Studies in Honour of Lammert Leertouwer*, Leiden: Brill, 2002. Although a *Festschrift* honouring an eminent Dutch scholar, this volume aims to provide a survey of the study of religion in Europe, North America, Middle East, Africa, and Asia. Given this geographically almost global outreach, it seems all the more surprising that there is no reference to women's, feminist or gender studies in religion at all!

[3] Greg Bailey and Ian Mabett (eds.), *The Sociology of Early Buddhism*, Cambridge University Press, 2003.

[4] Peter Antes, Armin W. Geertz and Randi R. Warne (eds.), *New Approaches to the Study of Religion*, Berlin and New York: Walter de Gruyter, 2004, Vol. I: *Regional, Critical, and Historical Approaches*; Vol. II: *Textual, Comparative, Sociological, and Cognitive Approaches*.

[5] Lisbeth Mikaelsson, 'Gendering the history of religions', in Antes et al., *New Approaches to the Study of Religion*, Vol. I, pp. 295–315, which includes a wide-ranging bibliography.

[6] Ibid., pp. 297–8.

[7] Ibid., p. 311.

Equally important is Mikaelsson's emphasis on the pluralism of epistemological and methodological approaches found in contemporary
gender studies in religion, so that these may be 'woman-centered,
man-centered, inclusive of both genders, or be more comprehensive,
investigating the wide ramifications of engenderment and polysemic
meaning construction in different types of religious and social phenomena'.[8] Nowhere is this great richness and pluralistic diversity of
scholarly approaches to gender and religion better illustrated than in
the numerous and amazingly wide-ranging contributions to the revised,
second edition of the *Encyclopedia of Religion* published in 2005.[9] The
composite entry on 'Gender and Religion' alone, consisting of 21
parts and dealing with nineteen different religious traditions presented
by as many different scholars,[10] covers 125 pages of the *Encyclopedia*.
This reflects the tremendous growth of scholarship in the last fifteen
years since this important reference work was first published under the
editorship of Mircea Eliade in 1987. The composite entry on 'Gender
and Religion'[11] is given special mention in the new Preface of the
Encyclopedia as the largest new addition to the entire work,[12] reflecting
the international emergence of a new field. May I be permitted to
mention that the Chair of our session, Professor Noriko Kawahashi, has
contributed the entry on 'Gender and Japanese Religions',[13] but there
will be quite a few other contributors present at this IAHR Congress,
especially when taking into account the many additional entries relating
to gender issues in religion.

Gender issues relating to religion are ubiquitous, and gender boundaries and segregations can be found within and across all different
religions. But religion and gender are not simply two analogues existing side by side; they are mutually embedded within each other across
different religion and cultures. This *embeddedness* means that gender is
initially difficult to separate out from other aspects of religion until one
consciously takes what the Canadian scholar Randi Warne has so aptly

---

[8] Ibid.

[9] See note 1 for publication details.

[10] Altogether, twenty religious traditions are examined with regard to gender in
the *EOR*, but the entry on 'Gender and African American Religions' is found in *EOR*
XV, pp. 10036–41.

[11] *EOR* V, pp. 3295–3420.

[12] See *EOR* I, p. xiv.

[13] Noriko Kawahashi, 'Gender and Japanese religions', *EOR* V, pp. 3345–50.

called 'making the gender-critical turn'.[14] It involves effort and agency, for its significance has to be recognised, and a new critical awareness has to be intentionally developed since gender-critical thinking is neither 'natural' in the current social context nor has it been historically available before the modern era.

The relationship between gender and religion is made more complex still through the presence of diversity, an additional factor of which our postmodern sensitivity has become so much more aware. Diversity is understood as 'otherness'. There is the multiple 'otherness' of religious differences within and across specific cultures; there is the 'otherness' of diverse methods and approaches in understanding such differences; there is the 'otherness' of one gender for another, especially the 'otherness' of women for men, as traditionally understood, and also the 'otherness' of race, class, and sexual orientation. The social and political violence exercised by the West towards the 'otherness' of 'non-Western' cultures, whether defined as imperialism, Orientalism or neo-colonialism, has now come under fierce criticism. This critique applies also to the 'epistemological violence' often practised by Western scholars when writing about cultures and religions other than their own. Some of these issues are examined in more detail by the anthropologist and co-respondent to this plenary paper, Professor Masakazu Tanaka, in his introduction on 'Writing on Gender, Sexuality and Religion in South Asia' to a book specially devoted to the study of Hindu traditions, edited by him and Musashi Tachikawa.[15] From a different perspective they are also raised in the volume on *Gender, Religion and Diversity* edited by Tina Beattie and myself, which includes wide-ranging discussions on gender, identity, race, culture and religious traditions with a special emphasis on research methodologies.[16] The great diversity and international

---

[14] Randi R. Warne, 'Making the gender-critical turn', in Tim Jensen and Mikael Rothstein (eds.), *Secular Theories on Religion: Current Perspectives*, Copenhagen University: Museum Tusculanum Press, 2000, pp. 249–60.

[15] See Masakazu Tanaka and Musashi Tachikawa (eds.), *Living with Sakti: Gender, Sexuality and Religion in South Asia*, Osaka: National Museum of Ethnology, 1999.

[16] See Ursula King and Tina Beattie (eds.), *Gender, Religion and Diversity: Cross-Cultural Perspectives*, London and New York: Continuum, 2004 (Paperback edition 2005). To mention just a few examples of the wide-ranging topics covered by the international contributors to this volume: Ch. 2: Morny Joy, 'Postcolonial and gendered reflections: challenges for Religious Studies'; Ch. 6: Mary Keller, 'Raced and gendered perspectives: towards the epidermalization of subjectivity in Religious Studies theory'; Ch. 9: Gulnar Eleanor Francis-Dehqani, 'The gendering of missionary imperialism: the search for an integrated methodology'; Ch. 13: Anne Sofie Roald, 'Who are the Muslims? Questions

dimension of contemporary gender research is also evident from several panels organised during this IAHR Congress. Without any attempt to provide a comprehensive list here, I only mention as examples such panels as 'Religion and Gender in Korea and Japan'; 'Gender in Buddhism'; 'Religion and Gender in an African Globalizing Context'; 'Christianity and Gender Relations in Japan'.

Many instances could be cited that indicate the current shifting of boundaries within the field of gender and religion. Professor Satha-Anand's paper is just such an example illuminating the underlying, often hidden, gender patterns representing the deep structures of religious life, the boundaries and segregations, which need to be historically excavated and analytically traced in all religions. This is only possible by closely researching foundational texts and investigating the history of powerful institutions with long established lines of authority. This challenging intellectual task cannot be accomplished without tremendous effort, but it can also have shattering implications for religious life and consciousness. Research into gender boundaries and segregations within different religious traditions shows clearly the versatile, fluid nature of the diverse methods used in current studies of religion and gender. But these issues also demonstrate that while methodological questions are an important academic concern for ensuring high quality scholarship and the advancement of knowledge, gender questions *cannot be entirely contained* within academic fields of enquiry but spill over into practical life. It is here that I most strongly disagree with a statement made in Lisbeth Mikaelsson's paper 'Gendering the History of Religions'[17] where she argues against my plea for a 'participatory hermeneutics' and a 'more empathetic involvement and personal concern in relation to one's studies'.[18] She reads this merely as an understandable 'enthusiasm' that is 'problematic', a mingling of 'one's scholarly, religious or existential concerns' which abdicates some of the traditional scholarly standards of theory and methodology (however these may be defined!) and goes on asking whether 'emphasis on researchers' religious subjectivity and demands for major changes in religion have worked against a general

---

of identity, gender and culture in research methodologies'; Ch. 14: Paul Reid-Bowen, 'Reflexive transformations: research comments on me(n), feminist philosophy and the thealogical imagination'; Ch. 18: Sharon Bong, 'An Asian postcolonial and feminist methodology: ethics as a recognition of limits'.

[17] See footnote 5; the quotations are from p. 310.

[18] See Ursula King, *Religion and Gender*, Oxford, UK and Cambridge, USA: Blackwell, 1995.

feminist paradigm shift in the discipline'. This observation invites further debate which cannot be pursued here, but I still wish to maintain that practical engagements with contemporary gender issues in religion are enormously important and must not be ignored by scholars, for they can truly make a difference to people's lives. Such engagement may express itself in a variety of ways, whether by working for greater sexual equality and tolerance, for the re-establishment of the full ordination of Buddhist nuns in Theravada countries, or engaging in political activism, in 'dialogue among civilisations', in inter-religious dialogue, in the search for eco-justice, social justice, and human rights, or getting involved in more gender-balanced appointment policies in the academy.

Some of the best and most innovative contemporary scholarship on gender and religion is precisely so challenging because it combines in such a creative way the rigorous canons of scholarship with engaged commitment and practical advocacy. Many examples could be given in support of this statement—and the rich entries on gender and religion in different religious traditions found in the second edition of the *Encyclopedia of Religion* provide ample evidence, on such a scale that the point hardly needs arguing any more.

I also want to make explicit reference to three recent Japanese examples, given that this Congress is meeting in Japan. These are the special number of the *Japanese Journal of Religious Studies*, devoted to 'Feminism and religion in contemporary Japan', with excellent contributions on very different research topics by mostly Japanese scholars, edited by Noriko Kawahashi and Masako Kuroki.[19] Last year, these two scholars also published a volume entitled *Mixed Graces: Religion and Feminism in a Post-colonial Age*,[20] which is written in Japanese and therefore one would hope to see it widely read in Japan. Yet another example is the volume on *Women and Religion*, based on an international symposium co-sponsored by Tenri Yamato Culture Congress and The

---

[19] See *Japanese Journal of Religious Studies*, vol. 30, nos. 3–4 (Fall 2003) for more information on the application of feminist perspectives to research on Japanese religions. See also the review article by Noriko Kawahashi, 'Religion, gender, and Okinawan studies', in *Asian Folklore Studies*, vol. 59, 2000, pp. 301–11. The same author has also published 'Folk religion and its contemporary issues', in Jennifer Robertson (ed.), *A Companion to the Anthropology of Japan*, Malden, MA/Oxford/Victoria, Australia: Blackwell Publishing, 2005, pp. 452–65, and 'Gender issues in Japanese religions', in Paul L. Swanson and Clark Chilson (eds.), *Nanzan Guide to Japanese Religions*, Honolulu: University of Hawaï Press, 2005, pp. 323–35.

[20] Noriko Kawahashi and Masako Kuroki (eds.), *Konzaisuru Megumi* (Mixed Graces: Religion and Feminism in a Post-colonial Age), Kyoto: Jinbunshoin, 2004.

Center for Women and Religion at the Graduate Theological Union at Berkeley University, California, organised in commemoration of the 200th birth-day of Oyasama, the foundress of Tenrikyo.[21] This book deals not only with women and men in Japanese religions but also looks at Korean new religions, at Hinduism, Islam and Christianity. In his brief reflections on several essays in this particular volume Professor Shimazono, President of the Japanese Association for Religious Studies, listed among his points the 'liberation of femininity from the historical oppression, or restoration of the humanity of women', an important feminist principle in the contemporary study of religions. He also pointed out the 'many-facedness of femininity', and the need to distinguish between the abstract ideas about women in religion as distinct from 'how those ideas are being realized in actual social lives'.[22] This is a very important point relating to a necessary distinction which is not always sufficiently noticed, but it is also a distinction which invites active engagement on the level of social and religious practice, once the abstract ideas about gender differences and boundaries have been analysed with more critical insight and discernment.

A striking example of the innovative processes of the contemporary 'gendering of religions' within Buddhism is Sakyadhita: International Association of Buddhist Women', a globally active network of Buddhist nuns and lay women that seeks to achieve both intellectual and practical transformations for women in Buddhist societies. This global Buddhist women's movement was founded in 1987 in Bodhgaya by and for Buddhist nuns and lay women in East and West. Its fourfold aims are:

1. to create a global network of communication among Buddhist women;
2. to educate women as teachers of Buddhism;
3. to conduct research on women in Buddhism;
4. to work for the establishment of the *Bhikkhuni sangha.*

So far, Sakyadhita has organised seven international conferences in different Asian countries, with the last one being organised in Malaysia in June 2006. Much effort goes into education and the reinterpretation of texts, but also into reforming unjust, non-egalitarian practices and

---

[21] *Women and Religion*, Tenri Yamato Culture Congress, 2003.
[22] Ibid., pp. 97–8.

into the development of socially engaged Buddhism, as the issues for Buddhist women in Asia are different from those of Buddhist women in the West. The clearly articulated aims show how social, religious and scholarly aims can be fruitfully combined.

The president of Sakyadhita, the Venerable Karma Lekshe Tsomo, an American Buddhist nun ordained in the Tibetan tradition, has edited the papers given at different Sakyadhita conferences in a series of volumes, entitled *Sakyadhita: Daughters of the Buddha* (1988),[23] *Buddhist Women Across Cultures: Realizations* (1999),[24] *Innovative Buddhist Women: Swimming Against the Stream* (2000),[25] and *Buddhist Women and Social Justice* (2004).[26] Although by no means an uncontroversial figure, Lekshe Tsomo perceives the Buddhist women's movement as 'Mahaprajapati's legacy',[27] that is, the legacy of the Buddha's aunt who, as the first nun in Buddhism, began the *Bhikkuni sangha*. Now that gender equality has become part of the demand for a new global ethic, the question is how can the Buddhist tradition be re-envisioned along egalitarian lines? Lekshe Tsomo argues that women's traditional roles in Buddhist cultures have been changed without any direct link to the women's movement in the West, and that these changes are virtually unknown to outsiders. But on closer examination it becomes clear that considerable parallels exist between Asian Buddhist women's and Western feminists' efforts in re-reading, re-conceiving and re-constructing foundational religious texts and other sources to recover women's voices and histories.

In most, although not all, Asian countries the number of Buddhist nuns is less than that of monks. In Taiwan, however, there are two thirds more nuns than monks; Korea also knows a large number of nuns whose experiences, like those of other nuns, have rarely been recorded in Buddhist texts nor have they been much investigated by scholars. This is changing now that Buddhist women have organised themselves to study their own history and activities, whether as members of Sakyadhita or

---

[23] Karma Lekshe Tsomo (ed.), *Sakyadhita: Daughters of the Buddha*, Ithaca, NY: Snow Lion Publications, 1988.

[24] Ibid. (ed.), *Buddhist Women Across Cultures: Realizations*, Albany, NY: State University of New York Press, 1999.

[25] Ibid. (ed.), *Innovative Buddhist Women: Swimming Against the Stream*, Richmond, Surrey: Curzon Press, 2000.

[26] Ibid. (ed.), *Buddhist Women and Social Justice: Ideals, Challenges, and Achievements*, Albany, NY: State University of New York Press, 2004.

[27] See Karma Lekshe Tsomo, 'Mahaprajapati's legacy: the Buddhist women's movement: an introduction', in Tsomo (ed.), *Buddhist Women Across Cultures*, pp. 1–44.

as independent scholars. More and more Buddhist women are researching Buddhist women's history and religious practice, as is evident from recent publications, especially from *Innovative Buddhist Women: Swimming Against the Stream*. In this volume several writers underline the need for equal opportunities for education, ordination and leadership for women in Buddhist cultures. The contemporary controversy over the higher ordination of Buddhist nuns in Theravada countries clearly illustrates how women from one major non-Western religious tradition are pressing for spiritual and practical equality.

Central to this controversy is the situation in Sri Lanka. The order of Sri Lankan nuns originally came from India in the third century BCE, and it was Sri Lankan nuns in turn who took the *Bhikkuni sangha* to China in the fifth century CE. The Sri Lankan chronicle *Dipavamsa* (4th century CE) records in detail the establishment of the nuns' order in Sri Lanka, the special *Vinaya* rules followed by the nuns, and the nuns' contribution to the expansion of Buddhism, which has been totally ignored by the dominant *Mahavamsa* or 'Great Chronicle' of the sixth century CE, nor has it been acknowledged in the writings of later scholars and commentators. The Sri Lankan woman scholar and activist Hema Goonatilake mentions that this first chronicle, the *Dipavamsa*, may even have been 'a compilation by the community of nuns'. She describes this 'nuns' tale' of the 'forgotten women of Anuradhapura' as 'the earliest example of a recorded "her story" in Sri Lanka, and perhaps anywhere in the world'.[28]

The lineage of fully ordained nuns no longer exists now in any Theravada country, but only in Mahayana countries, where the very legitimacy of the Chinese *bhikkuni* lineage, so important for reviving full ordination in Theravada countries, rests on their fifth-century foundation by Sri Lankan *bhikkunis*. The Chinese nuns established their own *Vinaya* tradition, the *Dharmagupta Vinaya*, and transmitted full ordination to nuns in Korea and Vietnam. The history of Buddhist nuns, and their contemporary struggle for equal ordination and participation in the Buddhist *sangha* is a fascinating story that provides numerous examples of 'fluid boundaries' between Buddhist men and women in different Buddhist cultures of East and West. Numerous Buddhists are

---

[28] Hema Goonatilake, 'The forgotten women of Anuradhapura: "her story" replaced by "history"', in Durre S. Ahmed (ed.), *Gendering the Spirit: Women, Religion and the Post-Colonial Response*, London and New York: Zed Books, 2002, pp. 91–102; see p. 92 for the quotation.

now working for the transformation of women's position in Buddhism, and that applies to both nuns and lay women. The contemporary struggles of Buddhist women who are 'swimming against the stream' by questioning many of the established customs and traditions, raise important questions of how Buddhism can be re-envisioned along more egalitarian lines. Karma Lekshe Tsomo is convinced that if the teachings of Buddhism are psychologically liberative for women, 'they should be socially liberative as well'.[29]

This brings me back full circle to where I began, with Professor Satha-Anand's paper on Buddhist boundaries and institutions in Thailand. Her wide-ranging and perceptive discussion has demonstrated to us that gender issues within Buddhism can be studied at many different levels of teaching and practice, revealing how these affect women and men differently. As we have seen, case studies of different Buddhist communities, of canonical texts and their interpretation, are now being more consciously examined from a critical gender perspective, highlighting the differentiated gender relations and representations in the Buddhist *sangha*. Buddhism and gender studies are growing surprisingly fast and use many different approaches.

To list some of these gender issues in Buddhism worldwide, there is the wider issue of the construction of Buddhist women's identity; then there is the Buddhist nuns' struggle to change and improve their status within Buddhist monasticism; and furthermore there is the question of women's role and participation in reforming monastic regulations. All of these issues are illustrated and touched upon in Professor Suwanna Satha-Anand's paper. A common theme running through many discussions on gender boundaries is the critical need for equal opportunities for education, ordination, and leadership for women in Buddhist cultures. Access to education, to studying Buddhist scriptures and philosophy, is the key issue here and, like for women in the West who had to struggle to gain access to professional training and university education, including the most advanced philosophical and theological education, many Buddhist lay women and nuns now seek the highest professional qualifications and higher degrees in the study of their own tradition.

The struggle for full participation in the practice of religion, and in scholarship on religion, go hand in hand, not only in Buddhism but

---

[29] Tsomo, *Innovative Buddhist Women*, p. 328.

in other religions too.[30] More than a struggle, this is a new tidal wave arising around the whole world, an entirely new development in human consciousness and culture, which is brilliantly captured in the description that we are witnessing everywhere 'a silent revolution' of women in religion.[31] Largely silent, yes, but a revolution nevertheless. It will have significant implications not only for the future of women and men, and the future of religion, but it will also deeply impact and transform the shape of the academic study of religion around the globe.

[30] Major themes in women's reinterpretation of Hindu and Muslim texts are dealt with in the collection of papers edited by Durre S. Ahmed, *Gendering the Spirit* (see note 28).

[31] This expression has been used by Pieternella van Doorn-Harder with regard to Muslim women in Indonesia. She shows how the new awareness about gender issues is an irreversible process, 'part of a silent revolution'. See her book *Women Shaping Islam: Reading the Qur'an in Indonesia*, p. 195. This comment can be extended to women in other religions than Islam. Hema Goonatilake has used this expression with regard to women in Buddhism; see her paper 'A silent revolution: the restoration of the *Bhikkhuni* Order in Sri Lanka', presented at the IAHR Regional Conference on the Study of Religions in India, December 11–14, 2003, New Delhi, India. Since writing this response, an excellent study of Buddhist women's ordination has appeared, which also contains an extensive discussion of the 'Eight Special Rules': see Wei-Yi Cheng, *Buddhist Nuns in Taiwan and Sri Lanka: A Critique of the Feminist Perspective*, London/New York: Routledge, 2007, esp. pp. 83–99.

FLUID BOUNDARIES, INSTITUTIONAL SEGREGATION AND BUDDHIST SEXUAL TOLERANCE: A RESPONSE (2)

Masakazu Tanaka

I thank Professor Satha-Anand for her stimulating paper on Thai Buddhism.

While Professor Ursula King has tried to place the paper in the wider context of gender studies in religion, I will focus more on the social implications of Buddhism in contemporary society and try to connect these to non-religious issues, with particular attention to feminist ones.

Social Implications of Buddhism in Contemporary Society

Professor Satha-Anand's paper starts with an account of the basic Buddhist teachings, ranging from ethics, through temporality to ontological truth. The point she makes in the first section of the paper is that Buddhism is a non-essentialising religion, and that tolerance is its main characteristic. As a social anthropologist, I am not qualified to criticise such a characterisation of Buddhist teachings. My question is, how far does it show tolerance towards other religions and ethnic groups in reality?

In the early 1980s, I conducted research in Sri Lanka, which is one of the few Theravada Buddhist countries in the world. In the 1970s, Buddhism had been given there the status almost of a state religion, and it still maintains this status today. My main interest was in a minority religion of Sri Lanka, that is, Tamil Hinduism. In Sri Lanka, there had been serious ethnic conflicts between the majority Sinhalese and the minority Tamils since 1956. So, even though, as a Japanese, I have great sympathy towards Buddhism, I am very suspicious of the idealist teachings of Buddhism. The Buddhist idea of fluid identity is no doubt more congenial to other religions than monotheistic religions are. But Buddhism is not free from providing grounds for state violence and discrimination against the minority Tamils.

I do not think that the nature of the present ethnic problems in Sri Lanka is religious as far as the Tamils are concerned. However, it shows that Buddhism has been of little use in bringing about change in the relationship between the majority Sinhala Buddhists and the minority Tamils. In Professor Satha-Anand's paper, a distinction is made between 'enemies' and 'opponents'. However, to refer to the theme of the paper, such a distinction is in reality rather 'fluid', as opponents tend to become enemies. This is my first observation.

Professor Satha-Anand's analysis of the past and present situation of the *sangha* is more objective, and her proposal is sound. Her argument is basically the same for both gender and caste. Through the institution of the *sangha,* secular differences or discrimination among castes or gender were alleviated.

This is a very important point, but I would like to raise another question. Professor Satha-Anand's has indicated that as the *sangha* was open to all castes, social distinctions among the people (in the *sangha*) were fluid in character. However, does this mean that the distinction between a householder and an ascetic became more fixed and absolute? This would mean that, as a result, the *sangha* would remain aloof from social issues. This is my second point.

My third observation concerns the nature of asceticism. Asceticism is the main aspect that distinguishes a monk or nun from a householder. Professor Satha-Anand has pointed out the critical difference between Buddhism and monotheistic traditions. However, in my understanding, most world religions, including religions such as Hinduism and Jainism, have institutionalised asceticism in one form or another. In its narrow sense, asceticism implies refraining from sexual intercourse, and, for me, it means refraining from contact with women. A typical threat against male ascetics takes the form of a demonic but seductive female, as the case of the Buddha shows us. In my view, the real basis of discrimination against women is in institutionalised asceticism. The female, whether ascetic or not, remains a threat for the male ascetic.

In spite of many reforms, asceticism still remains anti-secular and anti-sexual (and thus anti-female). It should be noted that Weber originally contrasted asceticism with ecstasy. I propose that the real alternative to the present situation of religions supporting secular discrimination against women lies not in reformed asceticism but in 'ecstatic religion'. The present-day goddess or wicca movements in the West have emerged from such critical reflections on the ascetic-Protestant milieu, though they take many forms.

Thus, I would argue that the contrast between the ecstatic and the ascetic is more important than that between Buddhism and monotheism.

It might be said that one possible solution is provided by a Japanese version of anti-ascetic Buddhism. By this I mean those Buddhist priests or monks who do not consider women as an obstacle to the path of salvation or for performing religious acts. But I do not wish to romanticise it.

The Monastery and the Military

Finally, I would like to comment on Professor Satha-Anand's paper in relation to my current research topic, that is, the military institution. This is not directly related to religion, but it may clarify my point. It is well known that the female soldier has been an important issue in the United States and other countries.

The monastery and the military have much in common. To use the sociologist Erving Goffman's term, they are 'total institutions'.[1] That is to say, they are concerned with every aspect of one's life. They want to control everything about the person. In the 1970s, after the transformation of the U.S. military into an all-volunteer force in 1973, the military had to turn their attention to women to compensate for the decreasing number of servicemen. Since then, many women have joined the U.S. military, but it also appears that the military was reluctant to accept female soldiers, and the sections of the military open to them were limited. The situation gradually changed after feminist interventions, which were of two kinds. Major feminist groups supported the policy of realising gender equality in the military. At the same time, some feminists were concerned with the nature of the military itself. The military aims to kill people and damage property. Are such jobs suitable for women and feminists? This is their fundamental question.

Professor Satha-Anand contrasts the traditionalists with feminists in her paper. I have noted that in the debate over the female soldier, there are two types of feminists, that is, those who support equal opportunity in the military and those who question the very existence of the military. The counterpart to the latter seems to be missing in Professor Satha-Anand's paper. Can we question the nature of asceticism itself, including in the Buddhist *sangha*? As I have suggested, the alternative

---

[1] Erving Goffmann, Asylums: *Essays on the Social Situation of Mental Patients and Other Inmates*, New York: Doubleday, 1961.

could be the ecstasy-seeking wiccas, or more secular-oriented (thus anti-religious) feminists.

To sum up, I have addressed Professor Satha-Anand's paper on three points. First, concerning the relationship between the basic teachings of Buddhism and the realities of the secular world. Second, regarding the nature of the boundary between the *sangha* and the world of the householder. Finally, I have raised some questions about the nature of asceticism. In raising these various points, I have referred to topics such as the ethnic conflict in Sri Lanka, the feminist spirituality movements in the West, and the anti-ascetic nature of Japanese Buddhism.

PART FIVE

METHOD AND THEORY IN THE STUDY OF RELIGION

METHOD AND THEORY IN THE STUDY OF RELIGION
INTRODUCTION

Armin W. Geertz

Whenever I think about method and theory in the study of religion, the wonderful dinosaur sketch by the British comic group Monty Python comes to mind. The scene is a television interview program. The host, played by Graham Chapman, introduces a Miss Anne Elk, played by John Cleese, who is a specialist on dinosaurs. The dialogue between the two runs like this:

> Host: Now, Miss Elk—Anne—you have a new theory about the brontosaurus.
> Elk: Could I just say, Chris, for one moment that I have a new theory about the brontosaurus?
> Host: Er...exactly. What is it?
> Elk: Where?
> Host: No, no, no. What is your theory?
> Elk: Oh, what is my theory?
> Host: Yes.
> Elk: Oh what is my theory, that it is. Yes, well you may well ask, what is my theory.
> Host: (slightly impatient) I am asking.
> Elk: And well you may. Yes my word you may well ask what it is, this theory of mine. Well, this theory that I have—that is to say, which is mine—...is mine.
> Host: (more impatient) I know it's yours. What is it?
> Elk: Where? Oh, what is my theory?
> Host: Yes!
> Elk: Oh, my theory that I have follows the lines I am about to relate. (Coughs) Ahem. Ahem. Ahem. Ahem. Ahem. Ahem.
> Host: Oh God.
> Elk: Ahem. Ahem. Ahem. Ahem. Ahem. Ahem. Ahem. Ahem. Ahem. Ahem. Ahem. Ahem. [Impatient noises from Host] The Theory, by A. Elk. That's A for Anne, it's not by a elk.
> Host: Right....
> Elk: This theory which belongs to me is as follows. Ahem. Ahem. This is how it goes. Ahem. The next thing that I am about to say is my theory. Ahem. Ready?
> (Host moans)
> Elk: The Theory by A. Elk brackets Miss brackets. My theory is along the following lines.

> Host: Oh God.
> Elk: All brontosauruses are thin at one end, much MUCH thicker in the middle, and then thin again at the far end. That is the theory that I have and which is mine, and what it is too.
> Host: That's it, is it?
> Elk: Right, Chris.
> Host: Well, Anne, this theory of yours seems to have hit the nail on the head.
> Elk: And it's mine.
> Host: (ironical) Thank you for coming along to the studio.
> Elk: My pleasure, Chris.
> Host: Er…Britain's newest wasp farm…
> Elk: It's been a lot of fun.
> Host:…opened last week…
> Elk: Saying what my theory is.
> Host: Yes, thank you.
> Elk: And whose it is.
> Host: Yes.…opened last week…
> Elk: I have another theory.
> Host: Not today, thank you.
> Elk: My theory number two, which is the second theory that I have. Ahem! This theory…
> Host: Oh look…shut up!
> Elk:…is what I am about to say…
> Host: Oh please shut up!
> Elk:…which, with what I have said, are the two theories that are mine and belong to me.
> Host: Look, if you don't shut up I shall shoot you.
> Elk: Ahem! My brace of theories, which I possess the ownership of, which belongs to me…
> (BANG!)
> (Pause)
> Elk: Ahem. The Theory the Second by Anne…
> (MACHINE GUN FIRE)[1]

Many non-academics feel this way about scientists and scholars. They are pompously possessive and proud about their theories which, often enough, are unworldly, commonplace or absurd. In fact, many academics feel this way as well about their more theoretically oriented colleagues. Theories are not scholarship, they claim. Theories are tolerated, but only in order to get on with the 'real job' of reading, translating and interpreting texts in their own contexts.

---

[1] Transcribed by Jonathan Partington, 14 May 1987, <http://www.skepticfiles. org/en001/monty33.htm>.

This stance, however, is not only wrong, it is poor science. Any academic study, whether in the natural or human sciences, must describe, interpret and explain the subject under consideration. This involves description, understanding the contexts and meanings of the subject and explaining or interpreting the subject in terms of broader issues. All three procedures: description, understanding and explanation are theoretical exercises. There are those who claim that description is independent of theory. This is patently untrue. Others claim that methods are independent of theory. This too is untrue. The philosophy of science has clearly shown that there is no activity or procedure in research that is independent of theoretical assumptions, not only about the subject at hand, but also about the questions that are asked and the methods that are used. These implicit and explicit theories are expressions of broader philosophical issues. And this goes for the natural sciences as well as the humanities. Therefore, the academic study of religion, which aspires to be more than pleasant conversation or simple reproduction of religious texts, must clarify its implicit concepts and make its implicit theories explicit.[2]

The academic study of religion attempts to describe, understand, interpret and explain the religious beliefs and behaviour of peoples and nations by using a wide variety of methods, disciplines and theories. The methods often used are analytical comparison, historical reconstruction and contextualisation, linguistics, sociology, psychology, iconography, literary and exegetical analysis and so on.

The comparative science of religion as it was formulated in the West by German expatriate Friedrich Max Müller during the mid-nineteenth century grew out of the meeting of cultures during the heyday of Romanticism and European colonialism. The major theme then was to extricate itself from theological agendas and Western provincialism. During the twentieth century, a number of important movements and

---

[2] I have argued more explicitly on this issue in Armin W. Geertz, 'Analytical theorizing in the secular study of religion', in Tim Jensen and Mikael Rothstein (eds.), *Secular Theories on Religion: Current Perpectives*, Copenhagen: Museum Tusculanum Press, 2000, pp. 21–31; and 'Definition, categorization and indecision: or, how to get on with the study of religion', in Christoph Kleine, Monika Schrimpf and Katja Triplett (eds.), *Unterwegs: Neue Pfade in der Religionswissenschaft: Festschrift für Michael Pye zum 65. Geburtstag*, München: Biblion Verlag, 2004, pp. 109–18. An excellent introduction to the complexities of the comparative science of religion in terms of the philosophy of science is Jeppe Sinding Jensen, *The Study of Religion in a New Key: Theoretical and Philosophical Soundings in the Comparative and General Study of Religion*, Aarhus: Aarhus University Press, 2003.

theories such as historicism, functionalism, structuralism, hermeneutics, literary theory, feminism and gender approaches, and post-colonialism have enriched the comparative science of religion and made it what it is today. Recent trends, furthermore, introducing cognitive theories and experimental methods add highly promising perspectives to our science.[3]

A crucial aspect of twentieth-century debate was the sustained effort by non-Western intellectuals to transform the study of religion into a truly global endeavour. It was not a question of becoming advocates of ethnic, religious or ideological agendas—it was a matter of equal cooperation between partners to deconstruct stereotypes and to question the supposed dualisms of East and West. These are therefore exciting times for the academic study of religion, in which important breakthroughs might occur.[4]

In the following, three scholars from different parts of the world and grounded in different cultures and languages offer their reflections on method and theory in the scholarly study of religion. The papers consist of a keynote presentation by Tomoko Masuzawa, situated at the University of Michigan but born in Japan, and responses to her paper by Chin Hong Chung at Hallym University in Korea and by Sylvia Marcos at Universidad Autónoma del Estado de Morelos in Mexico.

In her paper, Professor Masuzawa explores method and theory from

---

[3] See Armin W. Geertz and Russell T. McCutcheon, 'The role and history of methodology and theory in the IAHR', in Armin W. Geertz, Russell T. McCutcheon (eds.) assisted by Scott S. Elliott, *Perspectives on Method and Theory in the Study of Religion: Adjunct Proceedings of the XVIIth Congress of the International Association for the History of Religions, Mexico City 1995*, Leiden: Brill, 2000, pp. 3–37. On new approaches to the study of religion, see Peter Antes, Armin W. Geertz and Randi Warne (eds.), *New Approaches in the Study of Religion*, Berlin: Mouton de Gruyter, 2004, *Vol. 1: Regional, Critical, and Historical Approaches*, and *Vol. 2: Textual, Comparative, Sociological, and Cognitive Approaches*.

[4] See Armin W. Geertz, 'On reciprocity and mutual reflection in the study of native American religions', *Religion*, vol. 24, no. 1, 1994, pp. 1–7; 'Critical reflections on the postmodern study of religion', *Religion*, vol. 24, no. 1, 1994, pp. 16–22; 'Ethnohermeneutics in a postmodern world', in Tore Ahlbäck (ed.), *Approaching Religion, Part I: Based on Papers Read at the Symposium on Methodology in the Study of Religions Held at Åbo, Finland, on the 4th–7th August 1997*, Åbo: The Donner Institute for Research in Religious and Cultural History, and Stockholm: Almqvist & Wiksell International, 1999, pp. 73–86; 'Global perspectives on methodology in the study of religion', in Geertz and McCutcheon, *Perspectives on Method and Theory in the Study of Religion*, pp. 49–73; 'Can we move beyond primitivism? On recovering the indigenes of indigenous religions in the academic study of religion', in Jacob Olupona (ed.), *Beyond 'Primitivism': Indigenous Religious Traditions and Modernity*, New York and London: Routledge, 2004, pp. 37–70.

a historical perspective. More precisely, she is interested in the location of method and theory in the genealogy of discourse formation in the science of religion. Taking her point of departure in Jacques Derrida's discussion on the language of the human sciences, Professor Masuzawa calls for a systematic and historic questioning of foundational concepts. Such a study brings to light the conflicts, compromises, polyvalences and disunities of our science. The default 'destroy-and-preserve' (that is, the two-stage move of self-criticism and self-confirmation) tactics of normal science are brought into question. 'What if the task of critique', Professor Masuzawa asks, 'is to be configured altogether differently?' She argues for an archaeology of current practice in our field and the need for 'critical theoretical work that is not directly linked to methodology'. This approach is applied to what Professor Masuzawa calls the near opaque nucleus of the concept 'world religions'.

Professor Chin Hong Chung responds sympathetically to Prof. Masuzawa's project and demonstrates what it is like to be among the 'reshuffled rest' in the turbulent, although sometimes innocuous, European conceptualisations of 'world religions'. In his response, Prof. Chung examines the concept 'folk belief' in the topography of Korean religious culture. He argues that the Western term 'religion', which has been imported into Asian terminology, is both alien and inadequate to describing Korean experience. The term implies a type-casting series of judgements that are of little use in studies of Korean beliefs. He shows that much is lost by assuming the Western term.

Although in basic agreement with Prof. Masuzawa's project, Professor Sylvia Marcos asks whether there is another way of structuring a systematic analysis 'that goes beyond critiquing and nevertheless recuperating the analytic armature of binary categories?' By focussing on the concrete practices of Mesoamerican religious specialists, Professor Marcos argues that the shortcomings of the term 'religion' can be redressed. Relevant to the study of oral traditions is what she terms a 'hermeneutics of orality' that is different from historical and textual hermeneutics. In her response, Professor Marcos sketches out some of the salient features of a hermeneutics of orality. In the process she notes that binary conceptions such as nature/culture, sacred/profane, and human/superhuman are interlocking and reciprocal rather than prohibitive divides. The job of a scholar of religion in this case is to systematically conceptualise a particular religious tradition as it unfolds in a process of poetic imagery and historical change. The ultimate goal, Professor Marcos argues, is to develop a science that approaches the Other devoid of systemic premises that are demeaning, distorting and/or idealising.

Developments force us now, more than ever before, to remain academically vigilant in the face of religious and ideological attempts to undermine our field, theoretically sophisticated in the face of small-minded attempts to denigrate reflection, and methodologically skilled in the face of tendencies towards disciplinary isolationism. These are urgent areas for all scholars of religion in whatever part of the world they might be. And it is my fervent hope that coming generations of scholars will help us realise the somewhat lofty goals of a global, academic study of religion.

THEORY WITHOUT METHOD
SITUATING A DISCOURSE ANALYSIS ON RELIGION

Tomoko Masuzawa

In the fall of 2004, I received an invitation from the International Association for the History of Religions to speak at the upcoming World Congress scheduled for the following spring, and to speak specifically in a session entitled 'Theory and Method in the Study of Religion.' I accepted the invitation with only momentary reflection, that is, little more than to say to myself: Well, where else would I fit? A few months later, just as I turned my thoughts in earnest to the task of composing the paper, the rubric under which I was to speak gave me pause. In the frigid depth of the winter, reality dawned on me, and it took the form of this frosty thought: But, I *never* write on this subject, 'theory and method'.

True, I am regularly and willingly associated with many scholars who do write on the subject, and, true, I am on the editorial board of a journal roughly by that name,[1] and I have even published in it. Yet it is even more true that I am not a 'theory and method' specialist, for I have no particular expertise in general theories of religion, or even less, in the *methodology* of the study of religion. In fact, my vaguely guilty conscience leads me to admit that, in much of my career, I have managed to stay in business largely by skirting issues concerning methods and theorising, by respectfully declining, when asked, to speculate on the possible implications of what I write for various research practices prevalent in the study of religion. To put it more positively, what I do is to take a non-utilitarian interest—call it 'historical' or 'theoretical' interest—in the textual vestiges of certain authors now long dead, some of whom are considered by various contemporary scholars of religion as their disciplinary ancestors. None of those forerunners of the field, however, seems to be held as sacrosanct or canonical in any way; they seem to be remembered more for what was wrong with them than for what was supposedly great.

---

[1] *Method and Theory in the Study of Religion*, to be precise.

This said, a question looms ever more curiously: Why is the default position of someone like myself, whose research is customarily focused on the history of a particular human science, or a discipline—always 'theory and method'? What does history have to do with 'theory and method', when history in question is not a chronicle of improvements in methods of a science but simply—or not so simply—the genealogical investigation into discourse formation, of which a science undoubtedly constitutes a part, but only a part?

Allow me to suggest that this question, which may seem rather self-centred, might not be entirely about an object of idiosyncratic interest, namely, myself, but that the oddity of my situation here could be an indication of something more significant, more general, and deeply structural. In fact, this situation may be symptomatic of the peculiar location of 'theory'—or 'theory and method'—in the study of religion today, if not to say in the human sciences overall. By choosing to enter the question of 'theory and method' in this manner, it is not my intention to keep dwelling on the navel of this problematic as it rose to my own consciousness on this particular occasion. Instead, I propose to commence our deliberations by gazing into another navel, as it were, another knotted spot marking a site of origination; in this case of duly historic import.

I

In October 1966, an international conference was held at the newly established Humanities Center of the Johns Hopkins University. Officially entitled 'The Languages of Criticism and the Sciences of Man', this event came to be better known under another name: 'The Structuralist Controversy', for good reason. The impressive gathering of luminaries representing French philosophy and American criticism of the mid-twentieth century was one of the most memorable moments in the advent of so-called *post*-structuralism, thus amounting to a beginning of so much of what has since come to be garnered, cultivated, variegated, and multiplied under the term 'theory'. This is not to imply, of course, that all, or even most of what we refer to as 'theory' today comes from this particular Franco-American lineage, let alone from this particular event. Yet it remains a curiously under-analysed fact that the term theory is especially and tenaciously attached to some of the figures present at the conference and some others closely associated with them either through lateral affinity, pedagogic filiation and descent, or simply, influence.[2] I begin by recollecting this moment, not in the hope of assessing its general historic significance (yet again), but rather in order to gauge the extent to which the tradition of theoretical interventions symbolised by this event has been dislocated whenever 'theory and method' is evoked in the study of religion today.

On the last day of the conference, the late Jacques Derrida delivered what turned out to be an epoch-making speech entitled 'Structure, Sign, and Play in the Discourse of the Human Sciences', wherein he proceeded to address a thorny issue precipitated by structuralist anthropology. Early in this speech he announced the following thesis of far-reaching consequences, but with beguiling simplicity and economy of expression: 'Language bears within itself the necessity of its own critique'.[3]

The language in question—as we remember from the title of the conference—is the language of human sciences, but more specifically, Derrida is referring here to the language of Claude Lévi-Strauss. As Derrida points out, the binarism of the nature/culture divide, which seems so fundamental to the analytic strategy of structuralism, is beset by a 'scandal' when it is confronted with the fact of the incest taboo—that is, a phenomenon at once ubiquitous and universal on the one hand and particular and infinitely various among different societies on the other hand; in effect, the incest taboo is a phenomenon that seems to be at once natural and cultural, thereby confounding the most fundamental distinction of the analytic schema. The prohibition of incest therefore marks a bewitched spot, a crossroads that threatens to stall analysis, or, as Derrida memorably put it, 'a nucleus of opacity within a network of transparent significations'.[4]

---

[2] Richard Macksey and Eugenio Donato (eds.), *The Languages of Criticism and the Sciences of Man: The Structuralist Controversy*, Baltimore: Johns Hopkins University Press, 1970. Speakers and colloquists at the conference included, among others, Roland Barthes, Tzvetan Todorov, Lucien Goldmann, Jean-Pierre Vernant, Paul de Man, Jacques Lacan, Jean Hyppolite, Roman Jakobson, René Girard, and Jacques Derrida.

[3] First translated by Richard Macksey and published in Macksey and Donato, *The Languages of Criticism and the Sciences of Man*, pp. 247–65; reprinted in Jacques Derrida, *Writing and Difference*, translated by Alan Bass (University of Chicago Press, 1978), pp. 278–93. The quotation is from p. 284 of the latter edition.

[4] Derrida, *Writing and Difference*, p. 283.

What, then, could be a way out of this fix, so that the work of analysis—that is, any empirical study of the varieties of human community and social industry—could go on? What choices do we have when the operational—if not to say foundational—concepts or schematic apparatuses of a science hit a snag of this sort, momentarily—if not indefinitely—disabling the interpretive work, as the whole operation seems to be besieged by doubt, suspicion, and umbrage?

If we are to trust Derrida's formulation here, neither the cause of this arrest and disability nor the possible agent for its dissolution should be considered exterior to the language of science itself. In fact, the snag and the solvent may be located in one and the same conundrum— the navel, if you will—which halts the current of business-as-usual *and* offers decisive leverage. For, as Derrida goes on to claim, what is called critique here turns out to be at once a necessity and an opportunity:[5]

> Now this critique may be undertaken along two paths, in two "manners." *Once the limit of the nature/culture opposition makes itself felt, one might want to question systematically and rigorously the history of these concepts.* This is a first action. Such a systematic and historic questioning would be neither a philological nor a philosophical action in the classic sense of these words. To concern oneself with the founding concepts of the entire history of philosophy, to deconstitute them, is not to undertake the work of the philologist or of the classic historian of philosophy. (284; emphasis added)

---

[5] Strictly speaking, Derrida's argument here is considerably more complicated than this passage may suggest. For, in the context of Derrida's text, ethnography's double-bind embodied and exposed by the incest taboo is actually superimposed upon another form of structural contradiction, namely, ethnology as an essentially ethno-Eurocentric science that has become possible precisely on the condition that its centricity is already dislocated, thus de-centred, by the recognition of the plurality of cultures, i.e., Europe's recognition of itself as no longer the 'culture of reference'. In Derrida's estimation this condition of compounded double-bind makes ethnography a 'privileged' case, as it lays bare all the more obviously the necessity *and* the impossibility of the foundational structure. The most relevant passage in Derrida's clarification of this point reads as follows: 'Now, ethnology—like any science—comes about within the element of discourse. And it is primarily a European science employing traditional concepts, however much it may struggle against them. Consequently, whether he wants to or not—and this does not depend on a decision on his part—the ethnologist accepts into his discourse the premises of ethnocentrism at the very moment when he denounces them. This necessity is irreducible; it is not a historical contingency. We ought to consider all its implications very carefully. But if no one can escape this necessity, and if no one is therefore responsible for giving in to it, however little he may do so, this does not mean that all the ways of giving in to it are of equal pertinence. The quality and fecundity of a discourse are perhaps measured by the critical rigour with which this relation to the history of metaphysics and to inherited concepts is thought' (p. 282).

This 'systematic and historic questioning', or *de-constitutive* analysis—or what we have since grown accustomed to calling simply: deconstruction—is therefore not a mere etymological tracing of words or word usage; nor is it a philosophical rumination on concepts 'in the classic sense.' But Derrida does not specify this first mode of critique any further. His point, rather, is that this was not the path finally taken by Lévi-Strauss. Thus he goes on to say without pause:[6]

> The other choice (which I believe corresponds more closely to Lévi-Strauss's manner), in order to avoid the possibly sterilizing effects of the first one, consists in conserving all these old concepts within the domain of empirical discovery while here and there denouncing their limits, treating them as tools which can still be used. No longer is any truth value attributed to them; there is a readiness to abandon them, if necessary, should other instruments appear more useful. In the meantime, their relative efficacy is exploited, and they are employed to destroy the old machinery to which they belong and of which they themselves are pieces. This is how the language of the social sciences criticizes *itself.* Lévi-Strauss thinks that in this way he can separate *method* from *truth*, the instruments of the method and the objective significations envisaged by it. [...] Lévi-Strauss will always remain faithful to this double intention: to preserve as an instrument something whose truth value he criticizes.

I believe it is this second path, the manner of critique specifically ascribed to Lévi-Strauss in this context, that is generally, nearly automatically, assumed to be taken whenever the foundational concepts of a discipline are called to account, whenever an investigation into the history of these concepts is proposed or performed.[7] The other possibility—namely, the first option just mentioned (though unelaborated) by Derrida—does not seem to be recognised at all. This said, I am inclined to situate my study of the world religions discourse in analogy with this other manner of critique.

But why, it might be asked, is this other possibility not given any consideration in the usual framework of 'theory and method'? My

---

[6] Ibid.

[7] Derrida's ascription of this mode of critique to Lévi-Strauss here, I believe, should be understood as strategic rather than absolute. As would be evident to anyone familiar with the rudiments of post-structuralist practice, these ascriptions and positionings are always a matter of situated enunciation rather than a judgement pronounced from some imagined space *above* the situation. It is useful to remember in this context that the relation/distinction between 'structuralism' and 'post-structuralism' is highly mobile and strategically drawn, and that it can never settle into a matter of difference in period ('before' and 'after'), or difference in philosophical positions or opinions.

purpose here is not to pursue in earnest the undoubtedly complex reasons as to why this alternative path continues to be overlooked despite what looks like forty years of extensive publicity that post-structuralism has received, pro and con, in the human sciences. Suffice it to say that, whatever the reason for this state of neglect or wilful disregard, the present condition obliges me to return to this most elemental of theoretical points, and to make visible once again the space of critical theory arguably claimed by Derrida four decades ago, as he posited that space in strategic distinction from, and in tactical opposition to, 'Lévi-Strauss', such that it did make some sort of sense to call this stance *post*-structuralist.

A historical investigation, if done 'systematically and rigorously', would likely or perhaps inevitably bring to light the polyvalent, non-unitary, often conflicting and compromising formation not only of the operative concepts but of the discipline predicated on these concepts. This may prove unnerving. It is not very surprising at first brush, therefore, that such an investigation is perceived to have largely negative consequences for the constitutional stability and integrity of the science's status quo. Or, as Derrida himself remarked parenthetically in one of the passages quoted above, such a work is often anticipated to have 'sterilizing effects'. Now, within the confines of the second manner of envisioning critique (i.e., the one ascribed to 'Lévi-Strauss'), a historical analysis of concepts is understood as a *self*-criticism of the discipline, and as such, it is assumed to represent only a *negatively* retrospective moment, that is, as a preliminary procedure *before* something more redeeming or positively prospective could be delineated. This mono-schematic assumption, in effect, insists on bifurcating the work of theory into negative and positive moments, arranged in tandem. The grievance so often voiced against 'mere theory' or 'mere critique' evidently presupposes this arrangement as a matter of course; the indictment against 'theory' often boils down to the complaint that the second, constructive or restorative moment is insufficiently attended to or altogether lacking.

Within the constraints thus laid down by this two-stage framework, which remains silently and stubbornly lodged in the very idea of 'theory and method' today, a theoretical deliberation would be judged woefully incomplete if no measures were taken to conserve, reform, or reconstitute the vital instruments of scholarship, or if no new alternatives were proposed *after*, and *in addition to*, a critique. From this perspective it is easily understandable that the Lévi-Straussian double intention of destroy-and-preserve would be valued as a preferred working model for critical operation—i.e., as a (self)-critique that does not bring empirical investigation to a standstill. In fact, this appears to be the only path available to the practising human scientist who is trying to put in an honest day's work, as this mode of critique purports simultaneously to denounce the limits of 'old concepts' while conserving something of them in the meantime until better ones come along. Within the strictures of this framework, theoretical deliberations will be always and immediately answerable to the question of method; that is to say, under this regime, the work of 'theory' is permitted and deemed beneficial only to the extent that it can take on the responsibility of maintaining a healthy stockpile of functional tools and instruments for on-going empirical research.

But this is no way to start a historical investigation. The historian of a disciplinary discourse, no less eager for her honest day's work, might file a complaint rather than begin working under these conditions. What if the task of critique is to be configured altogether differently? What if we are to take the other path, that is, the first manner of critique that Derrida describes? It goes without saying that the possibility of de-constituting analysis—whether it is 'deconstruction' in the specifically Derridian sense, or more broadly including 'genealogies' in the Foucaultian sense as well[8]—depends on the availability of this alternative path, on the viability of this manner of critique, wherein concepts are not thought of as *instruments*.

As already mentioned, I prefer to think of my own recent preoccupation, historically analysing the concept and discourse of 'world religions', as a loose variant of this other kind of critique. It is an excavation project aiming at an archaeology of present discursive practice (focused on the science of religion, but also with an eye to understanding its ramifications in our everyday discourse and what it implies); it is not conceived as a methodological mission to protect or to improve upon the science of religion. To be sure, I am uncomfortably

---

[8] I might add parenthetically here that, at least in this alternate understanding of critique, Derrida's deconstructive endeavours and Foucault's genealogical projects are basically consistent. They differ from each other, I think, partly because the immediate objects of their critical attention are different, and also because their strategies for historical investigations are not the same. By and large, Foucault's projects are focused on certain institutional formations and constellations of recent centuries. By contrast, Derrida's lifework—as the above quoted passage already signals—appears to have taken 'the entire Western metaphysics' to task.

aware that such a juxtaposition of my own tediously empirical work
with historic pronouncements issuing from one of the patent holders of
post-structuralism might appear comically self-important. The analogy
here, indeed, is a limited one, and if I bother to draw it despite the
limitations, it is not in order to ennoble my project in the eyes of those
who are favourably disposed toward post-structuralism, and even less,
of course, to test the patience of those who are not. My purpose here
is to reclaim, with some clarity, a space for a critical theoretical work
that is not directly linked to methodology.

This said, I should note at the outset that I do not maintain that
'world religions' is a foundational concept for the study of religion in
any sense comparable to the way the nature/culture complex may
be said to be fundamental to the analytic operations of structuralist
anthropology. In fact, it is one of the main findings of this study that
the idea of world religions does not claim for itself any such foundational value. I would rather suggest that it is precisely this apparent
lack of value and authority, and the mercurial instability of its precise
meaning, that allow this concept to function most effectively, and that
it is this occlusion of its own operative principle that is the source of
its power, its truth-effect, its efficacy. The concept of world religions is
an utterly placid and innocuous (yet for that very reason all the more
potent) marker that is capable of containing—and hiding—a complex
logic and history of its own formation. Perhaps it is finally this capacity
for self-effacement that renders this particular concept something very
close to what Derrida termed 'a nucleus of opacity within a network
of transparent significations.'

In the next section, I will sketch out some moments from the discursive formation of 'world religions' and its comparative and classificatory logic, the topic that I have investigated in a larger study.[9]
Again, my aim here is to suggest that an investigation of this sort—an
empirical study of a concept or discursive scheme, which would not
fall apart into two neat halves of negative and positive moments—may
be construed as an instance of this alternative manner of critique, a

---

[9] The study has since been published as *The Invention of World Religions: Or, How
European Universalism Was Preserved in the Language of Pluralism*, University of Chicago
Press, 2005. What follows in this paper is a synoptic summary of its argument, and
the reference matters are kept to a minimum. The reader is kindly requested to refer
to the larger study for the full citation and for more specific arguments.

work of theory that does not concern itself with methodology, insofar as method is understood in the instrumental sense of 'tools' extrinsic to the 'truth' of science. Such a (non-methodological) critique would not simply disarm or disenfranchise the science; for it is not a negative moment of the science's self-criticism. Such a work of theory—call it a historical critique or a genealogy—does not take something away from the science, but it may hand over some new tasks.

II

In the broadest sense, this study concerns the formation of modern European identity, that is, a history of how Europe came to self-consciousness: Europe as a prototype of unity amidst plurality, Europe as a marker for the subject position of universal history. While this was the result of the study apprehended in retrospect, what initially set off the investigation was nothing more than the following historical fact. For many centuries and probably as far back as the medieval times, Europeans had a well-established convention for categorising the nations of the world, dividing them unevenly into four domains: Christians, Jews, Mohammedans (as Muslims were more commonly called then), and the rest (variously called heathens, pagans, idolaters, or sometimes polytheists). This conventional ordering of nations began to wane in the early decades of the nineteenth century, and in the early decades of the twentieth, there suddenly appeared an entirely new system, namely, a list of about a dozen 'world religions'. The list has become a convention prevalent in academic discourse today, and at the same time it has thoroughly infiltrated common parlance outside the academy. The list, in any event, has not been significantly altered or seriously challenged in the past hundred years. This project was an inquiry into to what happened in the nineteenth century to produce this momentous change.

For this purpose, historical interrogation unimpeded by methodological mandate was useful and necessary. For, without an actual historical examination, it might seem enough to settle into the comforting conclusion that this change from the old four-part classification to today's world religions list was simply a matter of adjustment and refinement, that is, a matter of sub-dividing the fourth category of the old system into specific, individual religions. In short, the new system might appear to be a direct result of finer differentiation of the 'remainder' category, made possible by a more exact and accurate state of empirical knowledge. Furthermore, whereas the earlier system was clearly a hierarchy of nations with European Christendom at the top, the world religions system is seemingly a lateral spread of multiplicity, and this fact may lead us to believe that this is an egalitarian advance.

This train of thought at once celebrates the achievements of modern knowledge and boosts its moral standing in comparison to the unenlightened past. It complacently presumes that the prevalence and stability of the world religions list today—and of the standard description of each religion that comes with this list—is but a consequence of a better science. (And where else but from this same seat of present-day science could a methodological mandate be issued?) An investigation into the historical actualities of the nineteenth century, however, puts a stop to this easy slippage of thought—a slippage that often passes as a narrative history of scientific progress, a history of improvements in theory and method, or what effectively amounts to a hagiography of that particular branch of knowledge culminating in the glorification of the present. Needless to say, a 'systematic and rigorous' questioning of the concept and of the epistemic regime endemic to it must handle 'history' in some other manner.

What, then, count as 'world religions' in today's meaning of the term? A customary list begins with Christianity, Buddhism, Islam, Hinduism, and Judaism; it also typically includes Confucianism, Taoism, and Shinto (though these are often grouped together as 'Chinese and Japanese religions' or 'East Asian religions') as well as Parsiism (or Zoroastrianism), Jainism, and Sikhism.[10] This list, though ubiquitous and familiar, is at

---

[10] In addition to these purportedly major religions, a typical world religions textbook or curriculum often includes discussion of traditions that are supposedly minor in scale, numbers, or world-historical significance. In the earlier times, these minor traditions were often referred to as 'savage' or 'primitive' religions, though nowadays these appellations are generally avoided and variously substituted by 'primal', 'preliterate', 'tribal', or even 'basic' religions. The content of this category, under whatever name, has remained constant; it always refers to those cultic practices, mythic lore, and cosmologies that fall outside of the above named major religions. Such small-scale religions are recognised generically as a type, and the examples of this type of religion are said to be found in profusion in Africa, the Americas, the Pacific islands, Oceania, Central and Southeast Asia, and other pockets of indigenous tribal life. Within this group, individual cases and examples are specified by their geographical location, or by certain sub-categories coined by European scholars in the eighteenth and nineteenth centuries, such as shamanism and animism. Whether these minor traditions *en masse*

bottom merely conventional, as *world religions* is by no means a technical term, nor has its employment been carefully deliberated upon by scholars. A little research into the nineteenth century nonetheless reveals that it did originate in certain academic contexts, and that it was indeed for a time a subject of considerable scholastic debate among certain European scientists and theologians. But those arguments are now largely forgotten, and their import has been obscured by present usage, which takes little account of past controversies. Nonetheless, the notion of world religions can be shown to sustain a complex relation to some earlier conceptual schemes.

As already mentioned, until the early nineteenth century, a well-established European convention had been to divide the world population into these four groups: Christians, Jews, Mohammedans, and the rest—this last comprising all others who were attached to countless varieties of idolatry. This four-part classification did not imply a recognition of four distinct religions as we might assume from such a list today; rather, it was a partition of the world's nations into, first, the correctly faithful believers in one true God (i.e., Christians of various sorts), then two distinctly identifiable groups who subscribed to either superseded or perverted opinions about God (i.e., Jews and Mohammedans), and finally, those who were entirely ignorant of God and therefore reduced to worshipping various inappropriate substitute objects, or idols. In effect, in this pre-modern to early modern frame of mind, there was only one religion—the true one, of course—and all others were but various ways of deviating from it. The multiplicity of what we call religion today—that is, divergence of ways in which different peoples and nations pay reverence to gods, spirits, and similar entities and manage their real or imagined powers—was understood essentially as a diversity of error. The plurality of religions presupposed by the idea of world religions, therefore, signalled a fundamental change in the way in which Europeans thought about themselves as a communion and about their relation to the rest of the world. The question remains, however, whether this transformation of the classificatory system from the hierarchy of nations to the striation of multiple traditions really amounts to progress in European knowledge

are treated as part of world religions, or as constituting a category in addition to world religions, depends on whether a given author defines the term world religions as all religions of the world or as major religions.

concerning the religions of the world, or perhaps even more wishfully, democratisation of religious values.

*   *   *

It is significant that the early occurrence of the term *world religion* was in the singular. In summarising the controversy over the concept in the late nineteenth century, the Dutch historian of religion P. D. Chantepie de la Saussaye (1848–1920) noted that the word was first introduced in 1827 by a prominent Catholic theologian from Tübingen, Johann Sebastian von Drey (1777–1853).[11] The coinage in German, *Weltreligion*, may partially account for the awkwardness of the phrase in English and the degree of indeterminacy to this day, which is sometimes rendered as 'world religions' or 'world's religions'. The appearance in early nineteenth-century German was probably not unrelated to the advent of similar terms such as *Weltgeschichte* (or world history, a concept especially associated with Hegel) and *Weltliteratur* (world literature, reportedly first coined by Goethe also in 1827), which began to circulate about the same time. The sudden prevalence of the notion of 'the world' as a conceivable, finite but unbounded totality may be a subject warranting a historical investigation of its own. More relevant to the present context than the origin of the phrase itself, however, is the specific determination of the term, that is, the fact that *Welt* (or *world*) religion was posited as a special entity, in contradistinction from some other kind of religion.

In the treatise entitled 'Von der Landesreligion und der Weltreligion' (which could be loosely translated as 'On the religion of a country and the religion of the world'), Drey argued that the Christian Church, in its true catholicity, was an institution pertaining to what was universally human, as opposed to any cult of a particular nation or locality, be it tribal, ethnic, or political. In effect, *world religion* was the term he applied uniquely and exclusively to Christianity (*Christentum*) as something utterly singular, as a phenomenon fundamentally different from all the indigenous religions of Europe and elsewhere, roundly called heathenism (*Heidentum*). What is most noteworthy about the appearance of the term here, therefore, is this pairing with its presumed other, which Drey called *Landesreligion* or, literally, 'religion of the land', meaning

---

[11] P. D. Chantepie de la Saussaye, *Manual of the Science of Religion*, London: Longmans, 1891, p. 54.

'religion of a country', or, in a translation that subsequently became more common, 'national religion.'[12]

Roughly fifty years after Drey introduced the pair of terms, they acquired another function and significance in the context of a controversy among certain Dutch and German scholars.[13] The debate had to do with the distinction between two supposedly different *types* of religion: on one hand, purportedly 'universalistic' religions, and on the other, religions that were said to be ethnically, nationally, or racially particular and confined. More specifically, it was a debate over which religions were universalistic *world religions*, and which ones were 'race'—determined or location-specific *national religions*. The important change at this historical juncture, then, was that the term began to appear in the plural. Behind this development was a deep background, a fundamental transformation of the discourse on human variety and diversity, to which subject we now must turn.

* * *

In the half century that elapsed between Drey's article and the Dutch/German debate, one of the most important things to occur was the European discovery of Buddhism. As Philip Almond has shown, it was only in the course of the nineteenth century that the opinion among the European scholars came to settle on the following ideas: (1) that certain traditions of ritual practice and cultic observance, philosophic systems, legends, and clerical institutions found in various parts of Asia actually constituted a single religion; (2) that the essential unity and identity of these greatly divergent and diffuse phenomena could be traced back to a particular historical moment and location in northern India and to a specific historical personage who lived several centuries before Jesus; and (3) that the dissemination of this religion in Asia was successful to such an extent that it either rivalled or possibly surpassed Christianity in the size of its adherents.[14]

---

[12] This also finds parallels in the pairing of 'world literature' and 'national literature', or 'world history' and 'national history', which latter for the most part is delineated in terms of individual nations.

[13] The protagonists of the Dutch debate included: C. P. Tiele (1830–1902), L. W. E. Rauwenhoff (1828–1889), and Abraham Kuenen (1828–1891). The German theologian Otto Pfleiderer (1839–1908) and the American Semitic philologist trained in Europe Morris Jastrow (1861–1921) made significant statements about the issue.

[14] Philip C. Almond, *The British Discovery of Buddhism*, Cambridge University Press, 1988.

The recognition of Buddhism as a distinct religion therefore implied an awareness that there was indeed another religion in some ways comparable to Christianity, and this meant that Christianity was seen, for the first time, as a member of a *class*, even if many of its adherents were intent on claiming that it was, in the last analysis, a class unto itself, hence beyond compare. From the very beginning of the discovery of Buddhism, Europeans with varying attitudes toward Christianity were keen on drawing a structural affinity between the two religions. For one thing, it was observed that, just like Christianity, which grew out of an older religion native to a particular people, Buddhism grew out of an indigenous religion of India, Brahmanism, of which the Hinduism of today was understood to be a direct descendent. Like Christianity, Buddhism was said to have begun as a reform movement initiated by a supra-human but historically real person, whose mission supposedly was to bring a universal moral message, and who had a spiritual appeal to all humanity. Like Christianity, it was noted in addition, Buddhism disappeared from the land of its origin but spread swiftly beyond national, ethnic, and regional boundaries, not to mention among people of different social classes. This historical fact presumably testified to Buddhism's intrinsically trans-national, universalistic character. For these alleged reasons, then, European scholars came to recognise in Buddhism a second world religion.

During the same period, however, there was a controversy over Islam—a religion with an indisputably trans-national spread well known to Christian Europe for many centuries. Rather than taking Islam's status as a world religion as a matter of course, however, some among the Dutch and German scholars argued that the actual presence of this religion in the broad and varied areas of the world was not a sign of its intrinsic universality; rather, they averred, its dominance was a glaring example of a national religion transgressing its proper boundaries. In short, according to their opinion, Islam's trans-regional and trans-ethnic prevalence testified to its blindness about its own essential limitations, its menacing proclivity to impose itself upon others by force, its inherent violence. This is as much as to say that, as soon as world religion became the name of a class and began to be used in the plural, the immediate outcome was a startling polarisation of the two non-Christian religions foremost in their candidacy for admission to the class. On the one hand, the case of Buddhism went more or less uncontested, on the other hand, that of Islam was energetically disputed. Whence comes this contrast, this asymmetry of their respective valuation in the eyes of

Europe? Behind this conundrum was a yet deeper background, which brings into view a broader context involving the rise of comparative philology and Orientalist scholarship.

*   *   *

The discovery of Buddhism was among the most important achievements of European scholarship on Indian language and philosophy. An important beginning of this scholarship is customarily attributed to Sir William Jones, a poet, Orientalist, and official of the British East India Company, then residing in Calcutta. In his 1786 presidential address to the Royal Asiatic Society of Bengal, Jones proclaimed the affinity—hence the likely commonality of origin—between the classical languages of India and of Europe. This amounted to the discovery of what was soon to be named the 'Indo-European language family', which was to be the basis of much philological speculation that animated the European imagination in the nineteenth century. With Friedrich von Schlegel's epoch-making essay, *The Language and Wisdom of the Indians* (1808) as a clarion call, there arose great enthusiasm for the study of Sanskrit and Indo-Persian languages, literature, and philosophy, and for the study of their possible relation to the legacy of the Occident.[15] The group of languages that Schlegel referred to as 'Sanskritic' included Sanskrit, Persian, Greek, Latin, and a few other related languages of antiquity, as well as all of the more recent languages derived from these ancient tongues, and they soon came to be called Indo-European, Indo-Germanic, or Aryan languages. The most broadly consequential of all the achievements of the emergent science of comparative philology was to have demonstrated the definitive genealogical relation among these languages. The Aryan family was henceforth set apart from another family, the Semitic (which included Arabic and Hebrew), as well as from all other languages, which could be grouped together as a tertiary estate of sundry tongues, sometimes collectively called the 'Turanian' (meaning 'Turkic') language group, or else more descriptively called agglutinative languages.

According to the majority opinion among nineteenth-century comparative philologists, Aryan languages were distinguished from all

---

[15] Friedrich von Schlegel, *Über die Sprache und die Weisheit der Indier: Ein Beitrag zur Begründung der Altertumskunde*, Heidelberg: Mohr und Zimmer, 1808. English translation by E. J. Millington, included in *The Aesthetic and Miscellaneous Works of Frederick von Schlegel* (London: Henry G. Bohn, 1849).

others by the excellence of their grammatical form, or more precisely, the purity of their inflection. It was speculated that, in the case of the allegedly 'pure' or 'originally inflectional' languages such as Greek or Sanskrit, in the prehistoric period of their development, each primitive root-word—a kind of primordial utterance, a sound infused with meaning—generated its capacity to form a syntax *from within*, as it were; that is to say, each proto-word articulated itself by generating its own word-ending, as an embryo shooting out its limbs, thus becoming capable of connecting up with other similarly developing proto-words to form a meaningful sequence of utterance. The mode of articulation that thus developed intrinsically and without external contrivance, it was claimed, was more organic, natural, and free, and at the same time, rational.

In contrast, the majority of other languages were said to have developed in a different way. In their case, primitive root-words were mechanically strung together, so to speak, by means of inserting some extraneous 'particles' in the interstices. (Chinese was considered to be a language that most faithfully retained this mode of syntactical formation, the epitome of the language consisting almost entirely of monosyllabic root-words, or so it was claimed. This is the basis of the opinion oft-heard in the nineteenth century that Chinese does not have a grammar in the proper sense of the term.) As this type of language changed over time, the particles—initially free-standing help-words—gradually became melded into the root-words as though attached by some glutinous substance; hence these language were called *agglutinative*. In comparison to the inflectional language formation, syntax based on agglutination was thought to be more mechanical, contrived, inchoate, and somewhat more constrained; and the grammar formed in this manner was thought to be more childish and primitive. To this judgement the philologists added a consolatory opinion to the effect that, for those languages that began so awkwardly, there was potential for gradual refinement, whereas those languages blessed with pure inflection from the beginning were always in danger of decay and loss of their original perfection.

In this polarised scheme of language development as theorised by nineteenth-century philologists, the Semitic languages were placed structurally in the middle, wedged between the two types. As Friedrich von Schlegel argued (and later Wilhelm von Humboldt and many others concurred), Arabic, Hebrew, and some other related languages of the ancient Near East were constitutionally marred by 'imperfect' inflection because, in the case of these languages, the agglutination had already taken place when inflectional development began.[16] In other words, their word-endings, rather than growing directly and naturally out of the primordial root-words, were generated from partially agglutinated incipient words. Moreover, it was argued that this compromised formation of grammatical form (that is, inflection belatedly begun from an amalgam) caused a serious impediment to the development of the 'spirit' of the nation, and this amounted to an even worse fate than that suffered by those allied with the simply agglutinative languages. It was as though the Semitic languages were stranded in the middle, hemmed in from both sides, unable to grow in either direction, to evolve or to refine; forever confined and constrained by their mean grammar, they were condemned to stagnate and calcify—or so the theory went.[17]

This general opinion, repeated throughout the nineteenth century in endless variations, was typically expressed by one of the foremost Semitic philologists of the time, Ernest Renan, in his last major work, *The History of the People of Israel*:[18]

> The languages of the Aryans and the Semites differed essentially, though there were points of connexity between them. The Aryan language was immensely superior, especially in regard to the conjugation of verbs. This marvellous instrument, created by the instinct of primitive man, contained in the germ all the metaphysics which were afterwards to be developed through the Hindoo genius, the Greek genius, the German genius. The Semitic language, upon the contrary, started by making a capital fault in regard to the verb. The greatest blunder which this race has made (for it was the most irreparable), was to adopt, in treating the

---

[16] 'An appearance of inflection is sometimes produced by the incorporation of the annexed particles with the primitive word. In the Arabic language, and those related to it, the first and most important modifications, as, for example, the persons of the verbs, are formed by the introduction of single particles, each bearing its own appropriate signification, and in these the suffix not being easily distinguished from the original root, we may conclude a similar incorporation to have taken place in other instances, although the foreign particles inserted may be no longer traceable', Friedrich von Schlegel, *Language and Wisdom of the Indians*, p. 448.

[17] It is noteworthy that Friedrich Max Müller (1823–1900), who has been regarded as one of the founding figures of the science of religion and a champion of 'Aryanism', sharply disagreed with this majority opinion concerning the syntactical development of different languages. Contradicting most other philologists of his time, Müller insisted that all languages without exception developed the same way, that there was no such thing as an originally inflectional language. (*Lectures on the Science of Language*, London, 1861.)

[18] Ernest Renan, *History of the People of Israel*, vol. 1, London: Chapman and Hall, 1888, pp. 7–8.

verb, a mechanism so petty that the expression of the tenses and moods has always been imperfect and cumbersome. Even at the present time the Arab has to struggle in vain against the linguistic blunder which his ancestors made ten or fifteen thousand years ago.

This articulation of the Semitic-Aryan divide in terms of *linguistic* difference—originally written in 1887—was a late example of the kind. For, by then, few scholars persisted in referring to such matters as grammatical forms, syntactical excellence, or inflectional purity as a way of delineating this difference, the reasoning that had been most important in the early decades of the nineteenth century. By its last decades, however, most educated Europeans had become familiar with the notion that something more physical, natural, and intractable than language accounted for the fundamental difference between the Semites and the Aryans. The stock characterizations of their contrast—blind loyalty and submission vs. freedom, creativity, and self-rule; calcification and fossilization vs. adaptability and infinite growth; rigid and exclusivist laws vs. all-encompassing love and felicity, etc.—were finding fresh support in the emergent theory of 'race'.[19] It is only to be added, however, that we can easily trace a direct line of descent from the earlier linguistic (if also highly speculative) explanation of differences among peoples and the later racialist theory. For, without a doubt, it was comparative philology that first gave to the new way of conceptualising Europeans as Aryans its incentives, its seemingly scientific cast, and its appearance of self-evidence. It was the new science of the origins of language that first made it possible to align contemporary Europeans with ancient Greeks, Indians, and Persians while separating them all from the Semites as well as from the Afro-Asiatics.

* * *

The necessity to reconfigure the origins of 'Europe' was felt with particular urgency, it may be further surmised, because of another emergent idea, also based on the new understanding of language, culture, and race. This was the idea that Christianity, insofar as it began as one of

---

[19] One of the most stark examples of this is Emile Burnouf's *La science des religions: Sa méthode et ses limites*, 2nd edition (Paris: Maisonneuve, 1872), originally published serially in the late 1860s in a Parisian journal, *Revue des deux mondes*. English translation by Julie Liebe was published as *The Science of Religions* (London: Swan Sonnenschein, Lowrey and Co., 1888). The author of this highly racist treatise—who was a younger cousin of the great Eugène Burnouf, the patriarch of modern Buddhology—was himself a Sanskritist.

the numerous Jewish messianic sects of late antiquity, was, or seemed to be, a Semitic legacy. This notion proved disquieting to many nineteenth-century Europeans who lately gained the awareness that they were Aryans, and who were increasingly inclined to attribute almost all of their patrimony of perceived greatness to their alleged Greek origin while at the same time claiming Christianity as their own. Thus the question presented itself for the first time, and with disturbing clarity: Was the source of European modernity fundamentally split, between 'Hellenism' and 'Hebraism', between 'Athens' and 'Jerusalem'?

In some quarters, the disquiet rose to such a level that various daring theories began to be advanced, all implying that Christianity was only incidentally and tangentially related to the religion of the ancient Israelites. Some argued that Christianity grew not so much out of ancient Judaism as out of Pan-Hellenism—that is, the widespread Greek culture of the Mediterranean world in late antiquity.[20] Others propounded a theory of the Indian origin of Christianity.[21] And some even went so far as to suggest that Christianity began in a community of Buddhist missionaries residing in Egypt.[22] Although these once widely popular speculations have been largely discredited by mainstream scholarship today, it is important to remember that such efforts to Hellenize and Aryanize Christianity, and to separate Christianity from its presumed Semitic parentage, were strong undercurrents in the latter half of the nineteenth century, and that this was the condition under which Buddhism was first recognised as a world religion. For, what was fascinating about Buddhism for Europeans was that it was *originally* Aryan, though now extant only among the non-Aryan nations of eastern Asia in variously corrupted and particularised forms. In view of the newly prevalent idea of Aryan Europe and, concomitantly, their possible ancestral relation to the 'noble race' ('Arya') of ancient India, the recognition of Buddhism as a world religion had implications far beyond the technical question of how to classify religions found in various parts of the world.

---

[20] For example, Emile Burnouf in *La Science des religions*, mentioned above. We might also consider the import of the modern fascination with Alexander the Great, whose short-lived empire appears to symbolise the actuality of the Pan-Hellenism stretching from Egypt to northern India, an idea so vital to this theory.

[21] Louis Jacolliot, *La Bible dans l'Inde: Vie de Iezeus Christna*, Paris: Librairie Internationale, 1869.

[22] Arthur Lillie, *Buddhism in Christendom, or, Jesus, the Essene*, London: Kegan Paul/Trench, 1887.

Meanwhile Islam, increasingly viewed as the epitome of the Semitic disposition, came to serve an important conceptual function in reconfiguring European identity in another way. Until the early modern period, Islam's dominion covered a large portion of the known world, and its power had been much feared and resented by the provincial inhabitants of Europe. By the late nineteenth century, however, the power relation of these two domains was dramatically transformed and transposed. Accordingly, in the eyes of the newly hegemonic Europe, the historical fact of Islam's erstwhile semi-global dominance came to be severely devalued, radically reinterpreted, if not to say altogether effaced.

It was no mere coincidence that the typical image of the Muslim was transformed at this time. Once typically represented as an Ottoman Turk—epitomised by the fabulously rich, indolent pasha, clad in silk, lounging in his harem and wallowing in all manners of opulent infidelity—this image of the 'Mussulman' was deposed, and a new image came to replace it. From this moment on, the quintessential Muslim was to be a camel-riding, sword-wielding desert nomad, zealously monotheistic, materially poor, mentally rigid, and socially illiberal—in a word, he had become an Arab. This equation of Muslim with Arab, and Arab with primitive nomadism, gained strength despite the widely acknowledged fact that the great majority of Muslims, then as now, were not Arabs.

Concurrent with this transformation, there was among Europeans one tendency regarding Islam which seemed to lead in an ameliorating direction: a fresh surge of interest in so-called Islamic mysticism. Sufism—evocatively symbolised by the whirling dervishes in dancing meditation—was said to be a contemplative, philosophically sophisticated, and speculatively inclined tradition within Islam, but as such, altogether atypical of the mainstream. It was thought that this mystical component was most probably Persian or possibly Indian or neo-Platonic in origin—in any case, Aryan. In effect, the precious kernel of Islamic mysticism was judged essentially alien to 'Islam proper'. Though often approvingly mentioned as the saving grace of this otherwise violent and unspiritual religion, the hyper-valuation of Sufism therefore reflected, and further reinforced, the devaluation of Arabian (Semitic) Islam.[23]

---

[23] Similarly, when modern Euro-Christians strongly valorise the prophetic tradition of the ancient Israelites as the truly transcendent element, it resulted in the devaluation

* * *

These newly emergent trends of thought were largely implicit yet essential to the scholarly debate about world religions that took place in the 1870s and 1880s. The scholars who engaged in this debate were uniformly of the opinion that Buddhism, in addition to Christianity, was a world religion (thus differing in their conception of the term from that of Drey half a century earlier). Their disagreements were above all over Islam's standing. Some scholars—such as C. P. Tiele—counted as a matter of course Christianity, Buddhism, and Islam as world religions, presumably on the grounds that all three were major religions, each with a trans-national spread, thus de facto demonstrating their 'universalistic' aspirations and capabilities. As mentioned earlier, however, some prominent European scholars of the late nineteenth century strenuously denied that Islam was a world religion on the grounds that it was a religion particular to the Arabs, and it should have remained so had it not been for its 'fanatical' tendency to impose itself upon others by coercion. These modern European scholars, pointedly critical of Islam and overwhelmingly negative toward its allegedly violent character, thus turned the fact of Islam's internationality against itself and effectively argued that this was but a result of border transgressions by a national/racial religion.[24] Thus it came about that such infelicitous features as political violence, forced submission, and blind obedience were expressly attributed to Islam as its essential nature, just at the historical juncture when various Christian evangelical missionary societies—the vanguard of Western Protestantism in the wake of a series of 'great awakenings'—began to mobilise their spiritual troops, united in their hope that their Lord Jesus Christ might at long last succeed in conquering the entire world in their own lifetime.[25]

Not surprisingly, these contentious arguments eventually led some scholars to question the cogency of distinguishing world religions from national religions in the first place, and to mitigate their earlier claims

---

of what was deemed the remainder, the Rabbinic Judaism—or 'Judaism proper'—as mere ritualism and legalism; and this lack of spirituality was supposedly a defining character of the Semites.

[24] Abraham Kuenen, *National Religions and Universal Religions* (Hibbert Lectures, 1882); translated from Dutch by P. H. Wicksteed (London: Macmillan, 1882); Otto Pfleiderer, *Religion und Religionen* (München: J. F. Lehmann, 1906); translated by Daniel A. Huebsch as *Religion and Historic Faiths* (New York: B. W. Huebsch, 1907).

[25] Cf. William Richey Hogg, *Ecumenical Foundations: A History of the International Missionary Council and its Nineteenth-Century Background*, New York: Harpers, 1952.

for the scientific usefulness of these categories.[26] There was no clear resolution to this continental European debate. In the absence of any definitive proclamation in favour of one or the other side, the following observation by an American Semitic scholar of the next generation, Morris Jastrow, who had studied in German and Dutch universities, may be regarded as a well reasoned last word on the debate itself:[27]

> Strictly speaking, there is no such thing as a universal religion, since there is no religion universally professed. There are a number which aim to be universal—as Buddhism, Islamism, and Christianity—and there are others—as Judaism and Zoroastrianism—which contain elements that might under given conditions become the universal property of mankind, but it is manifestly unjust to place tendencies and aspirations on a par with reality. The fact that the doctrines of a religion do not set up national or racial distinctions, does not make that religion universal; and while due allowance should be made for the remarkable scope attained by such religions as Christianity and Islam—accepted by a larger variety of races than any others—it is not proper to allow personal pride in achievement to get the better of one's judgment, and to proclaim a certain religion as containing the elements which are destined to make it universal.

By the early decades of the twentieth century when the use of the term *world religions* in the plural became well established, it seems to have been taken for granted that Christianity, Buddhism, and Islam were 'world religions' without, however, any specification as to what that meant, or what *else* may be so called in addition to these three. In 1897 Ernst Troeltsch, for example, in his essay entitled 'Christianity and the History of Religions', named all three as world religions; and by the time he wrote 'The Place of Christianity among the World Religions' in 1923, he included a few other religions in the ranks, but without any express effort to rationalise the revision. This probably signals the fact that the demarcation between world religions and national religions was effectively undermined, as the latter category dropped out of use entirely.

No one was more instrumental in making this turn definitive and authoritative than Max Weber. In the last decade of his life, he undertook an ambitious multi-volume project under the general title: *The Economic Ethic of the World Religions* (*Wirtschaftsethik der Weltreligionen*), which remained unfinished at his untimely death in 1920. As can be discerned from his introductory essay by the same name, originally

---

[26] Cf. L.W. E. Rauwenhoff, 'Wereldgodsdiensten' [in Dutch], *Theologisch Tijdschrift*, vol. 19, 1885, pp. 1–33; C.P. Tiele, 'Religions', in *Encyclopaedia Britannica*, 1885, pp. 1875–89.

[27] Morris Jastrow, *The Study of Religion*, New York: Scribners, 1901, p. 122.

published independently in 1915, he treated *world religions* strictly as a conventional nomenclature referring to the major religions of the world, and he included Hinduism and Confucianism in the list.[28] In addition, he found it necessary to consider 'Ancient Judaism' as well, though he refrained from calling it a world religion. As he announced matter-of-factly:[29]

> By "world religions," we understand the five religions or religiously determined systems of life-regulation which have known how to gather multitudes of confessors around them. The term is used here in a completely value-neutral sense. The Confucian, Hinduist, Buddhist, Christian, and Islamist religious ethics all belong to the category of world religion. A sixth religion, Judaism, will also be dealt with. It is included because it contains historical preconditions decisive for understanding Christianity and Islamism, and because of its historic and autonomous significance for the development of the modern economic ethic of the Occident—a significance, partly real and partly alleged, which has been discussed several times recently. References to other religions will be made only when they are indispensable for historical connections.

Weber's reasoning here seems entirely pragmatic. Apparently he was of the opinion that any numerically substantial or otherwise significant religion could be called a world religion, and moreover, such a religion was of interest to him precisely because of its uniquely characteristic ethos, each specific to the history of a particular people. In other words, all of those Weber called 'world religions' were, in his view, what the nineteenth-century scholars called 'national religions'.

* * *

The idea of universality that was originally central to the concept of world religions in the German and Dutch context thus came to be disputed, mitigated, and effectively abandoned by most scientists of religion by the beginning of the twentieth century. But in addition to this discursive tradition, there was another, roughly concurrent development in the anglophone world, which contributed equally significantly to the formation of the pluralist world religions discourse.

---

[28] Originally published in *Archiv für Sozialwissenschaft und Sozialpolitik* (1915), reprinted in *Gesammelte Aufsätze zur Religionssoziologie* (Tübingen: Mohr, 1921), vol. I, pp. 536–73. The English translators of the essay, however, unaccountably rendered the title of the essay as 'The Social Psychology of the World Religions'. See below.

[29] Max Weber, 'The Social Psychology of the World Religions', in *From Max Weber: Essays in Sociology*, New York: Oxford University Press, 1958, p. 267.

To begin the description of this development at a chronological mid-point, the use of the term world religions in English most probably dates back to C. P. Tiele's article, 'Religions', in the ninth edition of the *Encyclopaedia Britannica*.[30] This was a rather literal translation of *wereldgodsdiensten* of his native Dutch; for, until then and even sometime thereafter, the usual translation of *wereldgodsdiensten* and *Weltreligionen* was indeed 'universal religions', or, as Tiele himself sometimes preferred, 'universalistic religions'. Although the nineteenth-century Dutch and German scholarly debate over the notion of world religions did not extend to the English-speaking world, a parallel distinction between what continental European scholars called 'national religions' and 'world religions' had been drawn under different names. To mention two of the most prominent examples, the renowned Christian socialist and progressive Anglican, Frederick Denison Maurice argued in 1847 that, although all religions purported to unite and encompass all humankind in their aspiration to rise above the merely human, only Christianity actually achieved this goal, and that all other 'religions of the world' were but melancholy testimonies to the impossibility of fulfilling their ideals on their own terms.[31] In short, in his view, Christianity alone accounted for the whole and was therefore universal, while all other religions were limited and particularistic. A second example is from across the Atlantic: the distinguished Unitarian minister James Freeman Clarke of Boston published a series of articles in 1868,[32] where he drew the same distinction between the truly universal religion, which he termed 'catholic religion', namely Christianity, and all the rest, which he called 'ethnic religions'.

It was in this sense of 'universal religion' that the term *world religion*, in the singular, first came to be used by certain anglophone theologians toward the end of the nineteenth century. John Henry Barrows—American Presbyterian minister who served as the president of the World Parliament of Religions in 1893—lectured in India under the title: 'Christianity, the World-Religion', signalling his conviction that Christianity alone was the truly universal religion.[33] Similarly,

---

[30] Edinburgh, 1885 pp. 1875–89.

[31] Frederick Denison Maurice, *The Religions of the World and Their Relations to Christianity*, London: John W. Parker, 1847.

[32] They were later issued in a single volume as *Ten Great Religions: An Essay in Comparative Theology* (Boston, 1871) and reprinted many times.

[33] John Henry Barrows, *Christianity, the World-Religion: Lectures Delivered in India* (Barrows Lectures, 1896–97), Madras: Christian Literature Society for India, 1897.

William Fairfield Warren—the occupant of arguably the first chair of Comparative Religion at an American university and later president of Boston University—gave the same appellation to Christianity.[34] Far from being a synonym for the *religions of the world*, then, for these authors, *world-religion* (in their cases, hyphenated) signified one unique religion, namely their own, which, in their opinion, happened to be universally viable.[35] In effect, they viewed the contrast between Christianity and all other religions as Maurice and Clarke did, and at the same time, their usage of the term world-religion was consistent with Drey's original sense of *Weltreligion*.

It remains to be added that the advocates of Christianity were by no means the only religionists to capitalise on this notion of *the* world religion, that is, the idea of a singular religion that is allegedly 'uniquely universal', as the oxymoronic phrase much favoured by some theologians went. The distinguished German Jewish theologian Leo Baeck, for example, described the prophetic tradition of the ancient Israelites as an utterly new and unique phenomenon that erupted on the face of the earth at a specific time and place in the biblical era, which in time also became, as he claimed, the basis of 'other world religions', namely, Christianity and Islam.[36] Similarly, Swami Vivekananda, in his famous speech at the World Parliament of Religions, professed the idea that Hinduism, as an all-encompassing faith that had endured for millennia, surely was a universal religion beyond compare.[37]

Once the claim is made that a particular religion (i.e. Christianity) could be 'uniquely' catholic and universal, not surprisingly, it invited analogous claims from all *other* particular religions. In effect, the protective shield of Euro-Christian exceptionalism was breached by its own hand, and the result was an open field where any number of religions or so-called faith communities could, at least in principle, enter and compete for their own unique universality claims. Ironically,

---

[34] William Fairfield Warren, *The Religions of the World and the World-Religion*, New York: Methodist Book Concern, 1911.

[35] To complicate the matter further, however, there were cases where the term 'world religions' or *Weltreligionen* (in the plural) was used precisely in the opposite sense, that is, meaning religions other than Christianity. See for example, Martin Schlunk, *Die Weltreligionen und das Christentum: Eine Auseindersetzung vom Christentum aus*, Hamburg: Agentur des Rauhen Hauses, 1923.

[36] Leo Baeck, 'The Religion of the Hebrews', in Carl Clemen (ed.), *Religions of the World: Their Nature and Their History*, New York: Harcourt, Brace, 1931, pp. 265–98.

[37] Vivekananda, 'Hinduism', in Richard Hughes Seager (ed.), *The Dawn of Religious Pluralism: Voices from the World's Parliament of Religions, 1893*, La Salle, IL: Open Court, 1993 pp. 421–32.

then, this para-scientific discursive development—that is, the tradition of religiously-motivated uses of the term *world religion* in the singular, exclusivist sense—also led to the proliferation and indefinite pluralisation, even if its utterly contradictory logic made it inevitable that each member of the class was to persist in their own absolutist claim.

III

There is little doubt that both the scientists' use of the term and the religionists' use—each tradition rife with its own internal tension and indeterminacy—found their way into the enormous dense fog that is the contemporary body of meaning of the term *world religions*. For this and other structural reasons, the advent of the category 'world religions' does not lend itself credibly to a narrative of the 'origin and development' schema. It is not a story of facts and insights accruing in the realm of human knowledge, or of the vicissitudes of a particular scientific instrument that has been gradually refined though still in need of further improvements. What this history unfolds, instead, is a broad and ubiquitous network of discourse that has spun itself over time with no discernible central intelligence to control its destiny—though this is not to say that it is arbitrary—a network that has since become the very sinews of our thinking and the pathways for managing the aspect of reality that we call 'religion'. The extraordinary utility and ubiquity of the concept today may in fact derive from this unmasterable complexity, multivalence, and finally, opacity. In view of this polymorphous discursive history, then, the question as to how the concept of world religions may be improved upon for the benefit of a better scientific study may be one, but only one, of many issues that could be meaningfully addressed. To insist on this question alone while refusing to consider the far broader implications of the historicity of this discourse would be, to say the least, myopic. Indeed, the reduction and restriction of the scope of critical investigations to the concerns of methodology would be a move complicit with the occlusion of the strongly racialist manoeuvres of the nineteenth-century reconstitution of 'Europe', the concealment that the final twentieth-century establishment of the pluralist regime so effectively achieved.

How, then, might one delineate this history in such a way that it would render visible, rather than efface, the fibres and the viscera of this discursive formation, the veritable support system assuring the smooth and naturalised functioning of the concept today? How could a history of any such concept be narrated without repeating the very process of erasure that the history has already effected? In the case of the concept of 'world religions', this discursive formation may be schematically mapped in relation to two coordinates. One of the axes parallels the chronological order, as it plots a series of nested or overlapping transformations, namely: (1) from the four-part hierarchy of nations to the striated list of a dozen or so religions (a transformation occurring from early modern to early twentieth century);[38] (2) from the theory of human descent and diversity predicated on certain perceived characteristics of language and grammar to the theory predicated on the biological notion of race and bodily properties transmitted through sexual procreation (from the early nineteenth to the late nineteenth century); (3) from the overt racialism manifesting in these theories of descent to the occluded racialism appearing as a plurality of distinct and isolable 'religions' (from mid/late nineteenth to early/mid twentieth century) (*See Figure A*). What could be referred to as the establishment of the pluralist regime of the world religions discourse was the result of this third transformation; but this in turn came about in relation to, and as a direct outcome of, the earlier transformations. This chronological axis, in brief, delineates the emergence of the modern discourse on religion as intimately intertwined with the idea of racial difference and incommensurability.

The second axis is structured by the enduring and prolific ideology of what may be called 'historicism' for short, or self-exaltation of so-called historical consciousness and its allegedly emancipatory, universalist potential. What is most striking about the modern development of the pluralist epistemic regime, in fact, is the extent to which this latter (i.e., 'historicism') worked powerfully to dissimulate, obscure, and render nearly unrecognisable the otherwise glaring reality of the former (i.e., the thoroughly racialised and striated underpinnings of the discourse on religion). Furthermore, it is a cardinal achievement of this historicism to have fabricated the most powerful, compelling, and indispensable artifice that we know today, that is, the fiction that seemingly grounds the very condition of our knowing, namely, the West. 'The West'—*not*

---

[38] Another aspect of this transformation, which is not discussed in the present essay, is a shift in the conception of what religion consists of. Prior to the 19th century, a typical European treatise surveying 'religions of the world' identified them as 'customs and ceremonies', whereas, from the mid-19th century onward, religions came to be identified as distinct 'belief systems'. See *The Invention of World Religions*, pp. 61–4.

(1)

Middle Ages to early 19th century	→→→	Early 20th century to present
nations of the world (4)	→→→	world religions (normally 10–14)
Christians Jews Mohammedans ----- idolators (pagans, heathens, or polytheists)		Christianity Buddhism Islam Hinduism, Confucianism, Judaism, etc. ----- primitive (tribal, pre-literate, etc.) religions
centre-to-periphery/summit -to-base gradation (hierarchy)	→→→	system of striation (pluralism)
traditions of 'customs and ceremonies'	→→→	'belief systems'

Circa 1920

(2) Theory of Descent & Human Diversity

LANGUAGE --------------------→ RACE
'inflection' ---------------------→ 'blood'; 'genes'

OCCLUSION OF **RACE** THEORY
SURVIVAL OF COMPONENT IDEAS
(3)   AS **RELIGIONS**

Figure A

as a people, or a place, but as a capacious imaginary called *identity*—or, to put another way, what allows 'the West' to function as *the* identity, is a cooperation and collaboration between, on the one hand, those various systems of striation (taxonomy of religions arguably the most important among them), *and* on the other hand, the unrelenting belief in the power of historical consciousness to liberate 'Europe and the world'—that is, the totality of human communion configured as 'the West and the Rest'—from the iniquities of the recent past, and to deliver us all in due course to the sphere of true universality *as its own extension.*[39] In the last analysis, pluralism is but a name for this historicist

---

[39] One could point to a number of diverse instances in which a thoroughly natural-

project and its vitiated struggle, and as such, we are not in the position either to accept it as a solution or to discard it as a symptom and, either way, to be done with it.

In sum, these two coordinates conjointly constitute an analytic apparatus that allows us to chart (hence to make visible) the intricate movements of various finite factors and programmes crossing and intermeshing, as do warp and woof, the movements that produce our shared sense of time and plenitude. This cooperative function, complicity, and confluence of the two coordinates is manifest particularly vividly in the writings of Ernst Troeltsch.[40] As a Protestant theologian deeply affected by the historicism of the nineteenth-century German scholarship, he actively struggled with the ineradicable contradiction endemic to the pluralist-historicist project, whose only point of resolution, for him, appeared to be but an eschatological one, that is, something to be expected only at the end of time and history. With an illumination provided by Troeltsch's example, among others, we can retrace the diachronic coordinate, or the warp (that is, the formation of the racialist discourse of religion), all the while keeping a close watch on the shuttling of the woof, that is, numerous and various strategies devised by different authors at different times in order to account for the fact of the world's discordant multiplicity and diversity. These strategies were 'historicist' in the sense that each of them involved a specific way of distributing space-and-time unevenly across the world, while at the same time allocating relative degrees of blessedness to its different parts, from salvation to damnation, from enlightened rationality to benighted superstition. In this manner, we can *follow* and *repeat* this interweaving of history and discourse—or history *as* a discourse—in

---

ised notion of 'the West' and a claim on a particular self-consciously secularist 'historical thinking' are asserted as intrinsically connected. See, for example, Peter Burke's declarative essay, 'Western historical thinking in a global perspective—10 theses'; together with some keenly critical responses, for example, by Aziz Al-Azmeh, tellingly entitled 'The coherence of the West', in Jörn Rüsen (ed.), *Western Historical Thinking: An Intercultural Debate*, New York: Berghahn Books, 2002. For another example of effective intervention, see A. S. Mandair, 'The repetition of past imperialisms: Hegel, historical difference and the theorization of Indic religions', *History of Religions*, vol. 44, no. 4, 2005, pp. 277–99.

[40] Most notably, 'The place of Christianity among the world religions' (1923), in *Christian Thought: Its History and Application*, University of London Press, 1923; *Die Absolutheit des Christentums und die Religionsgeschichte*, 3. Aufl., Tübingen: J. C. B. Mohr [Paul Siebeck], 1929; 1st edition published in 1901. English translation by David Reid, published as *The Absoluteness of Christianity and the History of Religions*, John Knox Press, 1971.

the effort to make visible the workings of this production, this vanishing act, wherein the overt racialism and stratification disappear into the seemingly equanimous grid of scientific classification.

This is as much as to suggest that perhaps what should be calling our critical attention above all in the history of a concept—or more properly, the history of the epistemic regime embodied by a concept—may be precisely what disappears, or what becomes unrecognisable, rather than what finally comes to appear, or the question of the when, where, how, and why of such an appearance. By tracing the course of the latter only, our historical narrative would risk simply reproducing and reaffirming the logic of the prevalent and predominant discourse. (This is one reason a mere retracing of the term to its earliest manifestation, its prototype, its former incarnations, etc. would be inadequate.) Nor is this a matter of recovering and exhuming what was inadvertently forgotten and buried. For, at least in certain circumstances, such as in the case of the world religions, it may be precisely what is silent and occluded that guarantees the utterly naturalised and routinised function of our quotidian discourse.

*   *   *

At least two issues remain to be considered further, though neither of them can be adequately addressed in the present occasion. One is the question how a historical investigation such as the one I have described above may itself avoid becoming a historicist project and succumbing to the mendacious belief in the redemptive power of historical consciousness. There is, to be sure, no definitive preventive measure that could be applied to any given work of historical analysis in advance, so to speak, guaranteed to pre-empt the possibility of its turning into yet another present-glorifying triumphalist narrative that we all want to avoid, or even less plausibly, to neutralise its potential for fitting readily into, and thus lending strength to, some narrative system with a problematic agenda yet unforeseen or unrecognised.

This said, it may still be useful to remind ourselves of the obvious: it is not necessary or prudent to assume that any handling of the historical material would automatically entail passive compliance with a historicist narrative scheme. Slogging in the archives, registries, libraries of forgotten books, of books perhaps too familiar to be read seriously, or collections of things yet to be assembled and articulated in any discursive network that we can understand—engaging in this bread-and-butter routine of historical scholarship does not convert one into a member of the vast and invisible cult of historicism. In fact, it would hardly be a revelation to a historian—or more precisely, historian of the kind Walter Benjamin idiosyncratically called 'historical materialist' in contradistinction from 'historicist'—to be reminded that it is just such evidence from the past that can sound a wake-up call, rustling us out of the dogmatic slumber that is our present state of business-as-usual, our naturalised regime of 'historical consciousness'.

What has been rounded up here under the name of historicism—and its structural underside, pluralism—points to an immense problem area calling for a concerted and sustained attention. It would be indolence of historicism indeed to draw back from this problem region under the pretext that, in some hypothetical moment in the future, the levee will break at some other point and there will be an entirely different kind of flood. That may be so; but this is our breach—or at least one of several, or perhaps many, such pressure points of our time—and attending to the present and the immediate with some sense of urgency surely does not condemn us to a myopic, present-obsessed, 'lack of historical perspective'.

Second, and finally, it might be observed that this kind of 'historical questioning', however 'systematically and rigorously' it is to be carried out, bears little resemblance to what Derrida was possibly envisioning when he posited the possibility of an alternative critique, in sharp distinction from the 'Lévi-Straussian', destroy-and-preserve, dialectical-methodological critique. For the most part, critical projects often characterised as deconstructive, whether Derrida's own or otherwise, have focused less on the discursive practice at the level of ordinary (including academic) language; rather, they have tended to engage more directly the reputed powerhouse of 'Western metaphysics'—with relatively little expression of qualms over what the very idea of 'the West' might entail. They have typically engaged, in other words, those seminal philosophical texts, a close rhetorical scrutiny of which undoubtedly yields much critical thinking and proves a great resource for creative manoeuvres and leverage. Derrida himself, in the essay referred to earlier, indicated the direction as to how one might pursue the 'historical questioning' of the 'opposition between nature and culture' with these words:[41]

---

[41] Derrida, 'Structure, sign, and play in the discourse of the human sciences', pp. 282–3.

> Despite all its rejuvenations and disguises, this opposition is congenital to philosophy. It is even older than Plato. It is at least as old as the Sophists. Since the statement of the opposition *physis/nomos, physis/technē,* it has been relayed to us by means of a whole historical chain which opposes 'nature' to law, to education, to art, to technics—but also to liberty, to the arbitrary, to history, to society, to the mind, and so on.

This is compelling. Yet it seems eminently plausible that this opposing pair of concepts has been also caught up in other layers of discursive networks than philosophy and the literature of high seriousness, other chains of relays and disruptions that may have energised, transmogrified, and changed the stakes of the 'same' opposition, the 'same' concepts. Or, to state it differently and perhaps more appropriately, there are other, maybe less philosophically foundational, yet no less discursively intractable concepts constituting the very conditions of our experience, shaping the regime of the real today. And these, too, are histories demanding the labour of reading.

RELIGION-BEFORE RELIGION AND RELIGION-AFTER RELIGION

Chin Hong Chung

Reshuffled Rest

Professor Masuzawa suggests that the study of religion should conduct its own research with an alternative manner of critique, one that is quite different from the conventional ways of undertaking the study of religion. As an example, she demonstrates her work of investigation of a discursive history and its comparative and classificatory logic of the word 'world religion'. She calls it a work of theory that does not concern itself with methodology. Such a non-methodological critique, in her view, is not a deprivation of the integrity of conventional approaches but it may imply new tasks, and urge new alliances and inventions. Her explanation of this suggestion is that the 'world religions' have not only shaped the study of religion and infiltrated ordinary languages, but also included an aspect of the formation of modern European identity. It has done so not merely as a descriptive concept but also as a particular ethos, a pluralist ideology, logic of classification, and a form of knowledge.

While it is outside my ambition—to examine the emergence of 'world religions' in modern European thought—to comment on her project, I generally agree with her analytical critique on the issue of 'theory and method.' However, reading her article I realised that I have sympathy with the concerns and issues she raises from quite a different locus. Describing the fact that in Western intellectual history a new concept of religion has emerged in Christian Europe, as a consequence of the decline of monotheism and its rejection of plurality, Professor Masuzawa makes the point that in the commotion the rest of the world has also been reshuffled and recast to the extent of a new 'map' having been drawn. In this context, my finding is that I belong to the reshuffled 'rest.'

My response as such is not a comment on Professor Masuzawa's presentation. My aim is rather to demonstrate my own concerns in sympathy with hers. So, it is a practical and personal wish to be in her 'new alliance', even if I belong with different 'language' to the 'rest' of the world.

World Religions and Folk Belief

Let me draw attention to the word 'religion' (*jongkyo*) which we use nowadays in Korea. As vocabulary, the term 'religion' is quite generally used not only in Korea but also in China and Japan. Yet 'religion' is not a word that 'belongs' to our culture and tradition. It was instead an alien term that was imported by Japan from the Western countries in the late nineteenth century. In the Korean language we had no word that corresponded to the term 'religion'. However, we had no other way to accommodate it except by translating it as 'religion'. This was certainly in part the consequence of Japan's and the Western countries' pressure through armed power that forced us to open the door toward Western culture and 'modernity'. Therefore, the term religion existed as an enforced and indeed a never 'experienced' word until Korea became engaged in the process of modernisation in the late nineteenth century.[1]

Even though it has become domesticated in Korea through such a historical process, the translated word 'religion' soon entered everyday usage as an ordinary word. It became a useful conceptual term in building the apparatus of a modern epistemology in our academism. But the concept of religion never succeeded in incorporating our experience fully, and it has been utilised as an inappropriate measure and criterion in the description and understanding of our traditional belief culture. It is unavoidable, therefore, to reach the point where the empirical reality of traditional religious experience and its expression is distorted, devalued, and confused by such a newly enforced word as 'religion'. But we have to use the word to describe our religious experience, because the term has so effectively usurped upon our ordinary language in our daily life.[2]

---

[1] Suk Man Jang, 'Gaehangki Hanguk Sahoe-ui Jongkyo Gaenyeom Hyeongseong-ae gwanhan Yeongu' ('A Historical Study of the Concept of *Jongkyo* in Modern Korean Society'), Ph.D. diss., Seoul National University, 1992.

[2] Chin Hong Chung, 'Redescription and rectification of the modernity experience of Korean traditional religious culture', *Korea Journal*, vol. 41, no. 1, 2001, Korean National Commission for UNESCO, pp. 3–17.

It is interesting to see how a Western word, 'religion', becomes a 'nucleus of opacity within a network of transparent significations', including the issue of method and theory, as Professor Masuzawa quotes from Derrida. It is natural to follow the thread of the question she subsequently asks: 'What then could be a way out of this fix, so that the work of analysis could go on?'

Her suggestion is to trace the historical terrain that is traversed by the emergent European discourse on religion. Her rationale for it is that such a terrain is the womb of the 'world religions'.

Even though we may differ on the issue itself and the approach to it, I agree with her concept of a 'problem', fundamentally in terms of seeking an alternative manner of criticising and de-constituting conventional theory and methods. This is why I think it is more relevant to try and present my personal issue than to contend the subject of 'theory and method' here. For this, as an example, I would like to take the word 'folk belief' as a subject word in my work, as she did with 'world religions' in her project.

Topography of Religious Culture

If we try to sketch the topography of Korean religious culture, where will the locus of folk belief be, what will the extent of it be, and how will its geological features be coloured? The conventional answer to this is unexpectedly simple.[3] Most particularly, folk belief is regarded as a descriptive category of religious culture accomplished by referring to the social classification. Another understanding is to explain it as a foundation and archetype of our culture. Lastly, there is the idea of trying to treat it as equivalent to the kind of concrete performance that used to be called *musok*: a shaman-oriented conventional life style.

However, my concern is with the word 'folk belief' itself. The word is a rather technical term which is abstracted and invented to designate particular experiences. It is then unavoidable to ask about the descriptive criteria of the actual reality from which the abstracted concept appears. At this point let me draw attention again to a previous question about what Korean understandings concerning folk belief are. It is a logical necessity that if there were no religion of the ruling class, no folk

---

[3] Ibid., *Gyeongheom gwa Giyeok* (Experience and Recollection: Reading the Gaps in Religious Culture), Seoul: Dangdae Publishing Company, 2003, pp. 160–2.

religion could be present at all, and if there were no appearance and disappearance of religions in history, there would be no commentary on the remnant religions so far. And without the presence of other religions here and now, how could it be possible to say anything about *musok* as a particular reality in our daily life?

It may not be impossible, then, to say that folk belief is nothing but 'religion which is antithetic to religion'. However, here arises another problem, namely whether it is possible to incorporate 'folk belief' into 'religion' or exclude it from the category of 'religion'—which has now become an ordinary word designating religious experiences and culture in general, even if it is not the original one constructed in our history and traditional culture—because 'religion which is antithetic to religion' is nothing but to imply a hidden judgement on folk belief as 'a religion which is not religion'.[4]

Let me briefly deviate from the point. Human beings are in existential turmoil and seek an exit from it. Even if there are variously modified historical and cultural conditions, it is impossible to evade the agony and to abandon the longing for an answer. Diverse metaphorical descriptions have appeared and been used to denote the answers to intense personal conflict in our traditional culture throughout its history. Some of them include 'releasing' (*pullim*), 'saving from drowning' (*keonjim*), 'loosening of the knot' (*maedeubpulgi*), 'opening' (*yeollim*), 'no obstruction' (*mansahyeongtong*), 'there is the other shore' (*jeoseungsari*), and 'born again' (*wangsaeng*), etc.

The question is whether there is a single abstract word that embraces all such metaphorical expressions. If there is such a word, what exactly is it? When and how has it been formed and transferred in history? Would this word still have an appropriate role in describing and interpreting the agony and longing of people nowadays, effectively and meaningfully?

The word 'religion' has appeared, and it has been supposed to be useful to delineate the situation properly ever since it was 'imported' in the late nineteenth century in the turmoil of modernisation. Hence, the term is actually utilised in a description and explanation of 'our' religious experiences. But when we speak about 'religion', this is a translation from Western terminology, and as such is so alien that it

---

[4] Ibid., p. 167.

is essentially neither possible nor appropriate to designate our specific experiences.

In spite of this, we continue to use the word 'religion', and consequently it serves nothing but to confront our own 'religion' with the Western concept of 'religion.' In other words, it means that we are categorising our own religious culture according to an alien concept of religion. If we put it from a different perspective again, it means we have no 'religion' in Korea, but only 'religionised religion'. Our experiences are reduced to a newly adopted unfamiliar frame, and thereby these experiences are reshuffled and re-described through a type-casting judgement implicit in the use of the word 'religion'.[5]

Religion-before Religion and Religion-after Religion

One of the urgent issues of the study of religion in Korea is whether it is possible at all to write such a study under the title of 'Korean History of Religious Culture' or 'The History of Religions of Korea'. Conventionally, ambitious work has been done by editing each individual religion's history into a single copy. It must be considered, however, that the term 'individual religion' was only introduced after the word 'religion' had begun to be used. In other words, it is a consequence of a normative application of the concept of 'religion'. Therefore, it is not different from the description of 'religion-before religion' with the norms or criteria of 'religion-after religion.'

Hence, it may be a necessity to exclude, as a 'non-religion', some of the phenomena which were already included in 'religion-before religion' from the traditional religious culture, because of its inappropriateness to 'religion-after religion'. Folk belief is an example of that necessity. It is 'a religion which is not religion'.

The concept of 'religion-before religion', therefore, as well as of 'religion-after religion', is the most significant criterion in the description and interpretation of religion and folk belief in Korean culture. According to this criterion, 'religion-after religion' can be defined as a separated juxtaposition of diverse religions, and 'religion-before religion' can be defined as an amassment of possible religious experiences. In other words, contrary to the 'religion-before religion', which should

---

⁵ Chin Hong Chung, *Jongkyo Munhwa-ui Nolli* (Logic of Religious Culture), Seoul National University Press, 2000, pp. 241–98.

rather be called an 'aggregated religious culture,' the 'religion-after religion' should be referred to as a 'diffused religious culture'. If we use a more technical terminology, each of these cultures may be named 'soteriological ethos' and 'soteriological doctrine' respectively.[6]

In this context, it is necessary to consider once more why folk belief is regarded as so significant for the description and interpretation of Korean religious culture. Let me state again that, according to the above understanding of folk belief, Korean religious culture becomes 'a religion which is not religion' by the criterion of the 'religion-after religion'. But strictly speaking, 'a religion which is not religion' does not indicate an empirical reality. It is only an indication of a conceptual reality. What must be clarified then is the substance of the empirical reality from which a conceptual reality is abstracted.

Musok: *Empirical Reality*

We mentioned already three different conventional understandings of folk belief. Among them, only *musok* can be attributed to factual reality, because it constitutes a physical performance. Therefore, it is plausible to take *musok* as a substance of empirical reality, which can be done without much difficulty. And if *musok* can be investigated analytically and structurally, it becomes possible to make clear why folk belief is the subject of my concern in the study of religion in Korea.

However, even if *musok* is delved into, there can be different claims regarding the reason why this is a topic of concern, representing two different positions, namely the position of 'religion-after religion' and that of 'religion-before religion'. While the former expects that through studying *musok* an archetype and a foundation for Korean religious culture will be discovered,[7] the latter is out to recapture the lost empirical religious experience that has not been occluded by the alien concept of 'religion'.[8] In other words, the manner of the latter may be sketched as a form of nostalgia, a longing for an 'aggregated religious culture' in the situation of 'diffused religious culture'. It is, therefore, nothing

---

[6] Ibid., pp. 169–73.

[7] Dong Sik Ryu, *Hanguk Mugyo-ui Yeoksa wa Gujo* (History and Structure of Korean Shamanism), Seoul: Yonsei University Press, 1992.

[8] Heung Yun Cho, *Mu wa Minjok Munhwa* (Shaman and National Culture), Seoul: Minjok Munhwasa, 1994.

but an expression of deliberate intention not to have concern for a 'soteriological doctrine' but instead to depict a 'soteriological ethos.'

If it is a necessity to reflect theory and method in the analytical discourse concerning folk belief, it should be sufficient to refer to the fact that the epistemology used for the investigation into diffused religious culture is inadequate for studying aggregated religious culture. Also, the phenomena expressed through *musok* are not of a 'soteriological doctrine' type, but representative of religious culture itself as an organic whole. In that case it is natural to consider *musok* as an actual expression of a particular religious culture, furnishing the perspective that a conventional approach does not allow for the recognition of folk belief, which has long been experienced and continues to be experienced, here and now, by the Korean people.

Even if the perspectives are mutually different, an ideological cognition of social reality, an evolutionary comprehension of history, and a psychoanalytical description of culture have each contributed to a holistic understanding of human life. But whatever the perspective may be, no interpretation can disregard the empirical reality that constitutes the very concept. Therefore, none of the systems that have been constituted through the development of logical expansion of conceptual reality expose any practical experiences from which the concept has been abstracted. This does not mean that no concept is needed at all, but that a concept must be the object of introspection, not only into its contents but also into the presence of the concept itself.[9] It must be acknowledged that concepts are history-laden productions. Thus, our present project must progress towards the description and interpretation of *musok* as an empirical reality, to locate and mark folk belief in topography of Korean religious culture.

Throughout almost all of the last century, studies of *musok* have been continuously conducted and have been considerably strengthened in recent years. However, this research has arrived constantly at the point where *mudang* (shaman) is explained as a subject of a 'soteriology of doctrine', in other words, in terms of *musok* as a particular religion. This is because *musok* has been investigated, from the position of 'religion-after religion', as a 'religion which is not religion'.[10] Disregarding

---

[9] Chin Hong Chung, *Jongkyo Munhwa-ui Insik gwa Haeseok* (Epistemology and Hermeneutics of Religious Culture: Development of Phenomenology of Religion), Seoul National University Press, 1996, pp. 1–26.

[10] Yee Heum Yoon (ed.), *Hangukin-ui Jongkyogwan* (Understanding of Religion among the Korean People), Seoul National University Press, 2001, pp. 5–9.

empirical reality, this research has always stopped at a particular point, namely at analysis of *musok* as a conceptual reality. There is no explanation of the 'aggregated religious culture', which is a description of a 'soteriological ethos'.

As one example, it can be pointed out that in studying *musok*, the *mudang* has been the main object of research, which is to marginalise the clients who participate in the *gut* (shamanistic ritual).[11] There are plenty of studies on *mudangs*, including their initiation experiences, their functions as a mediator, their mystic experiences, the disciplinary processes, and so on. And it can be affirmed that it has been done from the point of view of 'a religion-after religion'. But if the viewpoint were to be changed into the 'religion-before religion' perspective, the concern for *musok* would be expressive of a soteriological ethos that is urgently demanded by the clients. In this regard, it is interesting to note that explanations or interpretations about the ritual process, various instruments used, and music and dance cannot move the clients in a meaningful direction. Their concern is simply to confirm if a transformation of their own mode of being has taken place or not.

Originally the function of the *mudang* is to suggest an answer for a client's problem. Therefore, if there were no client who urgently demands an answer, there would be no *mudang* at all. Hence, the search for *musok* in terms of 'a soteriological doctrine' was an accidental choice determined by historico-cultural conditions. There would be only a particular religion in terms of 'a soteriological doctrine' if one were concerned only with *mudang* and *gut*. However, if one focuses attention on the clients, it becomes possible to describe the contemporary religious ethos, in which they are participating as a subject.[12] It is now clear why folk belief is becoming our topic of contention in religion discourse. It is not because *musok* as a folk belief is a particular religion that can be juxtaposed with the other religions in Korea, but because it is 'a soteriological ethos' that is disclosing the empirical reality.

Therefore, focusing on the clients in the case of *musok* studies prepares for a good momentum not only to reflect on our conventional

---

[11] Tae Gon Kim, *Hanguk Musok Yeongu* (A Study of Korean Shamanism), Seoul: Jipmundang, 1987. Even though this book is evaluated as a pioneering and conclusive work on Korean shamanism, no concern for clients is found in it.

[12] Ok Sung Cha, *Hangukin-ui Jongkyo Gyeongheom: Mugyo* (Religious Experience of the Korean People: Shamanism), Seoul: Seogwangsa, 1997. Her work is one of the exemplary studies using the method of depth interviews with the clients.

understanding of 'religion', but also to invite and recapture the 'religion-before religion': the forgotten empirical reality that has been unwillingly isolated by the concept of 'religion-after religion'. At this point, finally, it can be possible to contend and develop our own discourse of religious culture, without reducing our own religious experiences to the alienated category of a 'religion' as a conceptualised category from Western experience.

Meteorology of Religious Culture

At the beginning of this response, I raised a question of the possibility of incorporating folk belief into the topography of religious culture. Now it is inevitable to give a negative answer to this, because folk belief does not have any particular locus, it has no extent or geological features, nor its own colouring. Folk belief is an ethos; in other words, it is an incessantly moving atmosphere surrounding, or streaming upon, the terrain. The only possible drawing of folk belief is not the topography of religious culture but meteorology of it. But it is another problem whether or not it is possible to draw it on an intellectual map.

So far, the established studies of folk belief or *musok* claim that the phenomenon has a constituted structure, implying and expressing a concrete system. Therefore, it is maintained that what should be confirmed is nothing but the meaning of the *musok* phenomenon itself. *Musok*, then, becomes 'a text that must be read', and *musok* discourse becomes the contents that we should learn from the 'read meaning'. In this way, 'a soteriological doctrine' of *musok* has been constructed. This may be called a 'theologisation' of *musok*.[13] When *musok* was termed as *mugyo* (shaman-religion), such an approach to folk belief or *musok* had reached its peak.

The 'religion-after religion' approach accepts *musok* positively in so far as it is theologised or religionised. However, this means that the practical experiences related with it have been changed into a conceptual reality. In other words, the experiences of the individual have been deliberately cut to pieces by systematised logic and cognitive structure. If this is regarded as a legitimate description and interpretation of folk

---

[13] Gun Ho Ko, 'Jongkyo doegi wa jongkyo neomeoseogi' ('Religionising and de-religionising'), *Jongkyo Munhwa Bipyeong* ('The critical review of religion and culture'), vol. 7, 2005, pp. 42–71.

belief or *musok*, the discourse of the study of religion about that issue could be described as an 'additional hermeneutics' for 'a theologised *musok*'. In spite of the rigidity and precision of its epistemology, or of its theory and method, such an interpretation of *musok* is merely an unrealistic description of religious culture, because it is loosing the 'ethos' and ensuring the 'doctrine' instead. Consequently, it is no more than a misapprehension that confuses a conceptual reality with an empirical one.

Now, let me sum up our issues. The first one concerns a problem of priority: what should be the primary object of the study of religion in Korea: a soteriological doctrine or a soteriological ethos? The other one concerns a problem of the locus of scholars with an interest in religious culture: which of the two—'religion-after religion' or 'religion-before religion'—should be the locus of their own perspectives?

Conclusion

I come to the conclusion that the discourse of religious culture which tries to confirm the locus of folk belief in a religious culture must start with analysing and reconsidering the very concepts of 'religion' and 'folk belief'. Moreover, it should even go further and make a deconstitutive analysis of the use of 'concepts' in general in the academic world. The cognitive concepts in academia have already been criticised, in the sense that such an academic 'language' so often distorts human life since it is constituted in a 'disciplinary horizon' that lacks a holistic view. Reflection on this reality is not the specific responsibility of someone who is in the 'default position', nor is it a limited problem of newly awakened Western scholarship. In the 'rest' of the world, the urgency of reflection is not different from the 'rest of the rest' of the world.

As Professor Masuzawa appropriately expresses it, choosing an alternative path of critique may disturb the peace and integrity of the study of religion. But I sincerely agree with her that, at the same time, it may stimulate a new imagination and urge a move towards a new invention, for the 'welfare of the study of religions'.

THEORY AND METHOD IN THE STUDY OF RELIGIONS
A RESPONSE

Sylvia Marcos

I would like to thank those who have invited me to formulate a response to Professor Tomoko Masuzawa's paper on theory and method in the study of religions. During the last few years I have been systematising a methodology for the study of indigenous religions in Mesoamerica.[1] Therefore, I can only welcome the opportunity to outline some comments based on her presentation.

I am with Professor Masuzawa when she says: 'I am not a specialist in general theories of religion' but, unlike her, I am willing to use the term 'methodology' for my humble proposal, that is decidedly pedestrian, but also terrestrially empirical. I also agree with her that with today's non-poststructuralist frame of mind prevalent, theoretical deliberations will always and immediately be answerable to the question of method; that is, the work of theory is held responsible for the maintenance of a healthy stockpile of good tools and functional instruments for empirical research and analysis.

I would like to draw the attention to an interesting intersection between Professor Masuzawa's investigation and my own area of study. While she explores the historical terrain traversed by the European discourse on religion, I would like to make a reference here to Jonathan Smith's review of the terms 'religion', 'religions', and 'religious'.[2] Smith examines how these terms have been changing, stretching their meanings across time. He points out that '...this technical vocabulary...gets first extended to non-Christian examples'...in the description of the complex civilisation of Mesoamerica. He specially refers to Hernán Cortez, the conqueror of Mexico, and his letters to the King of Spain, as well

---

[1] Sylvia Marcos, *Taken from the Lips: Gender and Eros in Mesoamerican Religions*, Leiden: Brill, 2006.

[2] Jonathan Z. Smith, 'Religion, religions, religious', in Mark C. Taylor (ed.), *Critical Terms for Religious Studies*, University of Chicago Press, 1998, pp. 269–84.

as to the learned Jesuit Joseph de Acosta who in 1590 compiled an encyclopedic work entitled *The Natural and Moral History of the Indies*.[3]

Quoting Derrida's deconstructive, or deconstituting critique, Professor Masuzawa asks what, then, could be a way out of the fix, so that the work of analysis—that is, any empirical study of the variety of religions in human society—may continue? What choices do we have when the foundational concepts or schematic apparatuses of a discipline are called to account, '…momentarily—if not indefinitely—disabling the interpretive work, as the whole operation seems to be besieged by doubt, suspicion, and umbrage?' Turning her gaze to Lévi-Strauss, she affirms Derrida's observation that, 'This is how the language of the social sciences criticizes itself. Lévi-Strauss will always remain faithful to a double intention: to preserve as an instrument something whose truth value he criticizes'. 'So much of the grievance against "mere theory" or "mere critique", she continues, 'has to do with the complaint that this constructive or restorative moment is insufficiently attended to or altogether lacking'. Thus she summarises the bases of post-modern deconstruction. This path of double intention of destroy-and-preserve *is* indeed frequently assumed to be the only path of critique.

The binarism of the nature/culture divide has been fundamental as an analytic strategy, not only to structural anthropology but in general to other social sciences. As Professor Masuzawa recalls, a memorable moment in the birth of post-structuralism, amounting to a beginning of what has since come to be garnered, cultivated, variegated, and multiplied under the term 'theory', occurred in October 1966, at the Johns Hopkins Conference 'The Languages of Criticisms and the Sciences of Man'. However, this 'new beginning' of theory has also been developed much further, beyond the critique of binarisms such as the nature/culture divide.

I would then pose the question: Is there another way of structuring a rigorous and systematic analysis that goes beyond critiquing and nevertheless recuperating the analytic armature of binary categories? Is there a more constructive or restorative moment?

I have no ready-made answers, but *preguntando caminamos: se hace camino al andar*. We find our path by walking on it, as an ancestral Mayan Tzeltal saying goes. May I suggest that another path could be feasible? Turning an ethnographic gaze to the concrete practices of locally bound religious specialists, could one not locate diverse forms

---

[3] Ibid., pp. 269–70.

of what Foucault calls an *episteme*?[4] I am speaking here of a cognitive frame that would transcend an all-pervasive binarism.

This approach has been inspired by my encounter with the ancestral knowledge and religious universe of the Mesoamerican peoples, which I would like to sketch briefly. An ethnographic investigation, a dialogic encounter, conducted systematically and rigorously, is likely to bring to light a polyvalent, non-binary, and often conflicting formation.

Mesoamerica did not 'discover' Europe before 1519. The term religion, which until today is not considered by the indigenous peoples of Mesoamerica as adequately reflecting the structure of their universe of beliefs and practices, was first used by Europeans arriving to this area of the world with a colonising thrust. Religion, as a category extrinsic to the indigenous peoples of contemporary Mesoamerica, can give us only a point of departure for systematizing the way in which these indigenous traditions can best be approached.

Indigenous Mesoamerican 'religious' traditions are mainly 'oral' traditions. Texts, even if they exist, are not at the core of their belief structure except, perhaps, as another iconographic element in the Mesoamerican pantheon. Ancient codices play this role in the contemporary community of Milpa Alta (a Nahua community near Mexico City), as Joaquín Galarza has noted.[5]

Any attempt to approach religions transmitted through oral traditions with the methods used for systematizing religions rooted in 'sacred' and other texts, will lead to distortion and misinterpretation. Historical and textual methods presuppose a fixed narrative as a basis for analysis. Oral traditions are essentially fluid, flexible and malleable. The subtle shifting and changing of words, metaphors, and meanings easily slip through the text cast by historical and textual analysis. In order to capture a tradition that is in continuous change, a 'hermeneutics of orality' is needed.

I will reflect briefly on a possible proposal derived from a much larger work of mine.[6] Armin Geertz has proposed a method called 'ethno-hermeneutics', which can be used as a complement and is related to

---

[4] Michel Foucault, *The Order of Things: An Archeology of Human Sciences*, New York: Vintage Books, 1970, p. xxii.

[5] Joaquín Galarza, 'El Codex Mendoza'. Paper presented at the Instituto de Investigaciones Antropológicas, UNAM, Mexico, November 1998.

[6] Sylvia Marcos, *Taken from the Lips*. See also from the same author 'Approaches to orality: a methodology'. Keynote address at the 'Conference on Orality, Gender and Indigenous Religions', Claremont Graduate University, School of Religion, Claremont CA, May 2001.

the hermeneutics of orality. Ethno-hermeneutics, he explains, 'attempts to correct the "fictive" product of the philological analysis by combining two perspectives: 1) the reflections of the student of a religion and 2) the reflections of the indigenous student of that religion. Two hermeneutical endeavours brought together, but located in diverse personal, social, and historical contexts. The end product will be greater than the two.'[7] The 'hermeneutics of orality' proposes instruments to comprehend, interpret, and systematize (indigenous) oral religious traditions through a focus on:

1) *The solidity and permanence of spoken words.* The Aztecs called the words of their ritual discourses 'a scattering of jades', explicitly evoking the density and permanence of this precious stone.[8] In oral traditions words are meaningful in particular ways. They are often generative rather than representative. Speech does not encode realities that might exist independently apart from the speakers. Words shape a reality coming into being.[9] Maria Sabina, a shaman from Oaxaca, a southern state of Mexico, speaks concretely of her experiences of healing with language: '...and I also see the words fall, they come from up above, as if they were little luminous objects falling from the sky'.[10] Precious and permanent as jade stones, words, in oral traditions, literally call the world into being.

2) *An imagery carried by abundant metaphoric usage.* In oral traditions, metaphors disclose the deep qualities of nature, people and events. Metaphor, as a transport (transfer) from a domain in which its meaning is literal to another where it becomes figurative, is often basic to the structuring of reality. Already in 1577, Fray Bernardino de Sahagun translated into Spanish his transcriptions of Aztec oral religious chants and collected them in his *Historia General de las Cosas*

---

[7] Armin W. Geertz, 'Global perspectives on methodology in the study of religion', in A. W. Geertz and R. T. McCutcheon (eds.), *Perspectives on Method and Theory in the Study of Religion*, Leiden: Brill, 2000, p. 71.

[8] Fray Bernardino de Sahagun, *Historia de las Cosas de la Nueva España*, Mexico: Porrua, 1982, [1577]. Cited in Thelma Sullivan, 'A scattering of jades: the words of the Aztec elders', in G. H. Gossen, (ed.), *Symbol and Meaning beyond the Closed Community: Essays in Mesoamerican Ideas*, Albany: Institute for Mesoamerican Studies, State University of New York, 1986, p. 9.

[9] Kenneth Morrison, 'The cosmos as intersubjective: Native American other than human persons', in Graham Harvey (ed.), *Indigenous Religions*, London and New York: Cassell, 2000, p. 34.

[10] Alvaro Estrada, *Maria Sabina: Her Life and Chants*, Santa Barbara: Ross-Erickson Publishers, 1983, p. 94.

de la Nueva España. He records the abundant use of metaphors and expresses his admiration for their beauty, expressiveness, and the skill of their rhetorical use.[11] In contemporary indigenous societies—as confirmed by many ethnographies—this usage is still common practice today. For instance, water is still called *la sangre de la tierra,* the blood of the earth, in many communities.[12] Miguel León Portilla calls *difrasismo* the juxtaposition of two words or ideas, each transferred from a distinct realm, which together evoke a third reality. Practically inexistent in European languages, *difrasismo* is one of the richest sources of metaphors—and thus guides—for the interpretation of the Nahuatl language and culture. Some examples are: *flower and song,* meaning poetry, art and symbol; *skirt and shirt,* meaning woman in her sexual character; *chair and mat,* meaning authority.[13]

3) *Rhythmically formulae meticulously remembered.* The rhythmical repetition of certain formulae in diverse parts of a ritual discourse, religious chant, or recited epic are royal paths to interpretation. Songs or sung tales are highly formalised in structure: they bear the mark of metaphorical and other remembering techniques that elicit creative interpretation on the part of the listener. Some of these verbal formulae should be studied as a vital expression of beliefs and practices of oral texts transcribed for the first time. Oral narratives are neither the recitation of a 'text' learned by memory, nor completely original creations of the narrator. It is in these that religious myths and symbols rest encapsulated. Remembering them—every time in a slightly different way—is a collective enactment. Every such re-enactment is the work of a *rhapsoidos,* a rhapsody according to Parry,[14] meaning a patchwork in Greek, a woven kind of composition, based on ever new combinations of traditional formulae.

4) *Redundancy as a mnemonic and musical strategy.* The repetition of words, apparently synonymous, but with different shades, is one of the most conspicuous characteristics of oral languages and traditions. This is a poetic enhancement of discourses and also a powerful mnemonic device. Redundancies articulate all discursive practices musically.

---

[11] See Sahagun, pp. 415–24.

[12] Author's notes.

[13] Miguel Léon Portilla, *Literaturas de Mesoamérica,* Mexico: SEP, 1984.

[14] Milman Parry, *The Making of Homeric Verse,* Oxford: Clarendon Press, 1971. Cited in John Miles Foley (ed.), *Oral Traditional Literature: A Festschrift for Albert Bates Lord,* Columbus, OH: Slavica Publishers, 1981, p. 29.

Some complex formulae are the basis of ritual discourses. Here are some examples of the alternating use of formulae with closely related semantic contents rhythmically repeated:[15]

¿Cuix nel timotlatiz?
¿Cuix timinayaz?
¿Cuix canapé tonyaz?
¿Cuix teixpampa tehuaz?

By chance in truth you will hide?
By chance you will conceal yourself?
By chance you will go away?
By chance you will flee?

5) *Fluid symbolic meanings.* The use of symbols is basic to oral traditions, their syntactic polymorphism and ambiguity facilitates autonomous re-appropriation. In oral religious traditions, symbols overlap and intertwine in multiple layers of meanings beyond the grasp of linear interpretations. They are polysemic and multivocal.[16] However, '... [w]hen a symbol is conventionalized it is deprived of its ambiguity and *ipso facto* of its capacity for leverage and maneuverability... [it looses] its syntactic looseness [that]facilitates manipulation and choice.'[17] The most common circumstance for the conventionalisation of symbols occurs when a popular myth or symbol is taken over by a learned scholar and thus narrowed down to give them limited and non-contradictory, linear meanings. Meanings do not inhere only in symbols, but must be invested in and interpreted by active social beings. Polysemic, 'non-conventionalised', symbols are abundant in oral traditions. The ethnographer who inquires about the meanings of symbolic events and/or of iconographic representations, will frequently encounter a profusion and ambiguity of responses. This occurs even when the questions are posed to the same person, in different moments, and when the rituals studied and their communitary contexts are identical. Polisemy, multivocality, and ambiguity

---

[15] Thelma Sullivan, *Compendio de Gramática Nahuatl*, Mexico: UNAM, 1983, pp. 16–7.

[16] Victor Turner, 'Encounter with Freud: the making of a comparative symbologist', in G. D. Spindler (ed.), *The Making of Psychological Anthropology*, Berkeley: University of California Press, 1978, p. 573.

[17] Gananath Obeyeskere, *Medusa's Hair: An Essay on Personal Symbols and Religious Experience*, University of Chicago Press, 1981, p. 51.

would come in hand, so the ethnographer does not feel obliged to reduce or simplify findings to what can be rendered in a 'learned' linear logic of interpretation.

6) *The analysis of gendered rituals.* Frequently women hold the patronage of collective re-enactments, where rhythmic formulae are ritually remembered and woven together, re-creating oral religious traditions. Symbols are taken over and re-signified in a continual process of re-appropriation. El *Cántico de las Mujeres de Chalco* is a well-known example of women's leadership in rituals where poetry, politics and religion fuse.[18] It combines narratives and performative devices by which women evoke the domain of the erotic and, through it, challenge Lord Axcayatl, the local ruler. In interaction with the audience, these female religious specialists guide the audiences, re-interpret the symbolic domain, and express a world where, more often than not, women are the respected authorities. Gendered rituals are classic of oral religious traditions.[19]

Some underlying concepts of these religious worlds—sketched briefly here—are: the pervading indigenous concepts of the divine, *of* and *in* nature; the unfolding (not in a binary sense) of the sacred/profane and/or the transcendent/immanent; and finally the interlocking, interdependent, reciprocal relationships between 'more than human' beings (or super-human beings according to H. Penner, quoted by Ivan Strensky)[20] and humans. These apparent disjunctions are fused into a distinct unity.[21]

The above analytical interpretative strategies are more apt for grasping the particularity of a religious tradition immersed in a process of change. How can we otherwise comprehend, interpret and render—in all justice and with an ethics of the encounter with this 'Other'—a tradition that is permanently reconfiguring itself?

The paradoxical juxtapositions exemplified in the ritual discourses from Mesoamerican ancient sources reveal a seamless unity, which can

---

[18] Portilla, *Literaturas de Mesoamérica*, pp. 164–6.

[19] Cf. Sylvia Marcos (ed.), *Gender/Bodies/Religions*, Mexico: IAHR-ALER Publications, 2000; Ibid., 'Beyond binary categories: Mesoamerican religious sexuality', in Stephen Ellingson and M. Christian Green (eds.), *Religion and Sexuality in Cross-Cultural Perspective*, New York and London: Routledge, 2002, pp. 111–36.

[20] Ivan Strenski, 'Hans Penner, Horatio, and the Terminator: a review essay of radical interpretation in religion', *Religion*, vol. 34, no. 1, 2004, p. 57.

[21] Marcos, 'Approaches to orality'.

only be discovered in the mytho-poetic, metaphoric context of these traditions' worldview, not through the application of purely Western standards of syllogism.[22]

I find Professor Masuzawa's paper very thought-provoking, particularly for her observations on theory and method and discourse critique. Her review of modern European intellectual history is very illuminating, demonstrating to us the various ways in which Europeans have been re-imagining themselves as 'the West' and have re-conceptualised their relation with 'the rest'. Oral religious traditions, implied in this 'rest' present a challenge to standard rational syllogistic critical norms of discourse.

I would like to conclude my comments by recalling that there exist no pure or pristine essences. Rather, there exists an interlocking of power-ridden historical, political, social and religious interactions. A hermeneutics of orality would enhance the possibilities of approaching the 'Other' without demeaning distortions or idealised appropriations.

---

[22] Willard Gingerich, '*Cipahuacanemiliztli*, the Purified Life in the Discourses of Book VI, Florentine Codex,' in J. Kathryn Josserand and Kaaren Dakin (eds.), *Smoke and Mist: Mesoamerican Studies in Memory of Thelma Sullivan*, BAR International Series 402, 1988, p. 517.

PART SIX

THE STUDY OF RELIGION IN JAPAN

RELIGIOUS STUDIES IN POST-WAR JAPAN

Noriyoshi Tamaru

Introduction

In his seminal work *Le mythe de l'éternel retour*,[1] based upon a careful analysis of ancient Babylonian myths, Mircea Eliade has shown that one of the universal motifs in the religious life of mankind is to return periodically to the primeval time of origin and to recreate the existing order of things anew. A further look reveals that the same pattern can be found not only in the area of religion but in other spheres of cultural activity as well. The academic study of religion—the subject matter of the present article—is no exception to the rule that from time to time we must examine and reflect upon the basic premises of our undertaking and ascertain its implications and contemporary relevance.

For Japanese researchers working in this field, the year 2005 offered a welcome occasion for such an exercise in self-appraisal, as it marked the 100th anniversary of the founding of a Chair in Religious Studies at the University of Tokyo, in 1905. This is generally recognised as the official start of modern academic studies of religion in Japan, though this institutional arrangement was preceded and facilitated by a series of preparatory stages and movements.[2] To commemorate this historical moment, the Japanese Association for Religious Studies (JARS) invited the International Association for the History of Religions (IAHR) to convene in Tokyo for its XIXth World Congress in 2005. The Japanese association, founded in May 1930 at the occasion of the 25th anniversary of the establishment of the chair at the University of Tokyo, also organised a large-scale symposium aimed at reviewing the achievements of religious studies in Japan during the last hundred years as a major

---

[1] Mircea Eliade, *Le mythe de l'éternel retour*, Paris: Gallimard, 1949.

[2] For a brief historical overview of Religious Studies in Japan, see the present author's article, 'Religious Studies in Japan: a preliminary report,' in: Ugo Bianchi (ed.), *The Notion of 'Religion'. Comparative Research: Selected Proceedings of the XVIth IAHR Congress*, Roma: Erma di Bretschneider, 1994, pp. 755–61; Cf. also Satoko Fujiwara, 'Study of religion: the academic study of religion in Japan', in *The Encyclopedia of Religion* (2nd. ed.), Farmington Hills: Thomson Gale, 2005, pp. 8775–80.

program of its 63rd annual convention in September 2004.[3] In this
symposium, a total of eight research fields, representative of modern
Japanese scholarship on religion, were singled out, and eight leading
specialists delivered detailed reports on each topic, followed by extensive
general discussion. These papers were subsequently published in the
Journal of Religious Studies.[4] At the same time, some parts of this symposium were rephrased and incorporated into the academic program
of the IAHR World Congress in the form of two organised panels,
entitled The Study of Religion in Japan, held in Japanese.[5] Some of
the papers presented in these panels have been worked into in short
essays in English and are published in the following chapters of the
present volume.

The following survey is based on an article by the present author that
was originally published in the above-mentioned number of the *Journal
of Religious Studies*. In conjunction with the more specialised reports of
the symposium it was meant to provide some additional information
about the major trends and features of religious studies in Japan in the
post-war period. Here, it has been slightly modified to meet the interest of non-Japanese readership, and the references, mainly concerning
Japanese sources, are accordingly simplified.

---

[3] Some basic documents related to the early history and development of JARS have
been compiled in a booklet, entitled *Fifty Years of the Japanese Association for Religious Studies*
(in Japanese: *Nihon Shukyo Gakkai Gojunenshi*), which was published to commemorate its
50th anniversary in 1980.

[4] *Journal of Religious Studies*, no. 353, March 2005. This included the following papers:
Toshimaro Hanazono, 'The comparative study of religions and the phenomenology
of religion for the last 100 years in Japan', Kiyotaka Kimura, 'One hundred years of
Buddhist studies in Japan', Hiroshi Tsuchiya, 'From theology to the study of Christianity:
the fundamental problem of Christian studies in Japan', Kojiro Nakamura, 'Islamic
studies in Japan', Shoto Hase, 'Japanese study of religion and Japanese philosophy of
religion', Masahiko Asoya, 'The scientific and theological study of Shinto', Hitoshi
Miyake, 'Study of the history of folk religion: aiming to identify religious traditions',
Shigeru Nishiyama, 'A hundred years of study of new religions and the sociology of
religion in Japan'. *Journal of Religious Studies* is the official English title of *Shukyo Kenkyu*,
a journal published by JARS mostly in Japanese. Somewhat confusingly, the *Japanese
Journal of Religious Studies*, published by the Nanzan Institute for Religion and Culture
in Nagoya, is an English journal aimed at foreign readers. The latter is referred to
in note 12.

[5] The first panel was convened and chaired by Shinji Kanai, with papers by Kiyotaka
Kimura, Toshimaro Hanazono, Kojiro Nakamura and Hiroshi Tsuchiya; the second
one was convened and chaired by Kazutoshi Seki, with papers by Masahiko Asoya,
Shoto Hase, Hitoshi Miyake and Shigeru Nishiyama.

Changes in the Overall Framework and Some Emerging Topics

As stated earlier, in the commemorative symposium altogether eight fields of research were chosen as the subject matter for appraisal and discussion, and the reports by specialists were full of useful information and penetrating insight into their respective topics. At this juncture, however, I will not concern myself with the content of these papers; rather, what strikes me is the fact that these eight and no others were selected for review. In other words, the organisers of the symposium clearly thought it worthwhile to call attention to these as constituting the corpus of religious studies in contemporary Japan. This may be regarded as symptomatic of the situation surrounding the study of religion in this country. A glance at the programme of similar projects on earlier occasions, for example, reveals the scope of the matter. In 1966, the Japanese Association for Religious Studies held a symposium on 'Methods of Studying Religon' as a major event to mark its 25th annual convention. In 1977 it organised another symposium, 'Rethinking the Concept of Religion' at its 36th annual convention, and in 1980 a series of public lectures was held in commemoration of the 50th anniversary of JASR to discuss some major issues in the course of its development.[6]

When one compares the titles of the papers presented at these occasions with the afore-mentioned eight ones, it becomes evident that while themes such as Japanese religion or Shinto, Buddhist studies, Christian studies and the methodology of religious studies have been repeatedly dealt with, Islamic studies, Japanese folk religion and the study of new religious movements and the sociology of religion were now taken up for the first time as quasi independent fields. Since the choice and the

---

[6] The names of panelists and the titles of their presentations on two these occasions were for the 1966 symposium on Methods of Studying Religion: Yoshikazu Ishida, 'The method of studying religious ideas: interpretation and understanding', Kenji Ueda, 'The method of studying religion: the history and problems of Religious Studies in Japan', Jikido Takasaki, 'Indian and Buddhist Studies, and Religious Studies: methodological considerations', Nobukiyo Nomura, 'Religious Studies and the structure of concepts and scientific facts', Junshiro Kawabata, 'Hermeneutical methods in Religious Studies'. In 1980, the public lectures series involved Norihisa Suzuki, 'Fifty years of Religious Studies (1980): From the Society for Comparative Religion to the Japanese Association for Religious Studies', Kenji Ueda, 'Shinto Studies and Religious Studies', Yoshikazu Ishida, 'A task of Buddhist Studies: on religious symbolism', Keiji Ogawa, 'The development of Christian Studies in Japan: historical theology and systematic theology', Tetsuo Yamaori, 'The bright and the dark side of contemporary religion'.

arrangement of programmes on such occasions is likely to be affected by many accidental factors, technical and otherwise, this fact alone cannot be taken as a faithful indicator of research trends. Still, it may safely be inferred that the emergence of some new topics reflects a change in the overall framework for religious studies in contemporary Japan.

In his review of Islamic studies in Japan, for example, Nakamura points out that after the first and short-lived rise of public interest in Islam around 1935, full-fledged academic research did not start until the late 1970s. He then goes on to indicate that this second wave of interest took place against the background of both the oil crisis connected with the fourth Arab-Israeli war in 1973 and the change in international relations with far-reaching influences, such as the Islamic revolution in Iran in 1979. By the same token, research on new religious movements and related topics in sociology of religion was clearly stimulated by the burgeoning of new movements in the post-war decades, a phenomenon that H. N. McFarland has termed 'the rush-hour of the gods'.[7] As for the emergence of research on Japanese folk religion, it is not easy to find an all-encompassing factor responsible for it. However, we may assume that it was motivated at least in part by a deep concern in certain intellectual circles for the traditional pattern of life that was threatened at the time by the rapid economic growth of the 1960s and subsequent years.

Religious Studies and Its Context

To be clear, I should stress once more that the above observations are made with regard to some fields of research or topic in their entirety and not concerning individual scholars or their personal achievements. My contention here is based on a simple recognition that any attempt to study religion in one way or another is undertaken in a particular historical, social and cultural setting and can therefore not be discussed without giving due attention to these aspects. In connection with this, it is perhaps not too much out of place to interpose a few methodological remarks on the nature and status of religious studies as a discipline. To my mind, religious studies (or any other discipline, for that matter) may best be regarded as a study composed simultaneously of both

---

[7] H. N. McFarland, *The Rush Hour of the Gods: A Study of New Religions in Japan,* Tokyo: Macmillan, 1967.

extra-scientific (or extra-disciplinary) and scientific (or intra-disciplinary) factors. The important task in theoretical reflection, then, is to elucidate the exact content and function of these factors as well as their mutual inter-relationships. Without going into any detailed argument here, we may assume that the historical, social and cultural context, as an extra-scientific factor, often figures as the background for various kinds of research activities and supplies stimuli for them.

The relationship between the setting and the research activities *per se* can also be illustrated in terms of the now widely accepted interpreta-tion theory. This theory holds that the academic study of religion may be compared to a 'text' that is placed in a certain 'context'. It goes without saying that for a correct interpretation a text must always be read in its proper context. Certainly, this is a mere metaphor, and obvi-ously research activities are not exactly the same as texts in the ordinary sense. Unlike most texts (documents), which, once put into a fixed form, merely await interpretation by others, research in some way and to a certain extent can counteract on its context. To uncover and explore this feedback effect is an important task of methodological reflection. As a hasty look reveals, the term 'context', used here in a figurative way, in practice covers a variety of phenomena and plays many roles in different connections. As a background or premise for research activities, it can exert some determinative influences on the people engaged in that effort, but at the same time it can be affected by this undertaking and its outcomes. In the case of 'living' religions, such as Buddhism or Christianity or Japanese folk religion, for instance, this will be readily intelligible without much explanation. Religious studies in these areas, accordingly, may be seen as a form of intellectual endeavour for self-recognition on the part of those who are engaged in it.

Here it is neither necessary nor possible to enumerate all the factors that constitute a context for those who study religion; perhaps we should content ourselves with a rough distinction between international-indirect and domestic-direct backgrounds, socio-cultural setting in general, and the religious situation in the narrow sense, not to mention the predomi-nant intellectual trends in the academic community and wider circles of society of a particular time. Appraising the achievements of specialists, both in past and present, should surely first of all be carried out along internal criteria. At the same time, however, these achievements should be analysed and interpreted in reference to such contextual factors.[8]

---

[8] The concept of 'text' itself, as is well known, has been elaborated and become

The Post-War Situation and the New Development of Religious Studies

After this somewhat abstract excurs, let me now come to our topic
and try to describe the background of religious studies in Japan in the
post-war period. Tot that end, however, we must first have some idea
of what this 'post-war' period was like.

From a contemporary point of view, World War II clearly was a
turning point in world history; probably no one will disagree as to
the relevance of this judgement. World War I, too, constituted a serious crisis, but it was essentially a conflict between several European
powers, the impact of which remained local and limited. By contrast,
World War II was not only of a global scale in terms of the areas and
nations involved, but it also marked an important step towards a total
rearrangement of the existing order in both international politics and
cultures. Of course, the sixty years since the end of the war have not
passed unchanging, and we have witnessed a number of historically
significant incidents in various parts of the world. For the purpose of
the present survey, though, I shall divide the post-war period into its first
and second halves, with the dividing line roughly in the early 1970s.

Recent discussions about 'globalisation' (world integration) seem to
confirm this view, which has now become a sort of consensus among
specialists. Some leading theorists, such as Roland Robertson, argue that
globalisation, understood as the diffusion of thickly modern-European
(and sometimes American) institutions, behaviour patterns and values,

----

somewhat diffuse as a consequence of structuralist and post-structuralist controversies
after the 1960s, and theorists like Julia Kristeva or Roland Barthes even started to talk
about 'inter-textuality'. Rather than tracing the complications of the terminology, however, here I would like to propose a simple scheme, which sees the focus of interpretation
in the dynamics of two opposing motives of correlation and differentiation between the
text and its context. If one puts more emphasis on the motive of differentiation and,
accordingly, on the autonomous character of the text, the resulting approach would
be some sort of intra-textualism that demands that the text must be read as text, i.e.
along its intrinsic logic, irrespective of external conditions. By contrast, if one puts
more weight on the motive of correlation, one comes out with a contextualism that
requires that the text must always be treated in close connection with its context. In
the latter case, furthermore, the two aspects of correlation must be distinguished and
carefully investigated, i.e. on the one hand if and how far a concrete text is affected
by contextual factors, and if and how a text exerts influence on its context on the
other hand. It seems neither appropriate nor necessary to further discuss this issue
here. I just want to add that from this perspective the long tradition of hermeneutics
since. Schleiermacher and W. Dilthey may be reorganised, as well as Michel Foucault's
concept of 'discourse' which, in the wake of the post-colonial critique by Edward Said
and others, is now widely applied in discussions about religion.

proceeded rapidly especially in the so-called liberalistic countries or areas during the first half of the post-war period. They go on to indicate that in the 1970s a counteraction in various forms set in, and at present these two movements, pulling in opposite directions, are taking place side by side and simultaneously. This complicated situation, no doubt, has been enabled and also accelerated by the increase in international exchange of persons, goods and information, beginning around that time with the development of communication technology. There may be differences of opinion as to the details of the arguments but, from this angle, it is clear that events with the semblance of religious revivals—such as the Islamic revolution in Iran as well as the many counter-culture movements that began appearing in developed societies from the 1960s and that were linked with an accompanying search for 'spirituality'—can be explained in a plausible manner. In light of this view, the anti-modernist tendency—so strong in some of these counter-movements—and the attempt to re-evaluate local traditions can also be rendered more intelligible.[9]

Now, what was the situation in Japan during those years? As far as Japan participated in the global trend, it naturally shared many of the above-mentioned symptoms. At the same time, however, there clearly were a number of factors peculiar to Japan. Most important among them, of course, were Japan's defeat and its occupation by the Allied Forces—the first such experience in the history of Japan—and the wide-ranging changes in its social structure that occurred as a result. The seriousness of the impact is evidenced by the fact that the events of 1945 and the ensuing years were dubbed by some historians 'the second opening of the country'; that is to say, this period was put on the same level as the Meiji Restoration in 1868, when the isolation policy of

---

[9] This description of the general trend of the post-war world is based on the works of specialists such as: R. Robertson, *Globalization: Social Theory and Global Culture*, London: Sage, 1992; Kuniko Miyanaga, *Gurobaruka to Aidentiti* (Globalisation and Identity), Kyoto: Sekaishisosha, 2000. The post-war years in Japan are often divided into several stages from a mainly socio-economic perspective: the stage of immediate post-war confusion and gradual recovery, from 1945 till the early 1950s; the stage of rapid economic growth, from the late 1950s through the 1960s; the stage of stabilised growth after the oil crises of the 1970s; and the stage of stagnation, beginning from late 1980s. Even when dealing with socio-cultural phenomena, some authors have adopted this scheme: e.g. Tamotsu Aoki, *Nihon Bunka Ron no Hen'you* (The Transformation of Views of Japanese Culture), Tokyo: Chuokoronshinsha, 1994. Here, however, in keeping with international trends, I prefer to talk about two major sub-periods divided roughly as indicated in the text.

two and a half centuries was abandoned and a total rearrangement of the internal administration was realised. Right now it is not possible to dwell on this point, but I would like to stress that in order to understand the historical position of modern and contemporary Japan, a careful examination of these two decisive events is indispensable.

Regarding the Meiji Restoration there can be little doubt that it marked the starting-point of modern Japan. Seen in relation to the over-all path Japan has trodden since, the year 1945 may best be regarded as a major turning-point on its way, if not the end of an era. For while in several sectors of its national social life, such as the economy, it is possible to interpret the periods before and after this date as a nearly continuous process, in many of its civil institutions, most notably in its religious policy, a fundamental revision was carried out. For one thing, so-called 'State Shinto' was discontinued. This term, though now widely accepted also in academic vocabulary, still remains somewhat ambiguous, and specialists are by no means univocal as to its exact meaning and application.[10] This point needs further exploration, but nevertheless we cannot overlook that by this radical shift of policy the 'pre-modern' remnants in the Japanese social system were removed to make room for a democratic structure based on the principles of religious freedom and the separation of church and state. As indicated earlier, the enormous activity of many new religious movements, especially in the immediate post-war years until the 1960s, was partially prepared for, and promoted by, these administrative measures.

The new phase in the social and cultural setting of post-war Japan, in this manner, affected not only the actual religious life of people to a considerable degree but also, we may assume, the research activities of

---

[10] 'State Shinto' is not an officially recognised term. It was originally derived from the 'Shinto Directive' issued on 15 December 1945 by the General Headquarters (GHQ) of the Allied Forces occupying Japan for some years after the World War II. The term still remains ambiguous and controversial among specialists as to its contents, application or time of origin. It is solely for convenience's sake that we have adopted it in this survey. Generally, researchers with a pro-Shinto orientation tend to focus their attention primarily on the legislative-institutional aspect and define it narrowly (e.g. Uzuhiko Ashizu, Koremaru Sakamoto). Sometimes they even regard its historical existence as dubious. By contrast, some noted scholars of intellectual history have tried to subsume wider trends of nationalism in Japanese society during these decades under the rubric of State Shinto (e.g. Shigeyoshi Murakami, Hiroshi Kozawa). Since in historical reality both aspects can be witnessed, we should somehow try to synthesise these two approaches and come to a more comprehensive and balanced interpretation. On my part, I propose to regard this as a typical case of what I would term 'formal (not substantial) state religion'.

academics, albeit indirectly. I would like to reiterate at this point that this concerns mostly extra-disciplinary factors, which do not always—or directly—determine the contents and results of research *per se*. Put differently, if a discipline has attained a certain degree of maturity—and Religious Studies certainly has—researchers working in the field usually share an awareness about the problems and methods of research, an awareness that is transmitted at least for a while. In other words, research normally develops relatively independent of real-life events; accordingly, the new themes or approaches that are triggered by a change in circumstances or that try to meet their new requirements usually do not replace the older, more traditional topics at once, but are pursued in addition and parallel to them.[11]

Studies of Religious Change

Seen in this light, we can notice that a number of new themes or genres in the field of religious studies came to the fore in the post-war period besides those already acknowledged. First and foremost among these are studies that broadly deal with the problem of 'religion and social change'. Clearly, this theme was highlighted due to the fact that the established religious systems in some developed countries began to crumble in the socio-cultural turmoil of the post-war years. It attracted many able students, especially in the first half of the period under consideration. Though this thematic concern was later also reflected in research on other areas or societies, it proved to be relevant primarily to some developed countries where similar change was evident, notably in Western Europe and Japan.

---

[11] The model of scientific development that Thomas Kuhn proposed in his *The Structure of Scientific Revolutions*, 1962, and which consists of the formula: 'old paradigm → normal science → anomalies → scientific revolution → new paradigm', is a kind of ideal-typical pattern based primarily on physics and related areas with which he was familiar and cannot be easily applied to most disciplines of the humanities or social sciences. In these fields, as I have tentatively proposed, a new interpretation or theory derived from a confrontation with a new situation (anomaly) usually does not replace the old paradigm immediately (accordingly bringing no 'revolution'), and is accepted only gradually after a time of concurrence and parallelism with the old one. In addition to this intra-disciplinary view, the same state of affairs may also be analysed with regard to the generational characteristics of researchers. On this point, some additional information is given below, in note 14.

Research on religious change is a complicated task that requires several different types of work: on the one hand empirical data must be carefully collected to show the actual state of change, and on the other theoretical reflection is needed to account for its cause, the details of historical processes, etc. Also, we should not forget that this theme is not only of purely academic interest, but also of practical importance to those with a personal or professional commitment to religion, for instance clerics of existing orders. Against such a background, the founding of the *Conférence Internationale de Sociologie Religieuse* (CISR) and the commencement of such research in Western Europe as early as in 1949 was rather natural.[12]

The topics that were treated in the CISR conferences that were held every second year, and in related journals, were manifold; however, there can be little doubt that by far most central among these was the issue of 'secularisation'. Certainly, in spite of its currency, this concept remained multivalent, even in scholarly language, giving rise to unnecessary confusion. But it is equally true that it stimulated discussions about the status and significance of religion in the modern and contemporary world.

In Japan, by contrast, where social change was also remarkable, this was discussed not so much in terms of 'secularisation' but in terms of 'modernisation' or 'rationalisation'. From time to time, surveys on the trends of 'urbanisation' or 'industrialisation' were conducted, but while these represented some partial aspects of the historical process of change, they did not suggest such a far-reaching process of secularisation that might imply the decline of religion *in toto*. This difference in the overall theoretical framework in Japan may be ascribed to a number

---

[12] As its official designation in French indicates, CISR (now Societé Internationale de Sociologie Religieuse, SISR) originally consisted of members from francophone countries mainly in southern Europe, though it later grew into a more international organisation. It is built on individual membership, while the IAHR that started nearly simultaneously in 1950 is an association of national groups. This, together with the fact that the IAHR in its early days tended to emphasise the 'historical' approach, as espoused in its name, made collaboration between the two difficult. Later, notably from the XVth IAHR Congress in Sydney 1985 onward, both organisations have been trying to entertain a relationship with each other. Since around 1970 JARS has also kept close contact with CISR through the regular participation in its conferences by influential members. In addition, in December 1978 a special study meeting was held in Tokyo to which a number of core members of CISR were invited; its proceedings were subsequently published in the *Japanese Journal of Religious Studies* (vol. VI, no. 1/2, 1979, Nanzan Institute for Religion and Culture).

of factors. First, this was due to the different structural characteristics of the traditional religious system that was exposed to change. Second, there was a different theoretical and ideological need to interpret the 'pre-modern' factors that were at work in the historical process of modernisation in Japan.[13] Thirdly, it may well be that research interest in Japan was drawn to the new religious movements that were making such an impressive appearance soon after 1945 (that is, earlier than in other countries).

Studies of New Religious Movements

The study of new religious movements is the second major area of religious studies that came to the fore in the post-war period. In a sense, it may be regarded as a counterpart to the studies of change, since it approaches the same historical phenomenon of change but from the opposite angle. In modern Japanese history there have been several waves of increased religious activity wherein a number of popular movements formed by incorporating various ideas and practices from the established systems of Buddhism and Shinto.

The first such wave came during the last decades of the Tokugawa Shogunate in the first half of the nineteenth century, and the second one around the turn of the twentieth century. In this connection, the years after 1945 may be counted as the third big wave. Until then, however, these movements were generally looked upon with suspicion, both by the administration and by intellectuals. Since the Meiji Era, religious policy aimed at establishing 'State Shinto' had severely

---

[13] In the early post-war years, historical studies in Japan—partly in reaction to, and as a critique of, the war-time 'imperial-national outlook'—were dominated by a socio-economic interpretation with a heavily ideological slant. In this atmosphere, most traditional ideas and customs, including religion, were branded as 'pre-modern', and the disclosure and explication of 'survivals from feudalism' was eagerly sought for. However, modernisation theory, coming to the fore in the late 1950s, has almost reversed that view of Japanese history. Robert Bellah's maiden work, *Tokugawa Religion* (1957), though presented by a foreign scholar, clearly signalled this new trend of revaluating the past, notably of the early modern times in Japanese history. In this context, it is noteworthy that the theme of modernisation was closely linked to the problem of rationalisation in history, a phenomenon that Max Weber made key to his comparative analysis of world religions on a grand scale. We may also notice that, from around this time, the acceptance and revaluation of Weber's ideas proceeded steadily among Japanese intellectuals, even partly preceding the so-called 'Weber Renaissance' that was to occur in his homeland.

constrained the movements themselves as well as research on them. The abolition of this restrictive policy in the post-war period, therefore, had a remarkably liberating and stimulating effect.

Research on these new religious movements—since they constitute a recent phenomenon and are changing continually—may well be classified as a branch of contemporary history. In practice, as we saw in the symposium quoted at the outset, such research is often thought to belong to the field of sociology of religion, mainly because of the procedures employed in dealing with its subject matter. The same broadly sociological approach also proved to be fruitful in studying traditional Buddhist orders, or folk beliefs such as ancestor veneration and other such practices. The naming and classification of research, after all, is largely a matter of convenience. More important is the fact that the research on new religious movements contributed much to refreshing Japanese religious studies as a whole.[14]

By the early 1970s the majority of new movements that appeared directly after the war became somewhat stabilised and succeeded in securing a place among the established religions. Thus, some of the leading groups formed the Union of New Religious Organizations in Japan, Inc., in 1951. The following year this Union became affiliated with the League of Religions in Japan, Inc., which consisted of representatives from shrine Shinto, the denominations of sectarian Shinto, various Buddhist orders, and the Christian Alliance. Interestingly, almost parallel to this process of stabilisation, another group of movements began to enter the scene, in the second half of the post-war period. This is sometimes counted as the fourth wave. Since the movements assembled in this group generally exhibited markedly different traits compared to their predecessors, in keeping with the global trend of the time described above, Shigeru Nishiyama has coined the term 'neo-new religions' to describe them. Whether we like it or not, it is a fact that the study of these movements with their predilection for 'spirituality'

---

[14] It must be pointed out that this trend was promoted primarily by younger researchers, belonging to the generation born after World War II. They formed, alongside JARS, several independent study groups and engaged themselves in energetic research. These groups included: the Shukyo Shakaigaku Kenkyukai (Study Group in Sociology of Religion, 1975–1990), its successor, the Shukyo to Shakai Gakkai (Association for the Study of Religion and Society), and the Shukyo Shakaigaku no Kai (Sociology of Religion Group) consisting mainly of members living in the Kansai area. This fact poses an intriguing question as to the generational characteristics of researchers in relation to their research activities.

gave a strong impetus to the attempt to rethink the very concept of religion, as is presently the case among specialists.

Studies of Alien Religion and Culture

Another type of research started was subsequently initiated that includes, apart from the Islamic studies already mentioned, the study of Meso- and South American religions, Oceanian religions, African religions, etc. Generally speaking, full-dress academic work on these themes was undertaken since the second half of the post-war period;[15] we saw already that this was prepared and stimulated by the spread of anti-globalism the world over. Among these topics, only Islam has the status of a great tradition, and its scriptures and other records are usually explored with the aid of conventional philology and historiography. In most other cases, the basic data and findings are acquired in anthropological fieldwork as a part of area studies.

At any rate, this type of research clearly marks a different phase than the preceding two, requiring careful consideration for its implications on the public life. For almost all these religions, at least at the present moment, lack an indigenous basis and remain alien to the majority of the Japanese. In such a case, we cannot help but ask the delicate question as to the inherent motivation and the significance of such research itself. Recently, it has become widely acknowledged that modern European ethnographic and historical studies of foreign cultures and religions, whether intentionally or not, in practice have turned out to be to some extent a by-product of colonialism and at times of dubious scientific quality. As is well known, this has been severely criticised by non-Westerners such as Edward Said in his book *Orientalism*.[16] A somewhat similar problem may be inherent in the ethnological investigation of Asian peoples undertaken by Japanese scholars in the pre-war decades. The question to be asked, then, is: What is the meaning of studying the cultures and religions of alien peoples if not to serve the interests of one's own country or culture, even indirectly?

---

[15] One example is the founding of the National Ethnological Museum following the 1970 International Exhibition in Osaka (EXPO). Generally speaking, institutional arrangements such as the creation of posts for research and teaching, the organisation of professional societies and the publication of academic journals may be regarded as useful indicators of the maturity of a particular discipline.

[16] Edward Said, *Orientalism*, London: Routledge & Kegan Paul, 1978.

It seems rather surprising that so far this important issue has rarely been tackled at full length. Although this is not the proper place to discuss it in detail, let me just state my personal view briefly. In my opinion, in talking about the significance of research on alien religions or cultures, three relevant aspects must be considered equally: the researcher's own culture or religion, the alien culture or religion under study, and human culture or religion in general, which is assumed to make both comprehensible. It goes without saying that to study an alien religion or culture, it is prerequisite to treat them as impartially as possible and to try to see them as they are. However, it is also true that every researcher is inevitably bound by the premises of his own culture and time, despite their efforts to be objective. Therefore, studying an alien religion or culture amounts, in the final analysis, to participating in the dynamic process of mutual penetration and transformation that takes place between the selfhood of the researcher and the otherness of the object. This is possible, ultimately, only on the basis of a third aspect of religion or culture in general, which is presumed to transcend the first two ones and make them comprehensible. We may refer to this aspect figuratively as 'a common space' or 'field'. The significance of the comparative method, which has always been central in Religious Studies, can be found in its capacity to create such a common space.

New Frontiers: Inter-religious Dialogue, Gender Studies, Thanatology

A quick overview of Religious Studies in post-war Japan reveals that, especially in the second half of that period, a few new themes appeared on the agenda. Some of these are mentioned here to demonstrate the trend; they have all been taken from the titles of special panels and thematic sessions at the annual conventions of JARS in recent years.[17] This also means that these themes have been acknowledged as worthwhile discussing by a large number of members, if not all. Outside the academic community and in the press, too, these topics seem to have become increasingly popular. At the moment, however, they cannot be regarded as established areas of research, with a clear outline. Each theme requires a multi-faceted work of historical documentation and analysis, together with policy-related research with a view to formulating concrete measures. This can only be performed through interdisciplin-

---

[17] Cf. note 6.

ary or cross-disciplinary cooperation. In other words, these themes represent the new frontiers of religious studies and offer rich potential for future exploration.

Traditional Research Themes and Their New Orientation

So far I have called attention mainly to some themes that newly appeared on the research agenda during the post-war period, since these reflect best the changed social and cultural context of the time. However, this by no means implies that other topics of religious studies deserve to be neglected. On the contrary, the works dealing with these other themes, here called 'traditional' for convenience's sake, comprise a large portion, both quantitatively and qualitatively, of the total achievements of researchers in religious studies in contemporary Japan.

This can easily be inferred from the number and content of individual papers presented at the annual conventions of JARS, which may serve as a useful indicator. The annual convention, one of the central projects of the association, together with the publication of its official journal, suffered for some time from the confusions of the war period. It took several years before the present format, consisting of different sections, was introduced. The consolidation of this trend became visible, after the IAHR World Congress Tokyo in 1958: from the 20th convention in 1961 onwards, individual papers were assigned to any one of six sections, and starting from around the 36th convention held in 1977, the number of sections were increased to eight or nine, with the total number of presentations amounting to some 300 or more.

The assignment of topics to particular sections partly changed from year to year, but in the course of time the following ones became more or less standard practice: method and theory in religious studies, philosophy of religion, Christian studies (including Western thought), Buddhist studies, and Japanese Religion (including Shinto and folk religion), while some topics were placed in two sections. In addition, especially in recent years, a few thematic sessions or special panels were organised to discuss new subjects. The programme of the symposium in 2004 quoted earlier was broadly based on this pattern, though it did not correspond exactly. At any event, this is roughly how the 'traditional themes' are covered.

As noted in the previous part of this survey, I am not so much concerned here with the specific contents of papers presented in each section as with the fact that these themes are sometimes treated as separate and parallel to each other. The sections format, having been in practice for a fairly long time, is often deemed to be an established fact and therefore seldom called into question. At a time that we are celebrating the 100th anniversary of the start of the modern academic study of religion, however, it seems necessary to express some thoughts on this state of affairs. Where does it come from, and what merit, or demerit, does it bring to the field of religious studies in Japan?

In response to the first part of the question, two factors can be pointed out. To begin with, the assignment of papers to sections on Shinto, Buddhist, and Christian studies is unmistakably based upon the actual distribution of religious organisations in Japan since the Meiji Era. This framework has been adopted in the Religion Yearbook, the only official statistical data-book issued since the 1950s by the Ministry of Education (now Education and Science). From our perspective, this religious pluralism provides one of the basic features of the social and cultural context for religious studies in contemporary Japan. At the same time, it also is closely related to the second, intra-disciplinary reason: the need for specialisation. For to enhance the quality of research, relevant materials, accumulated information as well as human resources, must be utilised as effectively as possible, which makes some degree of specialisation or focus on a more limited subject matter inevitable. I should add that this is a trend that can be observed not only within JARS but also in wider areas of academic inquiry regarding religion.[18]

The second part of the question—what merit, or demerit, does this bring to the field of religious studies in Japan—is more difficult to answer, since it presupposes a prescriptive image of Religious Studies as a whole that individual students may conceive. On this point, I am inclined to think that the above-mentioned trend toward specialisation, necessary and unavoidable as it is, may some day prove to be the source of a serious demerit, because of the ease with which specialised inquiry

---

[18] The differentiation and specialisation of research is a trend that has become markedly conspicuous in the post-war period. Until 1945, the Japanese Association for Religious Studies remained almost the only nation-wide organisation of researchers working in the field of religion. In the post-war years, however, a series of academic societies with a more limited research area were created, including: The Japanese Association for the Study of Shinto Religion (Shinto Shukyo Gakkai, 1947), The Japanese Association for Indian and Buddhist Studies (Nihon Indogaku Bukkyo Gakkai, 1951), and The Japanese Society for Christian Studies (Nihon Kirisutokyo Gakkai, 1952). Since then these organisations have co-existed with JARS as an umbrella organisation in a loose collaboration. It is now almost customary for most researchers, the present writer included, to belong simultaneously to several of such academic groups.

can become self-sufficient and lead to segmentation within Religious Studies. In view of this danger, it seems good to be reminded that Religious Studies originally started as Comparative Religion. Simply stated, Religious Studies should not confine itself to a single tradition, but rather try and keep an eye on wider areas of human religious experience to establish a universal framework even when studying concrete phenomena. It is this search for an integral vision of religion that distinguishes Religious Studies as an independent and autonomous discipline.

While this is the common and ultimate aim of Religious Studies as a whole, it is no doubt the case that from among the more 'traditional' branches or genres, phenomenology and philosophy of religion were primarily put to this task. Phenomenology of religion seeks to describe the core element of religion, based on and in close connection with concrete, historical materials. Philosophy of religion operates on a higher level of abstraction, but both genres are equally expected to elaborate a meta-theory of religion as required for the empirical study of religions. Mircea Eliade has exerted a lasting influence in this respect internationally during the post-war period, despite severe critique from various quarters, with his grand theory and concept of 'hierophany', perhaps because he was able to meet the need for such a meta-theoretical framework. Whether or not his ideas are still relevant in the contemporary situation is of course a different question and a point that requires careful examination. In any case, we will probably have to look for a new vision of religion in the context of a globalising world.

Without discussing the problem in full detail here, I would suggest that, in this respect, Religious Studies in Japan finds itself in favourable conditions and is endowed with a rich potential for future development. Although the Japanese context of religious pluralism is likely to be a source of segmentation of research, looked at from the reverse angle, this very context may well provide fertile soil for the endeavour to attain a new, universal perspective on human religiosity.

Modern academic research on religion in Japan has been able to produce a number of important results during the last hundred years.[19]

---

[19] From this perspective I have some reservations about the sub-title of the JARS symposium in 2004, referring to 'The Introduction of Western Scholarship on Religion and Its Further Development in Japan.' The modern academic study of religion in Japan, to be sure, has adopted many things from the West, such as research concepts, basic terms and methods, etc. These elements, though, were not merely transplanted;

For details, readers are referred to the report of relevant sections in this volume, especially the section on the philosophy of religion. To take just one example, Manshi Kiyozawa's (1863–1903) *Skeleton of the Philosophy of Religion*, the first systematic work in this field,[20] was able to amalgamate in a unique way Buddhist belief with Western-Christian concepts and succeeded to draw a new image of religion for contemporary scholars. Since then, similar efforts of synthesising Eastern and Western traditions and scholarship have been carried out by generations of researchers. Perhaps the best known among them are the works by members of the 'Kyoto School', but by no means do these exhaust past achievements, nor are they without their limitations despite their originality. The Kyoto School draws its basic inspiration for its vision either from Buddhism or Christianity, or from both, and it is mainly the more refined and elitist types of religiosity, so to speak, that underlie its views. In other words, it has not necessarily incorporated the basic religious insights of Shinto or popular religious beliefs. However, in order to acquire a new integral vision of, or a universal framework for, religion, these forms of religiosity cannot be overlooked. This is a task assigned to Japanese scholars of religion, who have inherited the legacy of former generations to contribute to international scholarship.

---

rather they must be regarded as a sort of catalyst that helped to fully develop an already existing basis. In other words, the modern academic study of religion in Japan is by no means a by-product of Western scholarship, and its early history is an important topic awaiting further exploration. On this point, readers are advised to consult the lengthy and careful introduction by Michael Pye in his English translation of Nakamoto Tominaga's (1715–46) *Shutsujo Kogo* (*Emerging from Meditation*, London: Duckworth, 1990, pp. 1–47).

[20] Manshi Kiyozawa, *Shukyo Tetsugaku Gaikotsu* (Skeleton of the Philosophy of Religion), Kyoto: Hozokan, 1893.

ONE HUNDRED YEARS OF BUDDHIST SCHOLARSHIP IN JAPAN

Kiyotaka Kimura

Introduction

Buddhist studies started in Japan at roughly the same time as the introduction of Buddhism to Japan in the sixth century, enjoying a history of 1500 years. In this article I will concentrate on the last one hundred years of scholarship, clarifying its particularities and problematic, and to indicate the future of Buddhist scholarship. In addressing these matters, I will be mainly concerned here, from a methodological point of view, with Western and modern Buddhist studies that were introduced to Japan since the opening of the country to the West at the time of the Meiji Restoration.

Before proceeding to the main issue, it is necessary to discuss the definition of *bukkyo*. Generally, the Japanese term *bukkyo* has been used, and widely accepted, since the Meiji Restoration as the translation of Buddhism in English or similar terms in other Western languages, such as the German word *Buddhismus*. However, the term Buddhism cannot be considered the proper word for representing the substance or the total aspects of *bukkyo*. Given that the Buddha stated that we should free ourselves from any attachments to 'isms' or other biased assertions, the suffix 'ism' may appear somewhat inappropriate. Furthermore, surveying the Buddhist world as a whole, we can see that some branches of Buddhism encourage people to become a *buddha*, while others seems to be antithetical to that idea. In this sense, we can see the limitation of the term 'Buddhism' to represent *bukkyo*, which basically means 'the Buddha's teaching' in Japanese.

Given the role of *bukkyo* in the formation and development of different cultures, the expression 'Buddhist cultures' (with the term 'Buddhist culture' as the general designation) might be more appropriate to represent *bukkyo* in English. In this sense, as I will discuss later, a diversified approach in Buddhist studies is needed. Moreover, when we consider Buddhism by focusing on its aspect as a core from which various cultures emerged, we would better refer to 'Buddhist thoughts' or 'the Buddhist thought' to define it. In this respect, a close reading of Buddhist texts is regarded as the most important part in Buddhist studies.

The Tradition of Buddhist Scholarship

As mentioned above, Buddhist studies have a long tradition in Japan. During the last 1500 years, many excellent Buddhist treatises have been produced. Among these, the works related to Indian thought that had been obtained in early modern times are amazingly magnificent both in the depth and breadth. Many Buddhist publications were in fact printed during that particular time. For example, only the books written in the Edo period by Kazuma Kawase can be counted up to over one hundred.

At the same time, research on Buddhism as well as Indology grew richer. Many great researchers appeared, such as Hotan (1659–1738) of the Kegon School, and Fujaku (1707–1781), and a lot of high-level works were produced. For example, Onko (1718–1804) wrote his great one-thousand scroll work, *Bongaku Shinryo* (Guidance to the Study of Sanskrit), which succeeded in forging a new basis for the study of Sanskrit in Japan. Another great work is the study by Nakamoto Tominaga (1715–1746), entitled *Shutsujo Kogo* (Emerging from Meditation), in which he made the assertion that 'the Mahayana Buddhism is not the Buddha's teaching.'

Finally, the scholars of that time debated, in various ways, the reason for the existence of Buddhism. For example, Shosan Suzuki (1579–1655) wrote a work entitled *Banmin Tokuyo* (The Merit of Everyone's Practice), in which he indicated that 'all activities can be regarded as a practice for becoming a buddha.' This assertion, based on the teaching of the Buddha, reminds us of Max Weber's detailed analyses of the role of the Protestant work ethic in the formation of capitalist society, which also clarifies the relation between belief and relief.

The Beginning of Modern Buddhist Scholarship[1]

When we turn to the stream of modern Buddhist scholarship which has been built on research of Sanskrit Buddhist scriptures, it appears,

---

[1] For a selection of modern Buddhist scholarship, see the relevant part of the bibliography at the end of this volume.

at least from the outside, that this scholarly tradition originated in a manner somewhat unrelated to other developments.

Under the Meiji government, a law was enacted calling for the separation of Buddhism and Shinto. Although there were differences in the extent to which the law was enforced, it was nevertheless part of a more general movement to abolish Buddhism. As a result, the Buddhist world in Japan was not completely wiped out, but it was dealt a severe blow in every respect. At the same time it was, as a consequence, stimulated to reform itself. The dispatching of students by the Nishihonganji temple—the main temple of the traditional Buddhist order Jodoshinshu—in order to study abroad is one example of this.

Among these Nishihonganji students was Bun'yu Nanjo (1849–1927), who is remembered for opening the door to modern Buddhist scholarship in Japan. In 1876, Nanjo was sent to the United Kingdom to study Sanskrit, Classics and Western philology in Oxford under F. Max Müller. He returned to Japan ten years later. Modern Buddhist scholarship in Japan dates from his introduction of Sanskrit and Pali scriptures to Japan. Already during his studies abroad with Max Müller, Nanjo was involved in the production of an edition of Sanskrit manuscripts written on palm leaves. He also compiled and published *The Catalogue of the Tri-pitaka edited in the Ming Dynasty*, a catalogue of Obaku Buddhist canons that were donated by Tomomi Iwakura to the India Office library at the time of Nanjo's studies in the U.K. After his return to Japan, Nanjo published the Sanskrit texts of the *Saddharma-pundarika-sutra*, the *Lagkavatara-sutra* and the *Suvarnaprabhasa-sutra*. These texts must have shocked the Buddhist world in Japan, where until then most of its scholars had only been dealing with Buddhist scriptures written in classic Chinese or Japanese.

After Nanjo, text-based modern Buddhist scholarship was further entrenched, most notably by Junjiro Takakusu (1866–1945). After attending an ordinary school run by the Nishihonganji temple, Takakusu too went to study Sanskrit and Sanskrit literature under Müller, in 1890. Four years later, he went to Germany to study under P. Deussen, where he also mastered Pali, Tibetan and other languages at various universities. In 1897 he returned to Japan, where he first became a lecturer at the University of Tokyo and two years later a professor in philology. Takakusu also became the first professor of Sanskrit and Indian literature when the study of Sanskrit literature was established for the first time in Japan in 1901 at the same university. Since then, the foundation of Sanskrit and Indian literature research has been firmly established in Japan.

During his stay in England, Takakusu translated *the Guanwuliangshou-jing (Amitāyur-dhyāna-sutra)*—a sutra that had so far only existed in its Chinese version—into English. In addition, he completed Kenju Kasahara's annotated translation of the *Nanhai-jigui-neifa-zhuan*, a travel record of India and some other southeast Asian countries written by Yijing (635–713) of the Tang dynasty, which had been left unfinished because of Kasahara's premature death (the two had studied together for some time in England). In 1904, Takakusu translated the *Jinqishi-lun*, an important Sāmkhya work that had hitherto only been available in Chinese, into French.

In this way, Takakusu tentatively offered to the world a Buddhist scholarship based principally upon a philological methodology. After returning to Japan and making the most of his university position, he drew together specialists of Indology and Buddhist scholars and poured his energy into collecting and organising foundational texts and documents, introducing ancient Indian literature and southern Buddhist texts. Examples include his Japanese translations of the manuscripts of Sanskrit texts discovered in Nepali, his editing of the one hundred volumes of the *Taisho Shinshu Daizokyo (Taishozo)*, and his translation of the nine volumes of the Upanishads and the seventy volumes of southern Buddhist canons.

The works produced by the activities centred around Takakusu have lost none of their significance even today. In particular, the work on the *Taishozo*, which he supervised jointly with Kaikyoku Watanabe (1872–1933), has been highly praised after its publication. Even today, this collection of publications on Chinese Buddhist scriptures is still depended on as the most reliable source of reference. However, from a contemporary perspective, it must be said that there are some problems with the compilation, transcription and punctuation of many of the texts that were written by hand by Chinese and Japanese Buddhists.

The Inheritance of Philological Scholarship and its Developments

The philological study, whose foundation was laid by Takakusu and others, has continued to occupy a central position in Buddhist scholarship in Japan. Taiken Kimura (1881–1930), Takakusu's successor at the University of Tokyo, produced some remarkable papers about early Buddhism and Abhidharma Buddhism, basically by comparing Pali scriptures and Chinese translations. At the same time, through the investigation of the relationship between science and religion, he developed the 'Fundamental Buddhism' espoused by Masaharu Anesaki, a famous scholar of religion, and advocated the idea of 'Original Buddhism'. As a consequence, Indian philosophy and religion were for the first time understood in terms of a general history. This provided a great stimulus to the academic world.

At the age of 49, Kimura suddenly died. He was replaced at the University of Tokyo by Hakuju Ui (1881–1930). After graduating from the University of Tokyo, Ui had studied abroad in England and Germany, where he came particularly under the influence R. von Garbe. At first, he directed his attention to the original forms of Buddhist logical thought that had developed within Indian philosophy. While studying abroad Ui had already completed an English translation of the Chinese version of one of the texts of the Vaiśesika school, the *Dazapadartha-zastra*. When he returned to Japan he wrote the *Sanko Ronrigaku* (For the Learners of Indian Logic), elucidating for the first time the idea of *Inmyo* (*hetu-vidyā*) in reference to Western logical thought. This work triggered the development of logical studies in Indian philosophy and Buddhism in Japan.

On the basis of his strong belief in the possibility of understanding 'Indian philosophy' as developments and transformations of Indian thought, Ui broadened the perspectives on Indian Buddhism, as well as on Chinese and Japanese Buddhism. Many great works were produced by him in these related fields. This type of literary and philological approach has become the fundamental basis for Japanese scholarship in the fields of Indian thought and Buddhism.

There are two trends that stand somewhat apart from this story.

The first of these is the Buddhist scholarship of the so-called Kyoto School, which draws heavily upon Nishida's philosophy. Scholars such as Shin'ichi Hisamatsu (1889–1980), Keiji Nishitani (1900–1990) and Shizuteru Ueda (1926–), while adopting the fundamentals of Nishida's philosophy, have each developed and founded their own subjective philosophies.[2]

The second trend, that originated from Ui's disciple Hajime Nakamura (1912–1999), is related to the field of comparative philosophy. Nakamura's approach developed out of his initial work on a series of

---

[2] More detailed information on these Kyoto School scholars can be found in the article by Shoto Hase in the present volume; see pp. 267–71.

Vedanta philosophies, in which he utilised methods inherited from Ui. However, unwilling to remain within these field-defined methodological frameworks, Nakamura introduced comparative methods and tried to develop this particular field of scholarship. Though perhaps somewhat naïve in character, the first fruit of this approach was his book *Ways of Thinking of Eastern Peoples: India, China, Tibet, Japan* (1955).

Nakamura's book is concerned with the differences within 'Buddhism' that were produced as it evolved in various ethno-geographical areas. In general, the book attempts to highlight indigenous thought in those areas. The book was heavily criticised, but Nakamura took the criticisms on board and began to develop a historical perspective and comparative theory of ideas that resulted in ever-expanding scholarly works. Ultimately, his work was aimed at producing what became the *Sekai Shisoshi* (History of World Thought). In his own words, this is a study that 'deals with the common problems that may be seen in the parallel developments of the world's various cultural traditions'. Its results provided a great stimulus to the world of philosophy. While relying on a comparative intellectual methodology, Nakamura's book inspired a new wave of Buddhist scholarship from a world history point of view. This approach came to take root in Japan.

Recent Trends

In recent years, a new viewpoint has appeared, which has given rise to a number of criticisms of the hitherto predominantly philological Buddhist scholarship. The catalyst for this was the so-called School of Critical Buddhism, representing a line of thought particularly promoted by Noriaki Hakamaya and Shiro Matsumoto. Proponents of this school have pointed out various problems, but basically their position is that Buddhism is precisely and essentially 'critical'. Consequently, according to Hakamaya and others, Buddhism that has been transformed into a Philosophy of Topos (*Basho no Tetsugaku*), in particular the Thought of Original Enlightenment (*Hongaku Shiso*) in Japan and the Tathagatagarbha theory (*Nyoraizo Shiso*) that is the root of the former, is no real Buddhism at all.

Recently, there have been similar voices, for example Masahiro Shimoda's assertions with respect to the 'Revitalization of the Living World' and Fumihiko Sueki's 'Buddhism as Method.'

While registering the above developments and challenges, it should be noted that the tradition of faith-based scholarship (Shugaku) present in each Buddhist sect and dating from the inception of the pre-modern era down to the present, is a deeply-rooted one. Having said this, and despite the fact that this tradition has been fairly remarkable in terms of its output, there is also a feeling that the quality of work is in decline. It may be that the Shugaku tradition itself finds itself at a crossroads.

The Future of Buddhist Scholarship

As outlined above, the history of Buddhist scholarship in Japan in the modern era has been one of development on the basis of philological research. Even today one can still perhaps make this claim.

However, what we call Buddhism is a cultural synthesis, which exhibits many aspects which must be approached from different directions, such as philosophy, ethics, religious studies, literature, art, psychology, and so on. Because of this not only are differing research methods required, but one might even say that Buddhism itself should continue to demand such different forms of consideration. Unless various scholars, with their respective differing approaches, pursue the matter rigorously and with true intention, the larger picture of Buddhism will certainly never come to light.

Buddhism, in its fundamental sense as the Buddha's teachings, or, in other words, what the Buddha is believed to have taught, is found in the sutras. At the core of Buddhist scholarship must be the attempt to articulate as fully as possible the 'law' that forms the guiding standard by which to put into practice the teachings or explanations contained in the sutras. In that sense we may say that the study of Buddhist scriptures should be put firmly at the centre of Buddhist scholarship. Furthermore, locating important texts within a historical-intellectual tradition is a desirable but—particularly in the case of India—a very difficult task indeed. Yet, without making every effort towards this end, the reality of the text and its true meaning will remain forever distant to us.

When we reflect upon the confusion and loss of values that one encounters in today's world, a further step is called for. There are 'living texts' that are relevant to the history of mankind inasmuch as they concern universal values or ideas, containing the seeds of their own realisation. Human society will surely be more secure in future if we take these as a basis for action and future intellectual engagement. I personally believe this to be one of the responsibilities of Buddhist scholars in today's society.

THE STUDY OF CHRISTIANITY WITHIN THE FIELD OF RELIGIOUS STUDIES IN JAPAN

Hiroshi Tsuchiya

Introduction

In order to open up future prospects, a retrospective view of Christian studies in Japan is not best framed as a simple chronological account of the leading theories. There is a prior need to consider some fundamental problems concerning Christian studies in Japan. Depicting the theories in chronological order would be useful if we were to suppose that there is a rational model of study in the West. In fact, whether consciously or not, within some fields of Christianity in Japan, the supposition of a rational model seems to have been present. This has cast various shadows over Christian studies in Japan, and has caused their stagnation and isolation in Japan's academic world. To break away from this convention, I think it necessary to try to investigate the matter, looking at the fundamental basis of Christian studies in Japan from a new angle.[1]

I would like to approach this problem from four angles. First of all, we must note that when researchers study Christianity, they are always asked how they understand themselves in relation to Christian doctrine. This supposes an implicit understanding that the researchers themselves must have adopted a Christian consciousness. This will be discussed later in detail, but it is a phenomenon unique in religious studies in Japan. Secondly, there is the problem of which dimension of Christianity is chosen as the object of study. This is a matter concerning the relationship between culture and Christianity. In Japan, it is not necessarily self-evident that Christian studies are linked to other academic fields. Thirdly, the relationship between the object of study and the place of study must be consciously discussed. To put it concretely, we should consider the issue of how universities and churches respectively have influenced Christian studies. This raises both a circumstance shared

---

[1] For a selection of scholarly works on Christian Studies in Japan, see the relevant part of the bibliography at the end of this volume.

with the West and a characteristic distinctive to Japan. Fourthly, we must realise that in Japan the idea of 'Kirisutokyogaku' ('the Study of Christianity'), which does not exist in the West, has been proposed, but that it has never been productively developed. In present circumstances, this creates interesting new possibilities that I will address in a concluding section.

The Subjectivity of Study

In the West, Christian studies are termed 'theology', and in this discipline, researchers' faith in Christianity is taken to be a basic premise that requires no special attention. In such an environment, even if research leads directly to apologetics, the matter does not create controversy. In Japan, however, being a Christian is rather an exceptional state of affairs, requiring personal initiation. Yet Japanese researchers of Christianity have conventionally adopted Western theology rather unquestioningly, without interrogating the cultural differences between Japan and the West; thus, even in Japan, it has been assumed that Christian studies have been pursued by scholars who also profess a personal belief in Christianity and are driven by their personal faith. This approach has something in common with theology in the West. As long as this situation continues, Christian studies in Japan cannot avoid becoming self-contained as a peculiar field of an imported scholarship, while other fields of research develop in their own ways. Moreover, because Christian-oriented values are a precondition for the study, sometimes inducing people to a belief in Christianity, ordinary Japanese often react to these values with scepticism. The more Christianity seems to be supported by a sense of Western cultural superiority, the more cautious Japanese become. When we compare studies of various religions undertaken by Japanese scholars, the unique characteristic of Christian studies becomes rather clear. In studies of Shinto or Buddhism, a researcher's religious affiliations are not discussed, even though these studies are also usually in fact carried out by the leaders of relevant religious organisations. Studies of Islam and Judaism in Japan are generally undertaken by outsiders, who are not affiliated to these two religions, with people having the conscious status of insiders joining the research community only at a later stage. A presumption that the researcher stands outside his or her subject is also the approach usually adopted in studying religions in developing countries and new religious movements.

These distinctive characteristics of Christian studies in Japan are possibly related to the way in which Christianity was originally received in Japan. Christianity was introduced into the country as a new and different system of thought or belief considering the cultural context of Japan, while also considered deeply connected to science and technology in the West. Japanese politicians, therefore, were cautious about associating themselves with Christianity, but at the same time they were attracted to science and technology, which they saw as being to the benefit of the Japanese nation. They therefore separated Christianity from science and technology, regarding it simply as an ideology, and left the study of Christianity to its own community of believers. The more interesting science and technology seemed to modern Japan, the greater seemed the risk of infection by Christianity as the ideology attached to these forms of knowledge. Quite apart from the question of ideology or doctrine, however, the knowledge of Christian history and documents has also been isolated from the mainstream of academic work, because they were thought to have direct links to Christian faith although their importance should have been widely recognised. Nevertheless, it remains difficult to treat Western culture separately from Christianity. It is ironic that one of the results of this situation has been that, inasmuch as studies on Western culture flourished in Japan, the Japanese were absorbing Christianity without defense.

The general attitude in Japan towards Christianity has been one of caution, but there was one Christian tendency that received a relatively warm welcome. This was 'Liberal Christianity', whose teachings had been transmitted from the West since the late nineteenth century. 'Fukyu Fukuin Kyokai', 'Unitarians' and 'Universalists' are among the groups in Japan considered as belonging to this trend. These groups originally had a rationalistic character, but were 'heretical' from the viewpoint of the Christian mainstream. However, the Unitarians in particular greatly influenced not only Christian studies but also the wider study of religion in Japan. One of the reasons for this is that Japanese politicians regarded Unitarianism as rather innocuous. Moreover, the Unitarians created an opportunity to develop research in 'Religious Studies' at Japanese universities. It is clear that, historically speaking, the activities of Unitarians contributed to the establishment of numerous societies and professorial chairs in this field. If we adopt the standpoint of the orthodox Christianity of the West, Religious Studies in Japan might seem to be sustained by heretical denominations, but in the context of Japanese society, we need to reconsider whether it was orthodox

Christianity or the Unitarians who were able to occupy the leading position in academic publications.

The problem of how to differentiate Religious 'Studies' from the inquirer's subjective involvement in religion as a part of human activity is a fundamental issue for researchers at all times. As stated above, this problem becomes even more serious in the case of Christian studies in Japan. One reason is that Christian studies in the West, which are the basic model of those in Japan, are in fact Christian theology; the essence of the matter is that there is no separation between faith and study of the faith. In Japanese society, where many religious phenomena co-exist, this kind of approach to Christian studies does not work easily. Nevertheless, researchers in the field of Christian studies in Japan often show no awareness of this and take a directly theological approach. It was the overwhelming weight of the tradition of Christian theology in the West that justified this theological approach to study in Japan, and motivated researchers in Japan to disregard Christian studies as a type of 'Religious Studies'. The modern study of religion has become independent from theology through the influence of the Enlightenment, although there was also a later move back toward theology. In Japan, however, these distinctions were never fully recognised in Christian Studies; since theology was introduced into the West directly and without any negative associations, it was hard for Japanese scholars to achieve any originality. It is almost impossible to define when and how authentic Christian 'Studies' began in Japan, because the researchers cannot even distinguish for themselves between their academic studies, on the one hand, and their own personal confessions of faith, on the other. In order to discern the starting point of Christian Studies in Japan, therefore, we have to introduce formal standards, such as the founding of university chairs, academic societies and learned journals. Prior to that, however, the object of study must be carefully ascertained when talking of Christian Studies.

The Object of Study

Methodology in Christian Studies will greatly vary depending on the perspective from which we deal with 'Christianity'. Religion itself is not something that can be captured in and of itself. It can be studied only when it is linked to forms of cultural phenomena. Many religious groups have thought doctrine to be the essence of religion, but to develop dogma and to study it involves an overlap with the study of thought and philosophy. The study of ritual, which is another important element of religion, is linked to the study of art, such as painting, music, architecture and so on. The study of religious groups, meaning specific groups of people who introduce religious activities into their actual lives, naturally belongs to particular fields of social studies. In some cases, even natural science has something to do with Religious Studies. In the end, every approach needs to have a historical perspective. Since Christianity in the West developed along with diverse cultural traditions, Christian Studies (theology in the West) is consistently in need of adjustment with other fields and must always be followed by the question of how to understand culture. Yet in Japan, an imported Christianity was divided from the beginning into separate fields of cultural studies, and both politicians and churches affirmed and encouraged this trend from different motives. This situation has prevented the development of comprehensive Christian studies in conjunction with cultural studies. It ultimately hindered Christian studies in Japan from being rooted in local traditions and from developing its own unique identity.

The study of the New and the Old Testament occupies a specific position in Christian studies in Japan. Although it is generally not easy to point out how Christianity has visibly influenced Japanese culture, an exception has to be made concerning the rapid diffusion of the Bible. A bible itself is only an object, so to have one is not necessarily to assimilate the idea of it. But, inasmuch as the Bible is a thing itself, once it is obtained and in one's hand, it can be considered from various points of view. There seems to be a greater chance now than previously of the Bible becoming the object of the positive studies of linguistics, bibliography, and history, with subjective thought or creed being put in brackets. The historical-critical method introduced into Japan in the twentieth century has encouraged this trend. In addition, Mu Kyokai Groups—a non-church movement originating from the thought of Kanzo Uchimura—specific to Japan promoted the Protestant tendency, which focuses on Bible studies rather than Church tradition. These groups have encouraged New and Old Testament studies. Moreover, this movement influenced not only Christian circles but also furthered, for example, publication, which is a cultural product. Later, their interests widened to include not only the New and Old Testaments but also the Apocrypha, Pseudepigrapha and various documents concerning early Christianity. The absorption with the Bible itself remains prominent in Christian studies in Japan. But in actual fact, the standard of 'study' is left to the researcher's personal sense of values.

Once we become aware of the above situation, we must inquire into academic systems and institutions, such as university chairs, academic societies and their journals, in order to discern the starting-point of Christian studies in Japan. The role played by these systems is important in that they created a single standard for both Christian Studies and Religious Studies. Furthermore, there was a tacit expectation that they would enlighten Japanese society. By investigating what kind of themes were chosen in research into Christianity in the early days of these academic systems, this assumption could be verified. In order to do so, it is necessary to look at the journal *Shukyo Kenkyu* (Journal of Religious Studies) from that period. Its early editions carried a large number of papers on Christianity, but seldom on theology. This shows us how the framework of Christian Studies in Japanese universities and societies was formed, and what the main themes of the studies were. At this point, I will discuss this more concretely from a systematic and institutional perspective.

The Place of Study

Systems of research and higher education have been changed significantly in Japan over the years, and the research environment of Christian Studies has consequently been becoming increasingly complex. Even in contemporary Europe, there has often been a rather uncomfortable relationship between Christian churches and universities, but nevertheless the situation in Europe has been fundamentally different from that of Japan. In Europe, universities have their origins in the Christian church, a situation fundamentally different from Japan where, generally speaking, Christianity originally had a rather marginal position in the universities, and from there gradually became an object of study rather than forming part of the institutional environment. This has led to the formation of a loose framework of 'academic Christian Studies'. This framework has not subsequently changed much, although the universities themselves have, resulting in an even greater distance between Christian churches and Christian Studies than before, and this gap has been growing ever wider. This situation, however, has enabled the standard of study to be maintained. Whether conscious or not, Christian studies in Japan could not but start from this standpoint.

In face of criticism of the pragmatism that rules at contemporary universities, in Europe it is customary to return to classical and traditional culture, which was the original background of the university. In the European case, Christianity is naturally regarded as an essential element of that culture. The same is true in universities in the United States, which have seen the development of a multi-polar system of values, but where the importance of traditional religious culture remains clear. Japanese universities, however (especially Imperial Universities) have existed at a greater or lesser distance from traditional Japanese culture. Those universities rapidly absorbed the cultures of the West, yet they always maintained their distance from Christianity. At the same time, religious tradition generally did not enter universities in Japan. Whether good or bad, this phenomenon has become one of the characteristics of universities in Japan. Nevertheless, there are a few private independent universities supported by specific religious bodies, where religious education is organised along denominational lines, and these have flourished. But even there, denominational education has not succeeded. As a result, these universities have to try to find a way that may lead to a breakthrough in advancing their secularisation. We can say that some Christian universities played a distinct role in the history of Japanese higher education, but all of them have faced problems in regard to religious education. As previously stated, Christian groups, especially the Unitarians and Mu Kyokai Groups, were exceptionally influential in the universities, and they also contributed to the national universities in their own ways. But I think this phenomenon is very closely connected to the non-religious (non-denominational) character of the Japanese universities.

The history of Japanese universities is divided into three periods. The first period, the foundational one, is from 1886, when Tokyo Imperial University was established, to 1918. The second period is from 1918, when the University Act was promulgated, to 1945, when World War II ended. The third period is that since the end of World War II. The aim of the first period was research and education. The aim of the second was education to train professionals, and the aim of the third has been the reconstruction of liberal arts. These changes in the function of the university can equally be seen in the universities in the West. The fact that Christian studies in Japan cannot be identified with theology is deeply rooted in this history of the university institutions. Doshisha, a school founded in 1945 in Kyoto by Jo Niijima and admitted as a university formally in the second of the three periods described above, was not only engaged in mission work, but also took science and applied science seriously. The spiritual legacy of its foundation was to educate a conscience that stood apart from the secular. It was one of the old Christian universities, but its spirit was rather liberal. This becomes more apparent, if we investigate how other universities in those days reacted toward Christianity. Most of the other Christian universities were raised to university status in the third period, after World War II, so Christianity there was connected to education or liberal arts rather than to academic study.

'Academic societies' were originally formed to encourage and promote research, yet because they became closely connected to the university system, any changes in the function of the latter brought non-academic elements into academic societies. Moreover, as the number of presentations at academic conferences was counted as a criterion of achievement and became important for each scholar's personal career academic, societies themselves had to change accordingly. In view of this background, after World War II there was a rapid increase in the number of academic societies for Christian Studies in Japan, which concurred with the establishment of various new universities, especially Christian ones. Some Christian universities independently formed their own academic societies, which in turn resulted in a great increase in the number of academic journals as well. In spite of this development, not all of these societies worked together for the overall advancement of Christian studies, nor were their communications with other religion-related academic societies, such as Nihon Shukyo Gakkai (Japanese Association for Religious Studies), very active. In short, the increase in the number of Christian-related societies did not necessarily mean a higher quality of Christian Studies.

In the case of Christian Studies in the West, the church—as an institution—is a formidable element. The church is not a place to study, but rather a place to evaluate the appropriateness of the result of study. Furthermore, the church encourages research. Researchers can relate both to the academic societies and the church. Lay persons can sometimes take part in the research. Through this process the relationship between Christian Studies and cultural fields is actually strengthened. To have a discrepancy between them accordingly induces the awareness of a cultural crisis. With the rise of secularisation in Europe, this has been repeatedly pointed out. In Japan, however, the situation concerning Christianity is quite different. Apart from the personal influence of some individual Christians, Christian churches have had little influence in Japanese society. As a consequence, churches in Japan have shown little interest in culture. The church never became a medium for progress in Christian Studies. It has been left as a place for small groups to undertake Christian Studies, attracting the allegiance of only some one per cent of the whole population of Japan.

The Possibility of Kirisutokyogaku *(The Study of Christianity)*

Long after the establishment of the Japanese Association for Religious Studies in 1930, the Nihon Kirisutokyo Gakkai (Japanese Society of Christian Studies) was founded, in 1952. In choosing this name, its founders expressed their expectations for the study of Christianity. But judging from a different perspective, we must note that they had a special idea about the concept of the study of Christianity that was rooted in the establishment of this society. Namely, some of those who were instrumental in establishing the society, found deep meaning in using the term 'the study of Christianity' instead of the term 'theology'.

The first place where the study of Christianity was formally admitted in any of the Imperial Universities in Japan was at Kyoto Imperial University, with the creation of a chair in 'Kirisutokyogaku' (the Study of Christianity). It was initiated after private donations were made to Kyoto Imperial University in 1919 and in 1921 to set up a new chair to promote academic research into Christianity. This was agreed in May 1922. The official purpose of this chair was to open Christian studies academically to the public, regardless of whether researchers were of the Christian faith or not, and indeed regardless of any religious allegiance of the researchers concerned.

The idea of 'the Study of Christianity' which was institutionally set up in the core centres of academic learning in Japan, along with 'Religious Studies', should be valued in its own way, even though it was in conformity with the policy of the Ministry of Education in those days. When studying Christianity in the context of Japanese culture, we must be aware of the differences with the study of Christianity in Western cultural contexts, and we should take care in selecting our research method accordingly. Methodologically, the concept of 'theology' is deeply related to a Christian sense of value and bears a long history, which does not fit well with other modern fields of study, even though there is a relationship between them. In Japan, as suggested above, for as long as 'theology' is taken to indicate Christian theology, it will be hard for it to establish itself independently in the academic world without the medium of Western culture. In view of this, it would be useful to discuss this difficult relationship from a new angle, even for traditional Christian theology. In other words, without regarding theology as belonging only to Christianity, we should try to grasp it as follows: when religious bodies try to explain their own concepts of value, a theology of some sort will come into being by itself. When we seize the meaning of theology in such a broad manner, investigating the relationship between religious phenomena and theology in its various phases becomes an essential theme of Religious Studies.

When considering Christian Studies in the context of Japanese culture, the term 'theology', and even more so the term 'philosophy of religion', does not fit well. Thus, the introduction of a new method that can be located in the extension of modern and contemporary Religious Studies should be expected for Christian Studies in Japan. When the idea of 'the study of Christianity' first arose, people unconsciously expected it to move in this direction. However, the Japanese term 'Kirisutokyogaku' ('the Study of Christianity') is difficult to translate into foreign languages; and if we compromise too much, it will go back to the conventional 'theology'. Yet, there is nothing unnatural about this term 'Kirisutokyogaku' in Japanese. Christian churches in Japan have regarded 'Religious Studies' as having a peculiarly Christian understanding connected to 'Liberal Christianity', and so have either denied it or viewed it with a sense of relativism at best. As stated earlier, the legacy of the Enlightenment lies in the background of contemporary Religious Studies, and, above all, Japanese religious studies are influenced by Unitarianism, which may still be regarded as being 'heretical' by the standards of more conventional Christian viewpoints in the West. However, the minority in the West is the majority in Japan. This situation, amplified by diverse influences of reality, has given birth to a completely new context. Christian Studies in this new context require a flexible approach that is not bound by the framework of existing Christian churches of Western origin but is able to move freely in and out of conventional boundaries. Christian Studies in Japan should contribute to this process by investigating its own foundational basis. It is necessary, in my view, to discover a new method for 'the Study of Christianity' that is open and relevant to other fields of study.

ISLAMIC STUDIES IN JAPAN

Kojiro Nakamura

The first time the Japanese came into contact with Islam was after the Meiji Revolution of 1868, when the country opened its door to the world. Since then, there have been some Japanese who have become exposed to the Muslim world overseas. Some of them converted to Islam and went on a pilgrimage to Mecca. Today, many more Muslims are coming to Japan from abroad, and Japanese converts to Islam have increased but their number is still very limited. In fact, Islam remains in Japan an unfamiliar religion of foreigners.

In any case, since the opening of their country, the Japanese have shown interest in the Muslim world. Japan has seen the publication of travel books and diaries, reports on local Muslim laws and customs, (re)translations of the Qur'an and biographies of the Prophet Muhammad from the mid-Meiji to the Taisho Era (late nineteenth to early twentieth century). Islamic studies in Japan reached a first peak in the early decades of the Showa Era (1935–45) and took hold until the end of World War II. The tide of Japanese overseas expansion, from the Manchurian Incident (1931) to the Pacific War (1941), made the Japanese aware of the importance of the actions and attitudes of the Muslims living in China, as well as those in central and southeastern Asia, and made them aware of the necessity of maintaining a good relationship and solidarity with them (the so-called 'Muslim Policy'). Research and studies with regard to the Muslim world were consequently encouraged as a national policy. Western studies on the Muslim world were introduced and several research institutions and organisations were established, whose findings were subsequently reported and published. The departments of Eastern and Western history in the former Imperial universities, such as the University of Tokyo and Kyoto University, provided researchers for those institutions. Japanese research on the Muslim world started as a part of the study of Chinese history, and was gradually expanded to cover Central Asia. Therefore, research activities were initially conducted mainly based on Chinese literature and other materials, but soon began to incorporate Arabic, Persian and Turkish sources and documents, both for historical studies and field work, producing unique outcomes.

After World War II, however, these research activities came to a halt, due to the loss of research facilities and sources, which caused many Japanese researchers to drop the study of Islam. Yet, once the post-war confusion settled in the 1950s, Islamic studies in Japan were resumed. It was a time of vitality, as many nations of Asia and Africa were becoming independent. Young Japanese researchers and students, who became interested in the movements and developments of Middle Eastern and Muslim peoples, acquired knowledge of Western studies on Islamic history and society, of tax and state systems and of Muslim literature, and proceeded soon with their own studies using Arabic, Persian and Turkish sources. At this time, too, some pre-war scholars started to publish their previous works.

Post-war studies on the Muslim world in Japan experienced a period of great advancement, reaching a second peak in the latter half of the 1970s. The backdrop was formed by the oil crisis, associated with the 1973 war in the Middle East, and the Islamic revivalist movements symbolised by the Islamic revolution in Iran. These events triggered Japanese interest in those areas, since Japan was dependent on Muslim countries in the Middle East for most of its energy resources. As a result, the systematic foundations for the study of the Muslim world at Japanese universities and in research institutions expanded during this time, despite some fluctuation in the interest in these areas in the post-war period.

Methodologies in Islamic studies did not remain restricted, as before, to the fields of history, language, and literature, but became diversified to include international relations and politics, cultural anthropology, comparative religion, law, linguistics, intellectual history, philosophy, and philology. Japanese scholarship began to become more internationally recognised, as fieldwork and the acquisition of primary sources became easier. Notably, several works on the historical study of Muslim society and history were published in English.

As Islamic studies broadened, historians of religions, too, took up Islam as an object of study.[1] They focused mainly on theology, philosophy, Sufism, and on modern and contemporary Islam. It is notable that especially in the study of Sufism some unique Japanese achievements can be found. Especially notable are: Toshihiko Izutsu, who studied

---

[1] For a selection of scholarly works on Islam in Japan, see the relevant part of the bibliography at the end of this volume.

Sufism—particularly Ibn Arabi—as an Eastern religion, based on his own linguistic theory, comparing it with Zen Buddhism, Taoism and Jewish mysticism; Yoshinori Moroi, who tackled the issue of the origin of religious mysticism by comparing Hallaj with the apostle Paul; and Kametaro Yagi, who did research on Sufism in Iran. Ever since, various researchers have continued the study of Sufism. Among them are the young scholar Yasushi Tonaga, who published numerous articles about the Sufi orders and on methodology for the study of Sufism; Kojiro Nakamura, the author of the present article, who studied Ghazali's theory on mystical practices with reference to prayer (*dhikr* and *du'a*). By analysing Ghazali's mystical cosmology he clarified his theological position as a neo-Ash'rite with heavy philosophical interest but nonetheless remaining a creationist. The particular interest of Japanese scholars in Sufism may be due to the familiarity of Japanese religious traditions (especially Buddhist ones) and Sufism.

Izutsu, who was already active in the pre-war period, translated in 1957–58 for the first time the Qur'an directly from the Arabic original into Japanese. He also published a series of semantic studies on the Qur'an and on Islamic theology in English. After Izutsu's translation, two other direct translations of the Qur'an appeared: one by Katsuji Fujimoto, Kosai Ban and Osamu Ikeda in 1970, and another one in 1972 by Ryoichi Mita, a Japanese Muslim. Several Japanese scholars were trained as linguists or in Arabic by Izutsu, such as Shin'ya Makino and Toshio Kuroda. Makino's accomplishments include a semantic analysis of the Qur'an (1970; Japanese version 1972), a biography of the Prophet Muhammad, and a translation of Bukhari's massive collection of *hadith* (1993–94). A group of Japanese Muslim scholars had already translated another important volume of *hadith* collected by b. al-Hajjaj al-Sahih (1987–89), himself a Muslim. Kuroda, on the other hand, aims as a scholar of Islam to involve himself more independently in contemporary Islam.

On the life of Muhammad, there have been several translations and original works since the pre-war period. After the war, Izutsu's *Mahometto* (Muhammad, 1952) preceded all others. The next one was Johei Shimoda's *Yogensha Mahometto* (The Prophet Muhammad, 1966) and Katsuji Fujimoto's *Mahometto: Yudayajin to no Koso* (Muhammad: The Conflict with the Jews, 1971). These were followed by the aforementioned biography by Makino. Earlier Makino had also translated W. Montogomery Watt's *Muhammad: Prophet and Statesman* (1970). Concerning the historical and cultural background surrounding the birth of

Islam, I refer to the works of Akira Goto and Yoshiharu Ogasawara.

Islamic law has long been regarded an indispensable factor in understanding Muslim society. The actual conditions and application of Islamic law have been studied in Japan since the pre-war period, mainly in history and law faculties. Beginning with the works of Shiro Tomine and Sayoko Fukushima, there are recent studies by Yoshiaki Sanada, Yukihisa Koga and Michio Yuasa. Noteworthy works are the studies by Hiroyuki Yanagihashi, including *Isuramu Zaisan Ho no Seiritsu to Hen'you* (The Formation and Transformation of Islamic Property Law, 1998), *Isuramu Kazoku Ho: Kon'in, Oyako, Shinzoku* (Islamic Family Law: Marriage, Parents, Children, and Relatives, 2001), and *A History of the Early Islamic Law of Property* (2004), as well as Satoe Horii's *Isuramu Ho Tsushi* (A Concise History of Islamic Law, 2004).

One of the greatest achievements in the study of Islam in Japan in the disciplines of theology and philosophy is *Isuramu Tetsugaku* (*Islamic Philosophy*, 2000). This is one of the volumes of *Chusei Shiso Genten Shusei* (Compilations of Primary Sources of Medieval Western Thought), a project undertaken by the Institute of Medieval Thought by Sophia University in Tokyo. *Isuramu Tetsugaku* provides translations of the major Arabic writings on Islamic philosophy and theology. The present writer also took part in this project and translated Ghazali's *The Middle Way of Islamic Theology* and *The Niche of the Lights*. The chief editor and translator of the project, Masataka Takeshita, whose academic orientation is close to Izutsu, wrote a Ph.D. thesis on Ibn Arabi, under the guidance of Fazlur Rahman at the University of Chicago.

In the same field we should mention Akiro Matsumoto, who published a book and several articles on Islamic philosophy, specifically on Shi'ah contemporary political philosophy (1993); Shigeru Kamada, a specialist in Iranian mystical thought, especially that of Molla Sadra; Kazuko Shiojiri, who majored in the ethical thought of 'Abd al-Jabbar, a medieval Mu'tazilite theologian; and Tatsuya Kikuchi and Shin Nomoto, who have conducted research on medieval Isma'ili thought. Kikuchi's recently published work *Isumairuha no Shinwa to Tetsugaku* (Isma'ili Mythology and Philosophy, 2005) is a major contribution to the study in this field.

Modern and contemporary Islam have been debated in Japan since the pre-war period, for example by Iichi Oguchi who wrote about the formation of Muslim social units from the standpoint of sociology of religion, and Chijo Akamatsu and others who studied pan-Islamic movements. After the war, many researchers and students became interested in contemporary Islam and Islamic movements. Yuzo Itagaki, Wataru Miki and Kan Kagaya are the leading figures in this field. Kagaya, in particular, conducted a comparative study of the modern Islamic movements in the political and economic context of Iran, India and Pakistan. Since the 1970's, Islam has been studied by younger scholars and researchers in the fields of history, political science, cultural anthropology, and others.

The above provides a summary overview of the development of Islamic studies in Japan, with a major emphasis on the 'religious' aspect of Islam. It is often said that Islam is a religion, but not a 'mere religion'; it is more than that. Therefore, all research dealing with any aspect of the Muslim world has been regarded as Islamic studies. Major participants have included historians, specialists in law, languages and literature, but they have recently been joined by anthropologists, political scientists, linguists and others. The involvement of scholars in comparative religion has been very limited. This may be explained by the particular nature of Japanese interest in the Muslim world and the lack of religious interest in Islam, except its modern trends and Sufism. Some scholars, such as Oguchi and Kagaya, have argued that it is necessary to bridge the 'mere' religious and the 'more than' religious aspect of Islam. As a sociologist of religion, Oguchi has tried to find a methodological solution to the typology of religions. I agree with him and support the comparative approach to Islam that he has suggested. This is particularly needed at a time when researchers are putting increasingly more emphasis on the uniqueness of Islam against the background of a rise of fundamentalism since the 1970s.

STUDIES OF RELIGION IN JAPAN AND
THE PHILOSOPHY OF RELIGION

Shoto Hase

Many people think that philosophy of religion, unlike descriptive studies of religion, takes a normative standpoint and has no point of 'reference' to serve as a foundation for objective knowledge. Such a restrictive understanding of this field does not apply to philosophy of religion in Japan, however, where investigations into religions have habitually been based on questioning as to the source from which, or through what kind of reality, examinations should be conducted. In other words, the fundamental issue of the philosophy of religion in Japan has been to explain what the point of 'reference' is.

Joachim Wach has argued that the philosophy of religion does not have any reference.[1] According to him, Religious Studies as a discipline examines religions from a descriptive viewpoint, on the basis of facts. The philosophy of religion, on the other hand, stipulates what religions should be from a normative viewpoint, according to rationality. The difference between these two viewpoints is that, while Religious Studies as an empirical field finds a clear referential dimension in particular facts that serve as a foundation for scientific knowledge, philosophy of religion does not have such a referential dimension. On this ground, philosophy of religion has widely come to be regarded as taking an abstract and fundamentalist stance of prescribing the essence and meaning of religions, regardless of facts.

This proposition by Wach follows the neo-Kantian tradition of defining reality in an extremely narrow manner by limiting the dimension of linguistic reference to the objective reality of the empirical sciences. Even though this neo-Kantian, narrow view of reality enjoyed a period of popularity, it is well known that it has been overtaken by later trends in phenomenology, as well as by the philosophy of Henri Bergson, and the hermeneutical and other schools in philosophy. Thus, even though Wach's view has been superseded, in Japan Religious Studies as a

---

[1] Joachim Wach, *Introduction to the History of Religions*, ed. by Joseph Kitagawa and Gregory Alles, New York: Macmillan, 1988.

discipline has continued to use Wach's paradigm for the sake of convenience in order to classify and understand the various divisions within the field by determining their relative positions and relationships.

It was the French philosopher Henri Bergson (1859–1941) as well as Kitaro Nishida (1870–1945), the central figure in the philosophy of religion in Japan, who challenged the neo-Kantian perspective. It is not an overstatement to say that after writing *Zen no Kenkyu* (An Inquiry into the Good),[2] Nishida's utmost effort was exerted in overcoming the limitations of the neo-Kantian view of reality and developing a more profound understanding of it. According to neo-Kantianism, the realm of meaning and value is separate from the realm of being and reality. Nishida, however, made clear that the things that had been distinguished from being and encapsulated in the realm of meaning, value, and norm are still reality, or rather a deeper reality. He therefore paid careful attention to 'intuition' (immediate perception) as the basis of objective knowledge, and to the 'principle of the given'. Nishida's exhaustive speculation concerning the view of reality cannot be overlooked, as it constitutes his philosophy of *basho* (place), which in turn has become the origin of his abundant religious reflections. For the philosophy of religion, Nishida's phenomenology meant a recovery of reality as an existing entity.

The reality that Nishida's philosophy of religion has reclaimed is inspirational, introspective, and formless, and thus cannot be seen in particularistic, empirical, or psychological phenomena. Nishida referred to it as 'experience', 'awareness', 'will', 'place', 'nothingness', or 'life', and he concentrated on pursuing it in the direction of *noesis* as an original referent within the philosophy of religion.

Keiji Nishitani (1900–1990) regards such a reference as 'self'. He asserts that it is the distinctive stance of the philosophy of religion to question religions in the light of 'present circumstances of self'. In this case, the 'present circumstances of self' does not signify a subjective and individualistic sense of self; instead, it indicates a comprehensive view of human experience that is being perceived inwardly.[3]

The reality that the philosophy of religion has highlighted as a reference point in the examination of religions has been termed by Wilfred

---

[2] Kitaro Nishida, *An Inquiry into the Good*, New Haven: Yale University Press, 1990.
[3] Keiji Nishitani, *Religion and Nothingness*, Berkeley: University of California Press, 1982.

Cantwell Smith 'faith', which he contrasts with 'belief'. According to him, 'faith' is a 'quality of human life' and a 'human potentiality'; therefore, it cannot be limited to subjective decisions or acts of individual commitment. Smith argues that, formerly, Religious Studies attempted to apprehend religion by focusing on the objective (*noema*) pole, but that it is necessary to focus on faith, which is the invisible subjective (*noesis*) pole. This does not mean defining normative standards concerning the meaning and substance of religions, or scrutinising religious concepts, but describing reality as it is encountered through religious traditions.[4]

It may seem that studying religions by setting 'belief' as the objective pole would cause researchers to lose sight of what religions are, instead of elucidating them. Studying religions in the direction of 'self' and towards the subjective pole of 'faith' would enable us to search for lost religions in present-day society and discover hidden religions in non-religious phenomena. Manshi Kiyozawa (1863–1903), Kitaro Nishida, and other thinkers involved in philosophy of religion in Japan take this unique standpoint of studying religions by consistently questioning the 'circumstances of self'.

Buddhism and Christianity are the two religious traditions in Japan that have been taken up as a subject of academic research in philosophy of religion. In Buddhism, it is particularly the Zen and Pure Land schools that have been studied. The representative philosophers of religion in Japan with regard to Buddhism include the above-mentioned Manshi Kiyozawa and Kitaro Nishida, as well as Daisetsu Suzuki (1870–1966), Hajime Tanabe (1885–1962), Keiji Nishitani, Yoshinori Takeuchi (1913–2002), Masao Abe (1915–2006), and Shizuteru Ueda (1926–). With respect to Christianity, these include Masahisa Uemura (1858–1925), Kanzo Uchimura (1861–1930), Seiichi Hatano (1877–1950), Kazuo Muto (1913–1995), Kakichi Kadowaki (1926–), Seiichi Yagi (1932–), and Isao Onodera (1929–). In the study of Buddhism, these scholars have drawn attention to the Buddhist creative force of life by reinterpreting the canon in a new language that links it to various Western concepts. As for Christianity, the philosophers named have worked as mediators to facilitate the acceptance of Christianity in Japan. All these accomplishments in the field of philosophy of religion in Japan have

---

[4] Wilfred Cantwell Smith, *Faith and Belief*, Princeton University Press, 1979.

been made possible by examining religions with reference to the 'self' as their external reference point.

Manshi Kiyozawa is a prominent figure who represents the role that the philosophy of religion as an academic discipline has played in the study of religion in Japan. The Meiji Era was a time of tension in Japan, when Western European and Oriental traditions clashed and Japanese Buddhism faced the danger of becoming detached from reality, due to its difficulty in adapting to the contemporary social order as it was being westernised. Under these circumstances, Kiyozawa took on the role of re-awakening and preserving the creative life force of Buddhism. It is worth noting here that Kiyozawa achieved this by anchoring his work in the philosophy of religion. Or, more precisely, he shed a new light on the Buddhist canon through the 'internal demand of self towards complete fulfillment', thereby enabling Buddhism to live and work within itself.[5] As a result, Buddhism was revived and became capable of asserting itself against the Western European tradition. Kitaro Nishida, Daisetsu Suzuki, Hajime Tanabe, and Keiji Nishitani, all basically agree in their work upon this point. They understand religion as 'faith' (*not* as 'belief') in a broad sense of the term, through which the self can orient itself in the world.

In this way, Kiyozawa's acute awareness of the conflict between the East and Western Europe was transmitted to Kitaro Nishida and Daisetsu Suzuki. The philosophy of religion in Japan has set a certain course for determining Japanese Buddhist tradition. In the case of Suzuki, he became involved in Zen Buddhism and aimed to turn it into a system of thought. His intention was not to regard Zen as Zen as such, but to re-examine it as something that lives and works in the 'heart'. Suzuki's aim was to infuse new life into people by making Zen appear in their hearts as spirituality, instead of analysing Zen literature. In the case of Nishida, his intent was to invent a 'logic' that expresses Eastern thought, Buddhism, or Zen, allowing us to discuss them conceptually.

With the historical situation of the Meiji Era, where the Western European and Eastern traditions clashed, the philosophy of religion in Japan has developed an inclination towards, and a central framework built on, being conscious of the Eastern tradition and asserting it against Western European tradition. This inclination became the basis of the on-going development of the concept of absolute nothingness among

---

[5] Manshi Kiyozawa, *Zenshu* (Complete Works), Tokyo: Iwanami Shoten, 2003.

Nishida's successors, such as Hajime Tanabe, Shin'ichi Hisamatsu (1889–1980), and Masao Abe.

However, Nishitani was the one who actually opened up a new dimension in the philosophy of religion in Japan. In this new dimension, the formula of Western Europe versus the East was overcome, and the potentialities of religion were pursued from a global perspective. This was done in the awareness that nihilism, lurking close to the heart of modern Western Europe, had permeated the East and had been eroding the entire world. Nishitani's exploration of religions through the 'present circumstances of self' is related to such a sense of nihilism.[6] In other words, nihilism has become the reference point for determining the direction of religions today. In this respect, it cannot be overlooked that the Buddhist category of *kū*(sunya) ('nothingness' or 'emptyness') and its religious potential are also pursued outside the framework of Buddhism.

The following points offer a summary of the main achievements of philosophy of religion in Japan:

1. Philosophy of religion in Japan, as an academic discipline, has liberated Buddhism from being preoccupied exclusively with its own sects and cults in order to make it more accessible to the general public. It has facilitated the acceptance of Christianity among the Japanese by seeking a reference point in the study of religions within the self or the human being.

2. Philosophy of religion has introduced Japanese religious traditions abroad by approaching them from the perspective of the world at large. Daisetsu Suzuki, Kitaro Nishida, and Keiji Nishitani are the main figures in this regard. The worldwide acknowledgement of their philosophies of religion is due to their spiritual background in Buddhist tradition.

3. Philosophy of religion also made possible a dialogue between religious traditions by providing a site for such occasions. This was done through searching for 'faith' instead of a 'belief system' that claims a uniqueness and untranslatable absoluteness. A common ground for inter-religious dialogue is attained when various religions come into contact with the indisputable origin of religion, namely human life, which fundamentally constitutes human beings. The foundation of philosophy of religion is the site known as 'faith'.

---

[6] Nishitani, *Religion and Nothingness*.

NOTE ON CONTRIBUTORS

GERRIE TER HAAR is Professor of Religion, Human Rights and Social Change at the Institute of Social Studies, The Hague (see below). She was Chair of the Academic Programme Committee of the XIXth IAHR World Congress, Tokyo, 2005.

YOSHIO TSURUOKA is Professor in the Department of Religious Studies at the Graduate School of Humanities and Sociology, University of Tokyo. Widely interested in Eastern and Western mystical thought, he mainly specialises in Spanish and French mysticism. His field of study also includes contemporary theories on mysticism and philosophy of religion. He is the author of *Jujika no Yohane Kenkyu* [Dark Night and Ardent Love: A Study of John of the Cross] (Tokyo, 2000). He has authored many articles on Christian mysticism, its influence on modern Japanese religious philosophers, and methodological problems in mystical studies.

SUSUMU SHIMAZONO is Professor in the Department of Religious Studies at the Graduate School of Humanities and Sociology, University of Tokyo. He has published widely on contemporary religious movements, as well as on modern Japanese religions in general. He is the author of *From Salvation to Spirituality: Popular Religious Movements in Modern Japan* (Melbourne, 2004) and co-editor of *Religion and Society in Modern Japan* (Berkeley, 1993). His work on Aum Shinrikyo, *Gendai Shukyo no Kanosei* [The Potential of Contemporary Religions] (Tokyo, 1997) has been frequently cited in the works of both Japanese and Western scholars. He is currently working in the new field of Death and Life Studies.

The Religious Dimension of War and Peace

MARK JUERGENSMEYER is Director of the Orfalea Center for Global and International Studies and Professor of Sociology and Religious Studies at the University of California, Santa Barbara. He is an expert on religious violence, conflict resolution and South Asian religion and politics, and has published more than two hundred articles and fifteen books. His widely-read *Terror in the Mind of God: The Global Rise of Religious Violence* (University of California Press, rev. edn. 2003), is based on interviews with violent religious activists around the world. A previous book, *The New Cold War? Religious Nationalism Confronts the Secular State* (University of California Press, 1993) covers the rise of religious activism and its confrontation with secular modernity. His book on Gandhian conflict resolution has been reprinted as *Gandhi's Way* (University of California Press, rev. edn., 2005). Among his edited books are *Global Religions* (Oxford University Press, 2003) and *Religion and Global Civil Society* (Oxford University Press, 2005). He is currently working on a book on religion and war, and is co-editing the *Encyclopedia of Global Religion* and an anthology of writings on religion and violence.

GERRIE TER HAAR is Professor of Religion, Human Rights and Social Change at the Institute of Social Studies, The Hague. Her areas of expertise are history of religions, comparative religion, African religious traditions, religion and politics, religious diaspora. She is the author of several books and numerous articles. Among her recent publications are *Bridge or Barrier: Religion, Violence and Visions for Peace* (ed. with J. J. Busuttil, Brill, 2005), and *Worlds of Power: Religious Thought and Political Practice in Africa* (with S. Ellis, Hurst & Co./Oxford University Press). She is Vice-President of the International Association for the History of Religions.

MANABU WATANABE is Professor of Religious Studies at Nanzan University and permanent research fellow at the Nanzan Institute for Religion and Culture. He is the author of *Jung ni okeru Kokoro to Taiken Sekai* [The Psyche and the World as Experienced in C. G. Jung's Psychology] (Tokyo, 1991) and *Jung Shinrigaku to Shukyo* [C. G. Jung's Psychology and Religion] (Tokyo, 1994). He has studied the works of the 12th-century Japanese Buddhist poet Saigyo, as well as new religious movements in Japan. He contributed to *Religion and Social Crisis: Understanding Japanese Society through the Aum Affair* (New York, 2001).

ROSALIND I. J. HACKETT is a Distinguished Professor in the Humanities at the University of Tennessee, Knoxville, where she teaches Religious Studies and Anthropology. She has published widely on religion in Africa, notably on new religious movements, as well as on art, media, gender, conflict, and religious freedom in the African context. In 2005 she was elected President of the International Association for the History of Religions (until 2010). Her edited book, *Proselytization Revisited: Rights Talk, Free Markets, and Culture Wars* will appear in 2008 (London: Equinox).

Technology, Life and Death

EBRAHIM MOOSA is Associate Professor of Islamic Studies in the Department of Religion and Duke University and Associate Director (Research) of the Duke Islamic Studies Center. Previously he taught at the University of Cape Town in his native South Africa and was also a visiting professor at Stanford University. He is the author of *Ghazali and the Poetics of Imagination* (University of North Carolina Press, 2005), which offers a new interpretation of the ideas of the major medieval Muslim thinker Abu Hamid al-Ghazali. The book was awarded the 2006 American Academy of Religion prize for the Best First Book in History of Religions. He also edited and published the work of Professor Fazlur Rahman, *Revival and Reform: A Study in Islamic Fundamentalism* (Oneworld, 1999). He has authored many essays, ranging from issues in ethics and law to historical studies that deal with questions of Qur'an exegesis and medieval Islamic law and philosophy. He is especially interested in the way religious traditions encounter modernity and the way new conceptions of history and culture dialogically engage with the Islamic heritage. He is currently working on a book on the *madrasas* of the Indian subcontinent.

WILLIAM R. LAFLEUR is the E. Dale Saunders Professor in Japanese Studies at the University of Pennsylvania. Among his books are *The Karma of Words: Buddhism and the Literature Arts in Medieval Japan* (University of California Press, 1986); *Liquid Life: Abortion and Buddhism in Japan* (Princeton University Press, 1992); *Awesome Nightfall: The Life, Times, and Poetry of Saigyô* (Wisdom Publications, 2003); and, most recently, *Dark Medicine: Rationalizing Unethical Medical Research*, co-edited with Gernot Böhme and Susumu Shimazono (Indiana University Press, 2007). A book in process compares bioethics in Japan and North America, paying considerable attention to religion and philosophy.

HARUKO K. OKANO is President of the Catholic Seisen University in Tokyo. As a feminist scholar she is interested in inter-religious dialogue, bioethics and issues of justice and peace. She has been a visiting professor in various universities in Europe. She is the author of *Die Stellung der Frau im Shinto: Eine Religionsphänomenologische und -soziologische Untersuchung* (Wiesbaden,1976) and *Christliche Theologie im Japanischen Kontext* (Frankfurt/M., 2002). She has widely written about religious studies, inter-religious dialogue and women studies, in Japanese as well as in German and English.

Eiko Hanaoka (-Kawamura) is Professor Emerita of Osaka Prefecture University and of its Graduate School and Professor of Nara Sangyo University. She is specialised in the philosophy of religion, but initially concentrated on Christian Theology and Zen Buddhism. She is the author of *Shukyo Tetsugaku no Kongenteki Tankyu* [A Fundamental Inquiry into the Philosophy of Religion] (Tokyo, 1998), *Jiko to Sekai no Mondai: Zettaimu no Shiten kara* [The Problem of Self and World: From the Standpoint of Absolute Nothingness] (Kanagawa, 2005) and many books and articles about the Kyoto school.

Global Religions and Local Cultures

Talal Asad is University Distinguished Professor of Anthropology at the Graduate Center of the City University of New York (CUNY). He has conducted extensive research on the phenomenon of religion and secularism and is an expert on religious revival in the Middle East, which is usually called Islamism in Western literature. He has published more than fifty articles and five books, and his work has contributed to anthropology, history, works on modernity, as well as religious studies. His well-known *Formation of the Secular: Christianity, Islam, Modernity* (published in the series 'Cultural Memory in the Present' by Stanford University Press, 2003) explores the notions, practices, and political formations of secularism, emphasising the major historical shifts that have shaped secular sensibilities and attitudes in the modern West and the Middle East. In his previous, widely-read book, *Genealogies of Religion* (Johns Hopkins University Press, 1993), he traces the ways in which the notion 'religion' has come to be constructed historically. He is currently working on the secularisation of law in the Middle East.

Vasudha Narayanan is Distinguished Professor in the Department at the University of Florida and a past president of the American Academy of Religion (2001–02). Her fields of interest are the Sri Vaishnava tradition; Hindu traditions in India, Cambodia and America; Hinduism and the environment; and gender issues. She is the author and editor of six books and numerous articles. Her publications include *Hinduism* (2004) and *The Way and the Goal: Expressions of Devotion in the Early Srivaisnava Tradition* (1987). She also helped create the Center for the Study of Hindu Traditions at the University of Florida.

Pablo Wright holds a Ph.D. in Anthropology (Temple University). He is currently Researcher of the Argentine National Council for Scientific Research (CONICET) and Professor of Symbolic Anthropology at the University of Buenos Aires. He is an expert in religious change, shamanism, ritual and history among the Argentine Chaco Qom or Toba people. He is also interested in interpretive and symbolic anthropology and the impact of post-colonial critique in Western social sciences. His recent works include an edited volume entitled *Periferias Sagradas: Heterodoxias socio-religiosas en la Argentina* (Biblos, in press). He recently completed a manuscript about Toba ontology.

P. Pratap Kumar is Professor of Hinduism and Comparative Religions in the School of Religion and Theology, University of KwaZulu Natal, South Africa. His publications include *The Goddess Lakshmi in South Indian Vaishnavism* (Scholars Press, 1997), *Hindus in South Africa: Their Traditions and Beliefs* (University of Durban-Westville, 2000), and *Methods and Theories in the Study of Religions: Perspectives from the Study of Hinduism and other Indian Religions* (Sundeep Prakashan Publications, 2004). He is also the editor of *Religious Pluralism and the Diaspora* (Brill, 2006).

Boundaries and Segregations

Suwanna Satha-Anand is Associate Professor in the Department of Philosophy in the Faculty of Arts of Chulalongkorn University, Thailand. She is currently the President of the Association of Philosophy and Religion of Thailand, and a research coordinator for the Humanities Research Forum Project, Thailand Research Fund. She is an expert in Buddhist Philosophy and Chinese Philosophy, and has published nine books in Thai and many articles, both in Thai and English. Her main published works are *New Essays Reconstructing Eastern Philosophy* (Chulalongkorn University Press 2004, in Thai) and *Mahayana Buddhism in Buddhadasa's Philosophy* (Chulalongkorn University Press 1993, in Thai). Both works deal with the philosophy of Theravada Buddhism, Thai Buddhism and Chinese Philosophy. Her recent works in English focus on religion in contemporary society and women studies, including 'Truth over convention: feminist interpretations of Buddhism', in *Religious Fundamentalisms and the Human Rights of Women*, edited by Courtney W. Howland (St. Martin Press, 1999) and 'Female ordination and women's rights in Buddhism', in *Humanitas Asiatica* (December 2001).

Ursula King is Professor Emerita of Theology and Religious Studies and Senior Research Fellow at the Institute for Advanced Studies, University of Bristol. She is also Professorial Research Associate at the Centre for Gender and Religions Research, School of Oriental and African Studies, University of London. She holds degrees from universities in three continents and has published widely on gender studies in religion, the thought of Teilhard de Chardin, method and theory, Indian religions, especially modern Hinduism, and on interfaith dialogue. She was consultant and contributor on Gender and Religion entries for the second edition of the *Encyclopedia of Religion.*

Masakazu Tanaka is Professor of Social Anthropology at the Institute for Research in Humanities of Kyoto University. His main interest lies in rituals and their relationships with violence, gender and sexuality. He has conducted anthropological research in Sri Lanka and South India. His publications include *Patrons, Devotees and Goddesses: Ritual and Power among the Tamil Fishermen of Sri Lanka* (Delhi, 1997), *Living with Shakti: Religion, Gender Sexuality in South Asia* (edited with M. Tachikawa, Osaka: National Museum of Ethnology, 1998). Some of his recent articles on Hinduism can be found in *The Oxford India Companion to Sociology and Social Anthropology* (2003).

Noriko Kawahashi is Associate Professor of Religion at the Nagoya Institute of Technology. She has published extensively on the subject of gender and religion in Japan and Okinawa, both in English and Japanese. She has co-authored with Masako Kuroki a book on religion and postcolonial feminism, *Konzaisuru Megumi* [Mixed Graces: Religion and Feminism in a Post-colonial Age] (Kyoto, 2004), and co-edited the *Japanese Journal of Religious Studies* Special Issue on 'Feminism and Religion in Japan' (Vol. 30, Fall 2003).

Method and Theory in the Study of Religion

Tomoko Masuzawa is Professor of History and Comparative Literature at the University of Michigan. She specialises in the history of the human sciences in the 19th and 20th centuries, and in Western discourses on religion. Among her publications are *In Search of Dreamtime: The Quest for the Origin of Religion* (1993) and *The Invention of World Religions: Or, How European Universalism Was Preserved in the Language of*

Pluralism (2005), both published by the University of Chicago Press. She is currently working on a book-length study exploring the condition of secularity in the development of biblical studies in the 19th century. Her other research and publication projects include: an edited volume on the genealogies of the study of religion; a collaborative project—together with scholars of religion in Japan and Korea—on religion, secularism, university and nation-building; and a study of the transformation of European conceptions of religion, with special attention to Bernard Picart's engravings in *Cérémonies et coutumes religieuses des tous les peuples du monde* (1723–37) and their subsequent reproductions in the 19th century.

CHIN HONG CHUNG is Ilsong Distinguished Professor at the Hallym Academy of Sciences, Hallym University and Professor Emeritus of Seoul National University. He is also Member of the National Academy of Sciences, Republic of Korea. He is the author of *Jongkyo Munhwa-ui Insik gwa Haeseok* [Epistemology and Hermeneutics of Religious Culture: Development of Phenomenology of Religion] (Seoul National University Press, 1996), *Jongkyo Munhwa-ui Nolli* [Logic of Religious Culture] (Seoul National University Press, 2000), and *Gyeongheom gwa Giyeok* [Experience and Recollection] (Seoul, Dangdae Publishing Company, 2003).

SYLVIA MARCOS is the Director of the Center for Psychoethnological Research in Cuernavaca, Mexico, where she is a practising clinical psychologist. She is Visiting Professor at the School of Religion, Claremont Graduate University, and the author and editor of many books and articles on the history of psychiatry, medicine and women's popular culture in pre-Hispanic and contemporary Mexico. She has conducted extensive research on the construction of gender and sexuality in indigenous, colonial, and post-colonial culture. She has published widely on gender issues. Her most recent book is *Taken from the Lips: Gender and Eros in Mesoamerican Religions* (Brill, 2006).

ARMIN W. GEERTZ is Professor in the History of Religions at the Department of the Study of Religion, University of Aarhus, Denmark. He served as Treasurer (1990–95) and General Secretary (1995–2005) of the IAHR. He is currently chair of a key area research project 'Religion, Cognition and Culture'. He is Secretary General (since 2006) of the International Association for the Cognitive Science of

Religion (IACSR). His main interests are cognitive theory in the study of religion; the religions of indigenous peoples; and method and theory in the comparative study of religions. He is the author/editor of over 300 publications.

The Study of Religion in Japan

Noriyoshi Tamaru is Professor Emeritus in Religious Studies at the University of Tokyo. He served as president for the Japanese Association for Religious Studies and is an honorary life member of the IAHR. He has widely explored theoretical issues alongside the history of Japanese religions, especially Buddhism. His authored works include *Shukyo Gaku no Rekishi to Kadai* [The History and Problems of Religious Studies], (Tokyo, 1987). He co-authored and edited *Religion in Japanese Culture* (Tokyo/Palo Alto, 1996), and is the author of many academic articles.

Kiyotaka Kimura is President of the International College for Postgraduate Buddhist Studies, Professor Emeritus of Tokyo University, and the chief director of the Japanese Association of Indian and Buddhist Studies. His scholarly expertise is in East Asian Buddhism, particularly Chinese Huayan thought. His field of study further includes comparative theories on Buddhist philosophy. He is the author of *Shoki Chugoku Kegon Shiso no Kenkyu* [A Study of Early Huayan Thought in China] (Tokyo, 1977) and *Higashi Asia Bukkyo Shiso no Kozo* [The Basic Structure of Buddhist Thought in East Asia] (Tokyo, 2001).

Hiroshi Tsuchiya is Professor of Religious Studies at Hokkai Gakuen University and Professor Emeritus at Hokkaido University. Widely interested in theories of modern religious studies, he mainly specialises in studies about early Christianity and Scriptures. He has authored many publications, among which *Bokkai Shokan* [The Pastoral Epistles] (Tokyo, 1990), *Seisho no Naka no Maria* [Mary in the Holy Scripture] (Tokyo, 1992), and *Kyoten ni Natta Shukyo* [Religion Realised as Scripture] (Sapporo, 2002). He has also widely published in academic journals and contributed to edited volumes.

Kojiro Nakamura is Professor Emeritus of the University of Tokyo and Obirin University. His major work is on Islamic mysticism, particularly that of Ghazali, about whom he has widely published. His books include *Ghazali and Prayer* (Kuala Lumpur, 2001) and *Isuramu no Shukyo Shiso: Gazari to sono Shuhen* [Religious Thought in Islam, with Special Reference to Ghazali] (Tokyo, 2002). He also translated some of Ghazali's works into Japanese. His field of study further includes modern trends in Islam. Recently he became interested in methodology with a view to developing an integral approach in the study of Islam.

SHOTO HASE is Professor Emeritus at the Graduate School of Letters at Kyoto University. He specialised in the philosophy of French spiritualism, from Maine de Biran to Henri Bergson, as well as in Pure Land Buddhism. He is the author of *Yokubo no Tetsugaku* [Philosophy of Desire] (2003), and *Kokoro ni Utsuru Mugen* [Infinity Represented in Mind] (2005), both published in Kyoto by Hozokan.

BIBLIOGRAPHY

I. *The Religious Dimension of War and Peace*

Adams, IV, Nathan A., 'A human rights imperative: extending religious liberty beyond the border', *Cornell International Law Journal*, vol. 33, no. 1, 2000, pp. 1–66.

Anderson, Benedict, *Imagined Communities: Reflections on the Origin and Spread of Nationalism*. London: Verso, 1983.

Appleby, R. Scott, 'Religions, human rights and social change', in Ter Haar and Busuttil, *The Freedom To Do God's Will*, 2003, pp. 197–229.

Barker, Eileen, 'Why the cults? New religions and freedom of religion and beliefs', in T. Lindholm, W.C. Durham and B. Tahzib-Lie (eds.), *Facilitating Freedom of Religion and Belief: Perspectives: Impulses and Recommendations from the Oslo Coalition*, Dordrecht, The Netherlands: Kluwer, 2004, pp. 571–94.

Brzezinski, Zbigniew, *Out of Control: Global Turmoil on the Eve of the Twenty-first Century*. New York: Scribner's Sons, 1993.

Castells, Manuel, *The Information Age: Economy, Society and Culture*. Oxford: Blackwell, 1997.

Ellis, Stephen, and Gerrie ter Haar, *Worlds of Power: Religious Thought and Political Practice in Africa*. London: Hurst & Co./New York: Oxford University Press, 2004.

Ginsberg, Faye, Lila Abu-Lughod and Brian Larkin (eds.), *Media Worlds: Anthropology on New Terrain*. Los Angeles and Berkeley: University of California Press, 2002.

Hackett, Rosalind I. J., 'Discourses of demonisation in Africa', *Diogenes*, vol. 50, no. 3, 2003, pp. 61–75.

——, 'A new axial moment for the study of religion?', *Temenos*, vol. 42, no. 2, 2006, pp. 111–29.

——, 'Devil Bustin' satellites: how media liberalization in Africa generates religious intolerance and conflict, in R. I. J. Hackett, S. Mahmud and J. H. Smith (eds.), *Religion in African Conflicts and Peacebuilding Initiatives: Problems and Prospects for a Globalizing Africa*, Notre Dame, IN: University of Notre Dame Press (in press).

Hall, John R., 'Religion and violence: social processes in comparative perspective', in M. Dillon (ed.), *Handbook for the Sociology of Religion*, New York: Cambridge University Press, 2003, pp. 359–81.

Herzfeld, Michael, *Anthropology: Theoretical Practice in Culture and Society*. Oxford: Blackwell, 2001.

Huntington, Samuel P., *The Clash of Civilizations and the Remaking of World Order*. New York: Simon and Schuster, 1996.

Juergensmeyer, Mark, *The New Cold War? Religious Nationalism Confronts the Secular State*. Berkeley, CA: University of California Press, 1993.

——, *Terror in the Mind of God: The Global Rise of Religious Violence*. Berkeley: Los Angeles: University of California Press, 2003 [3rd ed. revised and updated; originally published in 2000].

Keown, Damien, 'Paternalism in the Lotus Sūtra', *Journal of Buddhist Ethics*, vol. 5, 1998, pp. 190–207.

Lang, Andrew (collected and edited), *Arabian Nights*. Illustrated by Vera Bock, with a foreword by Mary Gould Davis. London: Longmans, Green, 1951.

Lifton, Robert Jay, *Destroying the World to Save It: Aum Shinrikyo, Apocalyptic Violence, and the New Global Terrorism*. New York: Henry Holt, 1999.

Lincoln, Bruce, *Holy Terrors: Thinking About Religion after September 11*. Chicago: University of Chicago Press, 2003.

Macdonald, Andrew, *The Turner Diaries*. Hillsboro, WV: National Vanguard Books, 1978.

Mack, Burton, 'Caretakers and critics: on the social role of scholars who study religion', *Bulletin of the Council of Societies for the Study of Religion*, vol. 30, no. 2, 2001, pp. 32–8.

Marty, Martin E., and R. Scott Appleby (eds.), *Fundamentalisms Observed*. Chicago: University of Chicago Press, 1994.

Meadows, Donella H. et al., *The Limits to Growth: A Report for the Club of Rome's Project on the Predicament of Mankind*. New York: Universe Books, 1972.

Miguez, Daniel, 'From open violence to symbolic confrontation: anthropological observations of Latin America's southern cone', in Ter Haar and Busuttil, *Bridge or Barrier*, pp. 81–118.

Niebuhr, H. Richard, *The Social Sources of Denominationalism*. New York: Meridian Books, 1960.

Orsi, Robert A., 'Is the study of lived religion irrelevant to the world we live in?', *Journal for the Society for the Scientific Study of Religion*, vol. 42, no. 2, 2003, pp. 169–74.

Richardson, James T., 'Discretion and discrimination in legal cases involving controversial religious groups and allegations of ritual abuse', in R. J. Ahdar (ed.), *Law and Religion*, Aldershot, UL: Ashgate, 2000, pp. 111–32.

Robbins, Thomas, and Susan J. Palmer (eds.), *Millennium, Messiahs, and Mayhem: Contemporary Apocalyptic Movements*. New York: Routledge, 1997.

Sassen, Saskia, 'Spatialities and temporalities of the global: elements for a theorization', *Public Culture*, vol. 12, no. 1, 2000, pp. 215–32.

Shimazono, Susumu, *Gendai Shukyo no Kanosei* (The Potential of Contemporary Religions). Tokyo: Iwanami Shoten, 1997.

Sullivan, Winnfred Fallers, *The Impossibility of Religious Freedom*. Princeton: Princeton University Press, 2005.

Taussig, Michael, *The Devil and Commodity Fetishism in South America*. Chapel Hill: University of North Carolina Press, 1980.

Ter Haar, Gerrie, 'Religion: source of conflict or resource for peace?', in Ter Haar and Busuttil, *Bridge or Barrier*, pp. 3–34.

Ter Haar, Gerrie, and James J. Busuttil (eds), *The Freedom to Do God's Will: Religious Fundamentalism and Social Change*. London and New York: Routledge, 2003.

—— (eds), *Bridge or Barrier: Religion, Violence and Visions for Peace*. Leiden and Boston: Brill, 2005.

The Skill in Means (Upāyakauśalya) Sūtra [trans. Mark Tatz]. Delhi: Motilal Banarsidass, 1994.

Victoria, Brian, *Zen at War*. New York and Tokyo: Weatherhill, 1997.

Watanabe, Manabu, 'Religion and violence in Japan today: a chronological and doctrinal analysis of Aum Shinrikyo', *Terrorism and Political Violence*, vol. 10, no. 4, 1998, pp. 80–100.

——, 'Opposition to Aum and the rise of the 'anti-cult' movement in Japan', in Robert J. Kisala and Mark R. Mullins (eds.), *Religion and Social Crisis in Japan: Understanding Japanese Society through the Aum Affair*, Basingstoke and New York: Palgrave, 2001, pp. 87–105.

Wickham, Carrie, 'The Islamist alternative to globalization', in Mark Juergensmeyer (ed.), *Religion in Global Civil Society*, New York: Oxford University Press, 2005, pp. 149–70.

Wuthnow, Robert, 'Is there a place for "scientific" studies of religion?', *The Chronicle of Higher Education*, 2003, 24 January, pp. B10–B11.

Yen-zen, Tsai, 'Ritual violence and communal sanity: the case of Hērem in Biblical Judaism'. Paper presented at the IAHR World Congress, Tokyo, March 2005.

II. *Technology, Life and Death*

Agamben, Giorgio, *Homo Sacer: Sovereign Power and Bare Life* [trans. Daniel Heller-Roazen, edited by Werner Hamacher and David E. Wellberry]. Stanford, CA: Stanford University Press, 1998.

Al-Jazari, Ibn al-Razzaz, *The Book of Ingenious Mechanical Devices* [trans. and edited by Donald R. Hill]. Islamabad/Dordrecht, The Netherlands: Pakistan Hijra Council, 1409/1989 [first published by D. Reidel Publishing Company, 1974].

Buber, Martin, *Gottesfinsternis: Betrachtungen zur Beziehung zwischen Religion und Philosophie.* Heidelberg: Verlag Lambert Schneider, 1962 [1953].

Buber, Martin, *I and Thou.* New York: Macmillan,1958 [1923 in German].

Connolly, William E., *Neuropolitics: Thinking, Culture, Speed.* Minneapolis: University of Minnesota Press, 2002.

Dogen, Kigen, *The Shobo-genzo.* Vols. 1–4 [trans. Yuho Yokoi]. Tokyo: Sankibo Buddhist Bookstore, 1986.

Dreyfus, Hubert L., 'Between techne and technology: the ambiguous place of technology in *Being and Time*', *Tulane Studies in Philosophy*, vol. 32, 1984, pp. 23–35.

Gilligan, Carol, *In a Different Voice.* Cambridge, MA: Harvard University Press, 1982.

Haker, Hille, 'Feministische Bioethik', in Marcus Düwell/Klaus Steigleder (eds.), *Bioethik*, Frankfurt/M.: Suhrkamp 2003, pp. 168–83.

Hanaoka (-Kawamura), Eiko, *Jiko to Sekai no Mondai: Zettaimu no Shiten kara* (The Problem of Self and World: From the Standpoint of Absolute Nothingness). Kanagawa: Gendaitosho, 2005.

Heidegger, Martin, *Die Technik und die Kehre.* Stuttgart: Neske, 1962.

——, *Einführung in die Metaphysik.* Gesamtausgabe Bd. 40. Frankfurt/M.: Vittorio Klostermann, 1976.

——, *The Question Concerning Technology and Other Essays.* [trans. William Lovitt]. New York: Harper & Row, 1977.

——, *Vorträge und Aufsätze.* Stuttgart: Neske, 1978 [1954].

Heyward, Carter, *The Redemption of God: A Theology of Mutual Relations.* Washington, D.C.: University Press of America, 1982.

Ishii, Seishi, *Iyashi no Genri*: Homo Curans *no Tetsugaku* (The Principle of Healing: The Philosophy of *Homo Curans*). Kyoto: Jinbunshoin, 1995.

Jonas, Hans, *Das Prinzip Verantwortung: Versuch einer Ethik für die technologische Zivilization.* Frankfurt/M.: Suhrkamp, 1984. [English trans. *The Imperative of Responsibility: In Search of an Ethics for the Technological Age.* Chicago: University of Chicago Press, 1984].

Kato, Hisatake, Bioethics *to wa Nani Ka* (What is Bioethics?). Tokyo: Miraisha, 1986.

Katz, Marion Holmes, 'The problem of abortion in classical Sunni fiqh', in Jonathan E. Brockopp (ed.), *Islamic Ethics of Life: Abortion, War and Euthanasia*, Columbia, SC: University of South Carolina Press, 2003, pp. 25–50.

Keller, Evelyn Fox, *Reflections on Gender and Science.* Chicago: Yale University Press, 1986.

Kuhn, Thomas, *The Structure of Scientific Revolutions.* Chicago: University of Chicago Press, 1962.

LaFleur, William R., 'Adjusting the body-clock: archaic aspirations and contemporary chemicals', in Walter Schweidler (ed.), *Zeit: Anfang und Ende*, Sankt Augustin: Academia Verlag, 2004, pp. 417–30.

——, Review of Julia Adeny Thomas 'Reconfiguring Modernity', in *Philosophy East and West*, vol. 56, no. 1, January 2006, pp. 172–8.

Manzei, Alexandra, *Körper-Technik-Grenzen: Kritische Anthropologie am Beispiel der Transplantationsmedizin.* Münster: LIT Verlag, 2003.

Mbembe, Achille, 'Necropolitics', *Public Culture*, vol. 15, no. 1, 2003, pp. 11–40.

Merton, Thomas, *The Collected Poems of Thomas Merton.* New York: New Directions, 1977.

Mies, Maria, *Patriarchy and Accumulation on a World Scale*. London: Zed Books, 1986.

Moosa, Ebrahim, 'Brain death and organ transplantation—an Islamic opinion', *South African Medical Journal*, vol. 83, no. 6, 1993, pp. 385–6.

——, 'Languages of change in Islamic law: redefining death in modernity', *Islamic Studies*, vol. 38, no. 3, 1999, pp. 305–42.

Nakagawa, Yonezo, *Igaku no Fukakujitsusei* (The Uncertainty of Medical Science). Tokyo: Nihon Hyoronsya, 1996.

Nishida, Kitaro, *K. Nishida's Complete Works*, Bd. 8–11. Tokyo: Iwanami Shoten, 1965.

Nishitani, Keiji, *Ku to Soku* (Emptiness and Sive), in *Keiji Nishitani's Work*, Vol. 13. Tokyo: Sobunsha, 1987.

Okano, Haruko, 'Moral responsibility in the Japanese context: a perspective from feminist theology', in: Jan Jans (ed.), *Für die Freiheit verantwortlich*, Freiburg/Wien: Herder, 2004, pp. 162–9.

Picht, Georg, *Hier und Jetzt: Philosophieren nach Auschwitz und Hiroshima*. Bd. I and II. Stuttgart: Kletta-Cotta, 1980.

Pieper, Annemarie, *Gibt es eine feministische Ethik?* München: W. Fink, 1998.

Postman, Neil, *Technopoly: The Surrender of Culture to Technology*. New York: Vintage, 1993 [1992].

Praetorius, Ina, *Skizzen zur Feministischen Ethik*. Mainz: Grünewald, 1995.

Ricoeur, Paul, *Das Selbst als ein Anderer*. München: W. Fink, 1996. [Originally published in French as *Soi-même comme un autre*, Paris: Edition du Seuil, 1990].

Ruether, Rosemary Radford, *Feminist Theology and Spirituality in Christian Feminism: Visions of a New Humanity*. New York: Harper & Row, 1984.

Scheper-Hughes, Nancy, *Death Without Weeping: The Violence of Everyday Life in Brazil*. Berkeley: University of California Press, 1993.

Schneider, Werner, *'So tot wie nötig—so lebendig wie möglich!' Sterben und Tod in der fortgeschrittenen Moderne*. Münster: LIT Verlag, 1999.

Shimazono, Susumu, *Toward the Construction of Death and Life Studies* [Bulletin of Death and Life Studies, Vol. 1]. Tokyo: University of Tokyo Death and Life Studies, 2005.

Suzuki, Daisetsu, *Manual of Zen Buddhism*. New York: Grove Press, 1960.

Swer, Gregory Morgan, 'The road to Necropolis: technics and death in the philosophy of Lewis Mumford', *History of the Human Sciences*, vol. 16, no. 4, 2003, pp. 39–59.

Thomas, Julia Adeny, *Reconfiguring Modernity: Concepts of Nature in Japanese Political Ideology*. Berkeley: University of California Press, 2001.

Tsujimura, Koichi and Hartmut Buchner, *Der Ochs und sein Hirte*. Stuttgart: Neske, 1958.

Virilio, Paul, *Speed and Politics: An Essay on Dromology*. New York: Semiotext(e), 1986 [1977].

Whitehead, Alfred North, *Process and Reality: An Essay in Cosmology* [corrected edition, ed. by David Ray Griffin and Donald W. Sherburne]. New York: Free Press, 1979 [1929, London: Collier Macmillan Publishers].

——, *Adventures of Ideas*. New York: Free Press, 1967 [1933].

III. *Global Religions and Local Cultures*

Amin, Galal, *'al-Taghrib wa-l-ightirab fi taqrir al-tanmiya al-insaniyya al-'arabiyya'* ('Westernisation and alienation in the Arabic Human Development Report'), in *Wajhat Nazar*, vol. 4, no. 46, November 2002.

Armstrong, Karen, 'Spiritual Prozac', *New Statesman and Society*, July 21, 1995.

Asad, Talal, 'Anthropological conceptions of religion: reflections on Geertz', *Man (New Series)*, vol. 18, 1983, pp. 237–59.

——, *Genealogies of Religion: Discipline and Reasons of Power in Christianity and Islam*. Baltimore: Johns Hopkins University Press, 1993.

——, 'On re-reading a modern classic: W. C. Smith's *The Meaning and End of Religion*', *History of Religions*, vol. 40, no. 3, 2001, pp. 205–22.

Benjamin, Walter, *The Origin of German Tragic Drama*. London: Verso, 1998 [originally published in German,1963].

Bennett, Jane, *The Enchantment of Modern Life*. Princeton: Princeton University Press, 2001.

Berger, Peter L, 'The desecularization of the world: a global overview', in Peter L. Berger et al. (eds.), *The Desecularization of the World: Resurgent Religion and World Politics*, Grand Rapids, MI: Eerdmans Publishing Company, 1999, pp. 1–18.

Bhagwati, P. N., 'Religion and secularism under the Indian Constitution', in Robert D. Baird (ed.), *Religion and Law in Independent India*, New Delhi: Manohar, 1993, pp. 7–21.

Bonfil, Guillermo Batalla, 'El concepto de indio en América: una categoría de la situación colonial', *Anales de Antropología*, vol. 9, 1972, pp. 105–24.

Bruce, Steve, *Religion in the Modern World: From Cathedrals to Cults*. Oxford: Oxford University Press, 1996.

——, *God is Dead: Secularization in the West*. Malden, MA: Blackwell, 2002.

Brunner, José Joaquín, *América Latina: Cultura y Modernidad*. Mexico: Grijalbo, 1992.

Butterfield, Herbert, *The Whig Interpretation of History*. New York: W. W. Norton, 1965.

Campbell, Colin, *The Romantic Ethic and the Spirit of Modern Consumerism*. Oxford: Blackwell, 1987.

Daston, Lorraine, 'Enlightenment fears, fears of Enlightenment', in: K. M. Baker and P. H. Reill (eds.), *What's Left of Enlightenment?*, Stanford, CA: Stanford University Press, 2001, pp. 115–28

——, 'Scientific error and the ethos of belief', *Social Research*, vol. 72, no. 1, 2005, pp. 1–28.

Friedman, Thomas L., *The Lexus and the Olive Tree*. New York: Farrar, Strauss and Giroux, 1999.

García Canclini, Néstor, *Culturas Híbridas: Estrategias para Entrar y Salir de la Modernidad*. Buenos Aires: Sudamericana, 1992.

Handoussa, Heba, 'Crisis and challenge: prospects for the 1990s', in H. Handoussa and G. Potter eds., *Employment and Structural Adjustment: Egypt in the 1990s*, Cairo: AUC Press, 1991, pp. 3–21

Harvey, David, *The Condition of Postmodernity: An Enquiry into the Origins of Cultural Change*. London/Cambridge, MA: Blackwell, 1989.

Henry, Clement and Robert Springborg, *Globalization and the Politics of Development in the Middle East*. Cambridge: Cambridge University Press, 2001.

Hollywood, Amy, 'Gender, agency, and the divine in religious historiography', *Journal of Religion*, vol. 84, no. 4, 2004, pp. 514–28.

Jackson, Michael, *At Home in the World*. Durham and London: Duke University Press, 1995.

Jameson, Fredric, 'Postmodernism, or the cultural logic of late capitalism', *New Left Review*, vol. 146, 1984, pp. 53–92.

Johansen, Baber, *Contingency in a Sacred Law: Legal and Ethical Norms in the Muslim Fiqh*. Leiden: Brill, 1999.

Kepel, Gilles, *The Prophet and the Pharaoh*. London: Saqi Books, 1985.

Kimanen, Anuleena, 'Explaining religious revivalism in a Northern Karelian village—A microhistorical approach'. Paper presented at the Sixth European Social Science History Conference, Amsterdam, 22–25 March 2006.

Kuhn, Thomas, *The Structure of Scientific Revolutions*. Chicago: Chicago University Press, 1962.

Martin-Munoz, Gema (ed.), *Islam, Modernism and the West*. London: I. B. Tauris, 1999.

Mignolo, Walter, *Local Histories/Global Designs: Coloniality, Subaltern Knowledges, and Border Thinking*. Princeton, NJ: Princeton University Press, 2000.

Mitchell, Richard, *The Society of the Muslim Brothers*. Oxford: Oxford University Press, 1969.

Norris, Pippa, and Ronald Inglehart, *Sacred and Secular: Religion and Politics Worldwide*. Cambridge: Cambridge University Press, 2004.

Oestreich, Gerhard, *Neostoicism and the Early Modern State*. Cambridge: Cambridge University Press, 1982.

Omar, Irfan A., 'Secularism and religious activism in India: a Muslim perspective'. Paper presented at the conference on 'The religions of Abraham concerning state and democracy', International Scholars Annual Trialogue (ISAT), Jakarta, Indonesia, 14–19 February 2000.

Ricoeur, Paul, *Freud: una interpretación de la cultura*. Madrid: Siglo XXI eds., 1983. [Originally published in French as *De l'interprétation: Essai sur Sigmund Freud*. Paris: Le Seuil, 1965].

Roy, Olivier, *Globalized Islam: The Search for a New Ummah*. New York: Columbia University Press, 2004.

Spinner-Halev, Jeff, 'Hinduism, Christianity, and liberal religious toleration', *Political Theory*, vol. 33, no. 1, 2005, pp. 28–57.

Tambiah, Stanley, 'Vignets of present-day diaspora', in Eliezer Ben-Rafael with Yitzhak Sternberg (eds.), *Identity, Culture and Globalization*, Leiden: Brill, 2002, pp. 327–36.

Trilling, Lionel, *Sincerity and Authenticity*. Cambridge: Harvard University Press, 1972.

Yasin, Sayyid et al. (eds), *al-Turāth wa tahadiyyāt al-ʿasr fi al-watan al-ʿarabi aw al-asāla wa al-muʿāsira* [Heritage and Contemporary Challenges in the Arab Homeland, or Authenticity and Contemporaneity]. Beirut: Markaz Dirasat al-Wahda al-ʿArabiyyah, 1985.

IV. *Boundaries and Segregations*

Ahmed, Durre S. (ed.), *Gendering the Spirit: Women, Religion and the Post-Colonial Response*. London and New York: Zed Books, 2002.

Antes, Peter, Armin W. Geertz and Randi R. Warne (eds.), *New Approaches to the Study of Religion*. Berlin and New York: Walter de Gruyter, 2004, Vol. I: *Regional, Critical, and Historical Approaches*. Vol. II: *Textual, Comparative, Sociological, and Cognitive Approaches*.

Bailey, Greg and Ian Mabett (eds.), *The Sociology of Early Buddhism*. Cambridge: Cambridge University Press, 2003.

Buddhadasa Bhikkhu, *The Lord Buddha with Other Religions*. Bangkok: Sukhapabjai Publisher, 2000.

Charnnarong, Bunnun, 'Female ordination in Thai society', *Journal of Buddhist Studies*, vol. 11, no. 2, 2004, pp. 81–96.

Cheng Wei-Yi, *Buddhist Nuns in Taiwan and Sri Lanka: A Critique of the Feminist Perspective*. London/New York: Routledge, 2007.

Collins, Steven, 'The discourse on what is primary (Agganna-sutta)', *Journal of Indian Philosophy*, vol. 21, 1993, pp. 301–93.

Dhamma-pitaka, Phra, *Looking at World Peace Through Histories of Global Civilizations*. Bangkok: Dhammasarn, 1999.

——, *The Buddhist Attitude toward Women and the Bhikkhuni Ordination*. Bangkok: Sukhapabjai Publisher, 2001.

Goffmann, Erving, *Asylums: Essays on the Social Situation of Mental Patients and Other Inmates*. New York: Doubleday, 1961.

Gombrich, Richard, *Theravada Buddhism*. London and New York: Routledge, 1988.

Gyatso, Janet, 'One plus one makes three: Buddhist gender, monasticism and the law of the non-excluded middle', *History of Religions*, vol. 43, no. 2, 2003, pp. 89–115.

Goonatilake, Hema, 'The forgotten women of Anuradhapura: "her story" replaced by "history"', in Ahmed 2002, pp. 91–102.

Hecker, Hellmuth, *Ananda: The Guardian of the Dhamma* (translated from German by Sister Khema). Kandy, Sri Lanka: Buddhist Publication Society, 1980.

Hick, John, *Philosophy of Religion*. New Jersey: Prentice Hall, 1983.

Horner, I. B. (trans.), *The Book of the Discipline (Vinaya-Pitaka)*. London: Pali Text Society, 1942.

Hurvitz, Leon (trans.), *Scripture of the Lotus Blossom of the Fine Dharma (The Lotus Sutra)*. New York: Columbia University Press, 1976.

Jones, Lindsay (editor-in-chief), *Encyclopedia of Religion* (second edition). New York/London/Munich: Macmillan Reference USA [Thomson Gale], 2005. 15 volumes (First edition by Micea Eliade, 1987).

Kabilsingh, Chatsumarn, *A Comparative Study of Bhikkhuni Patimokkha*. Varnasi: Chaukhambha Orientalia,1984.

Kalupahana, David J., *Causality: The Central Philosophy of Buddhism*. Honolulu: University of Hawaï Press, 1975.

——, *A History of Buddhist Philosophy*. Honolulu: University of Hawaï Press, 1992.

Kawahashi, Noriko, 'Religion, gender, and Okinawan studies', *Asian Folklore Studies*, vol. 59, 2000, pp. 301–11.

——, 'Folk religion and its contemporary issues', in Jennifer Robertson (ed.), *A Companion to the Anthropology of Japan*, Malden, MA/Oxford/Victoria, Australia: Blackwell, 2005, pp. 452–65.

——, 'Gender and Japanese religions', in *Encyclopedia of Religion*, 2005, Vol. V, pp. 3345–50.

——, 'Gender issues in Japanese religions', in Paul L. Swanson and Clark Chilson (eds.), *Nanzan Guide to Japanese Religions*, Honolulu: University of Hawaï Press, 2005, pp. 323–35.

Kawahashi, Noriko, and Masako Kuroki (eds.), *Konzaisuru Megumi* (Mixed Graces: Religion and Feminism in a Post-colonial Age). Kyoto: Jinbunshoin, 2004.

King, Ursula, *Religion and Gender*. Oxford, UK and Cambridge, USA: Blackwell, 1995.

——, 'General introduction: gender-critical turns in the study of religion', in King and Beattie 2005, pp. 1–10.

——, 'Gender and religion: an overview', in Lindsay Jones (ed.), *Encyclopedia of Religion* (second edition), New York: Macmillan Reference USA, 2005, Vol. V, pp. 3296–3310.

King, Ursula, and Tina Beattie (eds.), *Gender, Religion and Diversity: Cross-Cultural Perspectives*. London and New York: Continuum, 2004 (Paperback edition 2005).

Mikaelsson, Lisbeth, 'Gendering the history of religions', in Antes et al. 2004, Vol. I, pp. 295–315.

Satha-Anand, Suwanna, 'Truth over convention: feminist interpretations of Buddhism', in Courtney Howland (ed.), *Religious Fundamentalisms and the Human Rights of Women*, New York: St. Martin Press, 1999, pp. 281–91.

——, *Faith and Wisdom: A Philosophical Dialogue on Religion*. Bangkok: Chulalongkorn University Press, 2002.

——, 'Buddhist pluralism and religious tolerance in democratizing Thailand,' in Philip Cam (ed.), *Philosophy, Democracy and Education*, Seoul: The Korean National Commission for UNESCO, 2003, pp. 193–213.

Sharma, Arvind, *The Philosophy of Religion: A Buddhist Perspective*. Delhi: Oxford University Press, 1995.

Swaris, Nalin, *Buddhism, Human Rights and Social Renewal*. Hong Kong: Asian Human Rights Commission, 2000.

Tanaka, Masakazu, and Musashi Tachikawa (eds.), *Living with Sakti: Gender, Sexuality and Religion in South Asia*. Osaka: National Museum of Ethnology, 1999.

Tenri Yamoto Cultural Congress (ed.), *Women and Religion. Tenri International Symposium '98 in Commemoration of the 200th Birthday of Oyasama, the Foundress of Tenrikyo*. Tenri: Tenri Yamato Cultural Congress and Berkeley: Center for Women and Religion, Graduate Theological Union.

Thurman, Robert A., 'Monasticism and civilization', in Yoshinori Takeuchi (ed.), *Buddhist Spirituality: Indian, Southeast Asian, Tibetan, Early Chinese*, New York: Crossroad, 1995, pp. 120–34.

Tsomo, Karma Lekshe (ed.), *Sakyadhita: Daughters of the Buddha*. Ithaca, NY: Snow Lion Publications, 1988.

—— (ed.), *Buddhist Women Across Cultures: Realizations*. Albany, NY: State University of New York Press, 1999.

——, 'Mahaprajapati's legacy. The Buddhist women's movement: an introduction', in Tsomo 1999, pp. 1–44.

—— (ed.), *Innovative Buddhist Women: Swimming Against the Stream*. Richmond, Surrey: Curzon Press, 2000.

—— (ed.), *Buddhist Women and Social Justice: Ideals, Challenges, and Achievements*. Albany, NY: State University of New York Press, 2004.

Van Doorn-Harder, Pieternella, *Women Shaping Islam: Reading the Qur'an in Indonesia*. Urbana and Chicago: University of Illinois Press, 2006.

Warne, Randi R., 'Making the gender-critical turn', in Tim Jensen and Mikael Rothstein (eds.), *Secular Theories on Religion: Current Perspectives*, Copenhagen University: Museum Tusculanum Press, 2000, pp. 249–60.

Wiegers, Gerard A., in association with Jan G. Platvoet, *Modern Societies and the Science of Religions: Studies in Honour of Lammert Leertouwer*. Leiden: Brill, 2002.

V. *Method and Theory in the Study of Religion*

Al-Azmeh, Aziz, 'The coherence of the West', in Rüsen 2002, pp. 58–64.

Almond, Philip C., *The British Discovery of Buddhism*. Cambridge, UK: Cambridge University Press, 1988.

Antes, Peter, Armin W. Geertz and Randi Warne (eds.), *New Approaches in the Study of Religion*. Berlin: Mouton de Gruyter, 2004. *Volume 1: Regional, Critical, and Historical Approaches*, and *Volume 2: Textual, Comparative, Sociological, and Cognitive Approaches*.

Baeck, Leo, 'The religion of the Hebrews', in Carl Clemen (ed.), *Religions of the World: Their Nature and Their History*, New York: Harcourt, Brace, 1931, pp. 265–98.

Barrows, John Henry, *Christianity, the World-Religion: Lectures Delivered in India* (Barrows Lectures, 1896–97). Madras: Christian Literature Society for India, 1897.

Burke, Peter, 'Western historical thinking in a global perspective—10 theses', in Rüsen 2002, pp. 15–30.

Burnouf, Émile, *La science des religions: Sa méthode et ses limites*. Paris: Maisonneuve, 1872 (2nd edition). [English translation by Julie Liebe published as *The Science of Religions*, London: Swan Sonnenschein, Lowrey and Co., 1888].

Cha, Ok Sung, *Hangukin-ui Jongkyo Gyeongheom: Mugyo* (Religious Experience of the Korean People: Shamanism). Seoul: Seogwangsa, 1997.

Chantepie de la Saussaye, P. D., *Manual of the Science of Religion* [trans. Beatrice S. Colyer-Ferugusson]. London: Longmans, 1891. Vol. I of *Lehrbuch der Religionsgeschichte*, 2 vols. (Freiburg: J. C. B. Mohr [Paul Siebeck], 1887–89).

Cho, Heung Yun, *Mu wa Minjok Munhwa* (Shaman and National Culture). Seoul: Minjok Munhwasa, 1994.

Chung, Chin Hong, *Jongkyo Munhwa-ui Insik gwa Haeseok* (Epistemology and Hermeneutics of Religious Culture: Development of Phenomenology of Religion). Seoul: Seoul National University Press, 1996.

——, *Jongkyo Munhwa-ui Nolli* (Logic of Religious Culture). Seoul: Seoul National University Press, 2000.

——, 'Redescription and rectification of the modernity experience of Korean traditional religious culture', *Korea Journal*, vol. 41, no. 1, Spring 2001, Korean National Commission for UNESCO, 2001, pp. 3–17.

——, *Gyeongheom gwa Giyeok* (Experience and Recollection: Reading the Gaps in Religious Culture). Seoul: Dangdae Publishing Company, 2003.

Clarke, James Freeman, *Ten Great Religions: An Essay in Comparative Theology*. Boston: Houghton Mifflin, 1881 [1871].

Derrida, Jacques, 'Structure, sign, and play in the discourse of the human sciences', in Macksey and Donato, *The Languages of Criticism and the Sciences of Man* [trans. Richard Macksey], pp. 247–72; reprinted in Jacques Derrida, *Writing and Difference* [trans. Alan Bass], Chicago: University of Chicago Press, 1978, pp. 278–93.

Estrada, Alvaro, *Maria Sabina: Her Life and Chants*. Santa Barbara: Ross-Erickson Publishers, 1981.

Foley, John Miles (ed.), *Oral Traditional Literature: A Festschrift for Albert Bates Lord*. Columbus, OH: Slavica Publishers, 1981.

Foucault, Michel, *The Order of Things: An Archeology of Human Sciences*. New York: Vintage Books, 1970.

Galarza, Joaquín, 'El Codex Mendoza'. Paper presented at the Instituto de Investigaciones Antropológicas, UNAM, Mexico, November 1998.

Geertz, Armin W., a'On reciprocity and mutual reflection in the study of native American religions', *Religion*, vol. 24, no. 1, 1994, pp. 1–7.

—— 'Critical reflections on the postmodern study of religion', *Religion*, vol. 24, no. 1, 1994, pp. 16–22.

——, 'Ethnohermeneutics in a postmodern world', in Tore Ahlbäck (ed.), *Approaching Religion, Part I: Based on Papers Read at the Symposium on Methodology in the Study of Religions Held at Åbo, Finland, on the 4th–7th August 1997*, Åbo: The Donner Institute for Research in Religious and Cultural History, and Stockholm: Almqvist & Wiksell International, 1999, pp. 73–86.

——, 'Analytical theorizing in the secular study of religion', in Tim Jensen and Mikael Rothstein (eds.), *Secular Theories on Religion: Current Perspectives*, Copenhagen: Museum Tusculanum Press, 2000, pp. 21–31.

——, 'Global perspectives on methodology in the study of religion', in Geertz and McCutcheon 2000, pp. 49–73.

——, 'Definition, categorization and indecision: or, how to get on with the study of religion', in Christoph Kleine, Monika Schrimpf and Katja Triplett (eds.), *Unterwegs: Neue Pfade in der Religionswissenschaft: Festschrift für Michael Pye zum 65. Geburtstag*, München: Biblion Verlag, 2004, pp. 109–18.

——, 'Can we move beyond primitivism? On recovering the indigenes of indigenous religions in the academic study of religion', in Jacob Olupona (ed.), *Beyond 'Primitivism': Indigenous Religious Traditions and Modernity*, New York and London: Routledge, 2004, pp. 37–70.

Geertz, Armin W., and Russell T. McCutcheon (eds.) assisted by Scott S. Elliott, *Perspectives on Method and Theory in the Study of Religion: Adjunct Proceedings of the XVIIth Congress of the International Association for the History of Religions, Mexico City 1995*. Leiden: Brill, 2000.

——, 'The role and history of methodology and theory in the IAHR', in Geertz and McCutcheon 2000, pp. 3–37.

Gingerich, Willard, '*Cipahuacanemiliztli*, the Purified Life in the Discourses of Book VI, Florentine Codex', in: J. Kathryn Josserand and Kaaren Dakin (eds.), *Smoke and Mist: Mesoamerican Studies in Memory of Thelma Sullivan*, BAR International Series 402, 1988, pp. 508–26.

Hogg, William Richey, *Ecumenical Foundations: A History of the International Missionary Council and its Nineteenth-Century Background*. New York: Harpers, 1952.

Jacolliot, Louis, *La Bible dans l'Inde: Vie de Iezeus Christna*. Paris: Librairie Internationale, 1869.

Jang, Suk Man, 'Gaehangki Hanguk Sahoe-ui Jongkyo Gaenyeom Hyeongseong-ae gwanhan Yeongu' ('A Historical Study of the Concept of *Jongkyo* in Modern Korean Society'), Ph.D dissertation, Seoul National University, 1992.

Jastrow, Morris, *The Study of Religion*. New York: Scribners, 1901.

Jensen, Jeppe Sinding, *The Study of Religion in a New Key: Theoretical and Philosophical Soundings in the Comparative and General Study of Religion*. Aarhus: Aarhus University Press, 2003.

Kim, Tae Gon, *Hanguk Musok Yeongu* (A Study of Korean Shamanism). Seoul: Jipmundang, 1987.

Ko, Gun Ho, 'Jongkyo doegi wa jongkyo neomeoseogi' ('Religionising and de-religionising'), *Jongkyo Munhwa Bipyeong* (The Critical Review of Religion and Culture), vol. 7, March 2005, pp. 42–71.

Kuenen, Abraham, *National Religions and Universal Religions*. London: Macmillan, 1882. (Hibbert Lectures 1882). [Translated from Dutch by P. H. Wicksteed].

Lillie, Arthur, *Buddhism in Christendom, or, Jesus, the Essene*. London: Kegan Paul/Trench, 1887.

Macksey, Richard and Eugenio Donato (eds.), *The Languages of Criticism and the Sciences of Man: The Structuralist Controversy*. Baltimore: Johns Hopkins University Press, 1970.

Mandair, A. S., 'The repetition of past imperialisms: Hegel, historical difference and the theorization of Indic religions', *History of Religions*, vol. 44, no. 4, 2005, pp. 277–99.

Marcos, Sylvia (ed), *Gender/Bodies/Religions*. Mexico: IAHR-ALER Publications, 2000.

——, 'Approaches to orality: a methodology'. Keynote address at the 'Conference on Orality, Gender and Indigenous Religions', Claremont Graduate University, School of Religion, Claremont CA, May 2001.

——, 'Beyond binary categories: Mesoamerican religious sexuality', in Stephen Ellingson and M. Christian Green (eds.), *Religion and Sexuality in Cross-Cultural Perspective*, New York and London: Routledge, 2002, pp. 111–36.

——, *Taken from the Lips: Gender and Eros in Mesoamerican Religions*. Leiden: Brill, 2006.

Masuzawa, Tomoko, *The Invention of World Religions: Or, How European Universalism Was Preserved in the Language of Pluralism*. Chicago: University of Chicago Press, 2005.

Maurice, Frederick Denison, *The Religions of the World and Their Relations to Christianity*. London: John W. Parker, 1847.

Morrison, Kenneth, 'The cosmos as intersubjective: Native American other than human persons', in Graham Harvey (ed.), *Indigenous Religions*, London and New York: Cassell, 2000, pp. 23–36.

Müller, Friedrich Max, *Lectures on the Science of Language*. First Series, Delivered at the Royal Institution of Great Britain in April, May, and June, 1861. First American edition New York: Scribners, 1862 (Based on the second edition published in London, 1862).

Obeyesekere, Gananath, *Medusa's Hair: An Essay on Personal Symbols and Religious Experience*. Chicago: University of Chicago Press, 1981.

Parry, Milman, *The Making of Homeric Verse*. Oxford: Clarendon Press, 1971.

Pfleiderer, Otto, *Religion und Religionen*. München: J. F. Lehmann, 1906. Translated by Daniel A. Huebsch as *Religion and Historic Faiths*, New York: B. W. Huebsch, 1907.

Portilla, Miguel Léon, *Literaturas de Mesoamérica*. Mexico: SEP, 1984.

Rauwenhoff, L. W. E., 'Wereldgodsdiensten', *Theologisch Tijdschrift*, vol. 19, 1885, pp. 1–33.

Renan, Ernest, *History of the People of Israel*. Vol. 1 [trans. C. B. Pitman & D. Bingam]. London: Chapman and Hall, 1888.

Rüsen Jörn, (ed.), *Western Historical Thinking: An Intercultural Debate*. New York: Berghahn Books, 2002.

Ryu, Dong Sik, *Hanguk Mugyo-ui Yeoksa wa Gujo* (History and Structure of Korean Shamanism). Seoul: Yonsei University Press, 1992.

Sahagun, Fray Bernardino de, *Historia de las Cosas de la Nueva España*. Mexico: Porrua, 1982 [1577].

Schlegel, Friedrich von, *Über die Sprache und die Weisheit der Indier: Ein Beitrag zur Begründung der Altertumskunde*. Heidelberg: Mohr und Zimmer, 1808. English translation by E. J. Millington, included in *The Aesthetic and Miscellaneous Works of Frederick von Schlegel*, London: Henry G. Bohn, 1849.

——, *Language and Wisdom of the Indians*. In *The Aesthetic and Miscellaneous Works of Frederick von Schlegel*, ed. by E. J. Millington. London: Henry G. Bohn, 1849. Originally published as *Über die Sprache und die Weisheit der Indier: Ein Beitrag zur Begründung der Altertumskunde* (Heidelberg: Mohr und Zimmer, 1808).

Schlunk, Martin, *Die Weltreligionen und das Christentum: Eine Auseindersetzung vom Christentum aus*. Hamburg: Agentur des Rauhen Hauses, 1923.

Smith, Jonathan Z., 'Religion, religions, religious', in Mark C. Taylor (ed.), *Critical Terms for Religious Studies*, Chicago and London: University of Chicago Press, 1998, pp. 269–84.

Strenski, Ivan, 'Hans Penner, Horatio, and the Terminador: a review essay of radical interpretation in religion', in *Religion*, vol. 34, no. 1, 2004, pp. 53–64.

Sullivan, Thelma, *Compendio de Gramática Nahuatl*. Mexico: UNAM, 1983.

——, 'A scattering of jades: the words of the Aztec elders', in G. H. Gossen (ed.), *Symbol and Meaning Beyond the Closed Community: Essays in Mesoamerican Ideas*, Albany: Institute for Mesoamerican Studies, State University of New York, 1986, pp. 9–17.

Tiele, C.P., 'Religions', in *Encyclopaedia Britannica* (9th edition), Edinburgh: A.& C. Black, 1885, pp. 1875–89.

Troeltsch, Ernst, *Christian Thought: Its History and Application*. London: University of London Press, 1923. Edited with an introduction and index by Baron F. von Hügel.

——, *Die Absolutheit des Christentums und die Religionsgeschichte*. Tübingen: J. C. B. Mohr [Paul Siebeck], 1929 (3rd. edition; 1st edition published in 1901). English translation by David Reid, published as *The Absoluteness of Christianity and the History of Religions*, John Knox Press, 1971.

Turner, Victor, 'Encounter with Freud: the making of a comparative symbologist', in G. D. Spindler (ed), *The Making of Psychological Anthropology*, Berkeley: University of California Press, 1978, pp. 558–83.

Vivekananda, Swami, 'Hinduism', in Richard Hughes Seager (ed.), *The Dawn of Religious Pluralism: Voices from the World's Parliament of Religions, 1893*, La Salle, IL: Open Court, 1993, pp. 421–32.

Warren, William Fairfield, *The Religions of the World and the World-Religion*. New York: Methodist Book Concern, 1911 [Boston, 1892].

Weber, Max, 'Wirtschaftsethik der Weltreligionen', originally published in *Archiv für Sozialwissenschaft und Sozialpolitik* (1915), reprinted in *Gesammelte Aufsätze zur Religionssoziologie*, Tübingen: Mohr, 1921.

——, 'The social psychology of the world religions', in *From Max Weber: Essays in Sociology* [trans. H. H. Gerth and C. Wright Milles], New York: Oxford University Press, 1958, pp. 267–301.

Yoon, Yee Heum (ed.), *Hangukin-ui Jongkyogwan* (Understanding of Religion among the Korean People). Seoul: Seoul National University Press, 2001.

VI. *The Study of Religion in Japan*

Religious Studies in Post-War Japan

Aoki, Tamotsu, *Nihon Bunka Ron no Hen'you* (The Transformation of Views of Japanese Culture). Tokyo: Chuokoronshinsha, 1994.

Barthes, Roland, *Image, Music, Text* [trans. Stephen Heath]. New York: Hill & Wang, 1997.

Bellah, Robert, *Tokugawa Religion: The Value of Pre-industrial Japan*. Glencoe: Free Press, 1957.

Eliade, Mircea, *Le mythe de l'éternel retour*. Paris: Gallimard, 1949.

Foucault, Michel, *L'ordre du discourse*. Paris: Gallimard, 1971.

Fujiwara, Satoko, 'Study of Religion: the academic study of religion in Japan', in *The Encyclopedia of Religion* (2nd edn.), Farmington Hills: Thomson Gale, 2005, pp. 8775–80.

Journal of Religious Studies, no. 353, March 2005. Vol. LXXVIII-4, no. 343, March 2005. (The Proceedings of the Sixty-third Annual Convention of the Japanese Association for Religious Studies)

Kiyozawa, Manshi, *Shukyo Tetsugaku Gaikotsu* (Skeleton of the Philosophy of Religion). Kyoto: Hozokan, 1893.

Kristeva, Julia, *Desire in Language: A Semiotic Approach to Literature and Art*. New York: Columbia University Press, 1980.

Kuhn, Thomas, *The Structure of Scientific Revolutions*. Chicago: University of Chicago Press, 1962.

McFarland, Horace Neill, *The Rush Hour of the Gods: A Study of New Religions in Japan*. Tokyo: Macmillan, 1967.

Miyanaga, Kuniko, *Gurobaruka to Aidentiti* (Globalisation and Identity). Kyoto: Sekai-sisosha, 2000.

Robertson, Roland, *Globalization: Social Theory and Global Culture*. London: Sage, 1992.

Said, Edward, *Orientalism*. London: Routledge & Kegan Paul, 1978.

Tamaru, Noriyoshi, 'Religious Studies in Japan: a preliminary report,' in: Ugo Bianchi (ed.), *The Notion of 'Religion'. Comparative Research: Selected Proceedings of the XVIth IAHR Congress*, Roma: Erma di Bretschneider, 1994, pp. 755–61.

Tominaga, Nakamoto, *Emerging from Meditation* [Translated with an introduction by Michael Pye]. London: Duckworth, 1990. [Original title in Japanese *Shutsujo Kogo*].

Wakimoto, Tsuneya (editor-in-chief), *Nihon Shukyo Gakkai Gojunenshi* (Fifty Years of the Japanese Association for Religious Studies). Tokyo: Japanese Association for Religious Studies, 1970.

One Hundred Years of Buddhist Scholarship in Japan

Editorial Board of the Faculty of Literature at the University of Tokyo, 'History of the Faculty of Literature' [Part of 'Recent One Hundred Years of the University of Tokyo'], Tokyo: University of Tokyo, 1986, pp. 524–53.

Hakamaya, Noriaki, *Hongaku Shiso Hihan* (A Criticism of Hogaku Thought). Tokyo: Daizo Shuppan, 1990.

Kawase, Kazuma, *Kokatsujiban no Kenkyu* (A Study of Ancient Printings). Tokyo: Antiquarian Booksellers Association in Japan, 1962.

Kimura, Kiyotaka, 'Hara Tanzan to Indo Tetsugaku no Tanjo' ('Hara Tanzan and the birth of "Indian Philosophy"'), in *Higashi Asia Bukkyo: Sono Seritsu to Tenkai* (East Asian Buddhism: Its Occurrence and Development), edited by Kimura Kiyotaka Hakushi Kanreki Kinen Kai, Tokyo: Shunjusha, 2002, pp. 5–30.

Kimura, Taiken, *A Complete Collection of Taiken Kimura*. Vol. 1. Tokyo: Daihorinkaku, 1978.

Nakamura, Hajime, *Ways of Thinking of Eastern Peoples: India, China, Tibet, Japan* (revised English translation) [ed. by Philip P. Wiener]. Honolulu: University of Hawaii Press, 1964.

——, *Sekai Shisoshi* (History of World Thought). Tokyo: Shunjusha, 1998–9.

Nanjo, Bun'yu, *The Catalogue of the Tri-pitaka edited in the Ming Dynasty*. Tokyo: Nanjo Hakase Kinen Kanko Kai, 1929.

Matsumoto, Shiro, *Engi to Ku: Nyoraizo Shiso Hihan* (Pratītya-samutpāda and Cūnyatā: A criticism of tathāgata-garbha). Tokyo: Daizo Shuppan, 1989.

Sueki, Fumihiko, *Nihon Bukkyo Shisoshi Ronko* (A Treatise on the History of Japanese Buddhism). Tokyo: Daizo Shuppan, 1993.

——, *Kindai Nihon to Bukkyo* (Modern Japan and Buddhism). Tokyo: Transview, 2004.
Shimoda, Masahiro, *Nehangyo no Kenkyu: Daijo Kyoten no Kenkyu Hoho Shiron* (A Study of the Mahāparinirvāna Sūtra: With a Focus on the Methodology of the Study of Mahāyāna Sūtras). Tokyo: Shunjusha, 1997.
Suzuki, Shosan, *Banmin Tokuyo* (The Merit of Everyone's Practice). [Edited and annotated by Yusho Miyasaka]. Tokyo: Iwanami Shoten, 1964.
Takakusu, Junjiro, *A Complete Collection of Junjiro Takakusu*. Vol. 1. Tokyo: Daihorinkaku, 1978 (Tokyo: Kyoiku Shinchosha, 1982).
Tokiwa, Daijo, *Meiji Bukkyo Zenshu Gohohen* (A Complete Collection of Buddhist Works on Protecting Buddha's Teaching). Tokyo: Shun'yodo, 1935.
Tominaga, Nakamoto, *Shutsujyo Kogo* (*Emerging from Meditation*; trans. and introduction by Michael Pye, London: Duckworth, 1990).
Ui, Hakuju, *Sanko Ronrigaku* (For the Learners of Logic). Tokyo: Hakubunkan, 1913.

The Study of Christianity within the Field of Religious Studies in Japan

Ariga, Testutaro, *Kirisutokyo Shiso ni okeru Sonzairon no Mondai* (Ontological Problems in Christian Thought). Tokyo: Sobunsha, 1969.
Ebisawa, Arimichi, *Nihon no Seisho: Seisho Wayaku no Rekishi* (A History of Translation of the Bible in Japan) [revised and expanded edition]. Tokyo: Nihon Kirisutokyodan Shuppankyoku, 1981.
Hanzawa, Takamaro, *Kindai Nihon no Katorisizumu* (Catholicism in Modern Japan). Tokyo: Misuzu Shobo, 1993.
Hatano, Seiichi, *Hatano Seiichi Zenshu* (Complete Works of Hatano Seiichi). Tokyo: Iwanami-shoten, 1969.
Ishihara, Ken, *Nihon Kirisutokyoshi Ron* (A Treatise on the History of Christianity in Japan). Tokyo: Shinkyoshuppansha, 1968.
Kumano, Yoshitaka, *Nihon Kirisutokyo Shingaku Shisoshi* (History of Christian Theology in Japan). Tokyo: Shinkyoshuppansha, 1968.
Mizugaki, Wataru, *Shukyoteki Tankyu no Mondai* (Problems in Religious Quest in Ancient Christianity). Tokyo: Sobunsha, 1984.
Mullins, Mark R., *Christianity Made in Japan: A Study of Indigenous Movements*. Honolulu: University of Hawaï Press, 1998.
Muto, Kazuo, *Shingaku to Shukyo Tetsugaku no Aida* (Between Theology and Philosophy of Religion). Tokyo: Sobunsha, 1961.
Nagai, Michio, *Nihon no Daigaku* (Universities in Japan). Tokyo: Chuokoronsha, 1965.
Reid, David, *New Wine: The Cultural Shaping of Japanese Christianity*. Berkeley: Asian Humanities Press, 1991.
Suzuki, Norihisa. *Meiji Shukyo Shicho no Kenkyu* (A Study of Religious Thought in the Meiji Era). Tokyo: Tokyo Daigaku Shuppankai, 1967.
The Japan Society of Christian Studies, *Nihon no Shingaku* (Theological Studies in Japan), vols. 1–44, 1962–2005.
Tsuchiya, Hiroshi, *Kyoten ni Natta Shukyo* (Religion Realised as Scripture). Sapporo: Hokkaido Daigaku Toshokankokai, 2002.
Yagi, Seiichi, and Ulrich Luz (eds.), *Gott in Japan: Anstösse zum Gespräch mit japanischen Philosophen, Theologen, Schriftstellern*. München: Chr. Kaiser, 1973.
Yoshinobu, Kumazawa, and David L. Swain (edited and compiled by), *Christianity in Japan, 1971–90*. Tokyo: Kyo Bun Kwan, 1991.

Islamic Studies in Japan

Fujimoto, Katsuji, *Mahometto: Yudayajin to no Koso* (Muhammad: The Conflict with the Jews). Tokyo: Chuokoronsha, 1971.
Horii, Satoe, *Isuramu Ho Tsushi* (A Concise History of Islamic Law). Tokyo: Yamakawa-shuppansha, 2004.

Hanada, Nariaki, *Japanese Studies on West Asian and North African History (Pre-Ottoman Period): 1973–1983*. Tokyo: The Centre for East Asian Cultural Studies, 1987.

Izutsu, Toshihiko, *Mahometto* (Muhammad). Tokyo: Kobundo, 1952.

——, *Ethico-Religious Concepts in the Qur'ān*. Montreal: McGill University Press, 1966.

——, *A Comparative Study of the Key Philosophical Concepts in Sufism and Taoism: Ibn 'Arabī and Lao-Tzŭ, Chuang-Tzŭ*. 2 vols. Tokyo: The Keio Institute of Cultural and Linguistic Studies, 1966–7.

Kamada, Shigeru, 'Mullā Sadrā between mystical philosophy and Qur'ān interpretation: through his commentary on the "Chapter of Earthquake"', *International Journal of Asian Studies*, vol. 2, no. 2, 2005, pp. 275–89.

Kikuchi, Tatsuya, *Isumairuha no Shinwa to Tetsugaku* (Ismā'īlī Mythology and Philosophy: A Historical Study of a Muslim Minority). Tokyo: Iwanami Shoten, 2005.

Makino, Shin'ya, *Mahometto* (Muhammad). Tokyo: Kodansha, 1979.

——, *Creation and Termination: A Semantic Study of the Structure of the Qur'ānic World View*. Tokyo: The Keio Institute of Cultural and Linguistic Studies, 1970.

Matsumoto, Akiro, *Isuramu Seiji Shingaku: warāya to wirāya* (Political Theology of Islam: Walāyah and Wilāyah). Tokyo: Miraisha, 1993.

Miura, Toru, 'The past and present of Islamic and Middle Eastern Studies in Japan: using the Bibliography of Islamic and Middle Eastern Studies in Japan 1868–1988', *Annals of Japan Association for Middle East Studies*, vol. 17, no. 2, 2002, pp. 45–60.

—— 'Survey of Middle East Studies in Japan: historical development, present state, and prospects', *Annals of Japan Association for Middle East Studies*, vol. 19, no. 2, 2004, pp. 169–200.

Nakamura, Kojiro, *Gazari no Kito Ron: Isuramu Shinpishugi ni okeru Shugyo* (Ghazali's Concept of Prayer: Religious Exercises of Islamic Mysticism). Tokyo: Taimeido, 1982.

——, 'Early Japanese Pilgrims to Mecca', *Orient*, vol. 22, 1986, pp. 47–57.

——, 'Islam in Japan: A historical overview', *Echoes of Peace*, no. 18, 1987, pp. 4–6.

——, *Ghazali and Prayer*. Kuala Lumpur: Islamic Book Trust, 2001.

——, *Isuramu no Shukyo Shiso: Gazari to sono Shuhen* (Religious Thought in Islam, with Special Reference to Ghazali). Tokyo, Iwanami Shoten, 2002.

Shimoda, Johei, *Yogensha Mahometto* (The Prophet Muhammad). Tokyo: Kadokawa Shoten, 1966.

Takeshita, Masataka, *Ibn 'Arabī's Theory of the Perfect Man and Its Place in the History of Islamic Thought*. Tokyo: Institute for the Study of Languages and Cultures of Asia and Africa, 1987.

—— (ed.), *Isuramu Tetsugaku* (Islamic Philosophy). Tokyo: Heibonsha, 2000.

Tonaga, Yasushi, 'Sufism in the past and present based on the Three-axis Framework of Sufism', *Annals of the Japanese Association for Middle East Studies*, vol. 21, no. 2, 2006, pp. 7–21.

Yanagihashi, Hiroyuki, *Isuramu Zaisan Ho no Seiritsu to Hen'you* (The Formation and Transformation of Islamic Property Law). Tokyo: Sobunsha, 1998.

——, *Isuramu Kazoku Ho: Kon'in, Oyako, Shinzoku* (Islamic Family Law: Marriage, Parents, Children, and Relatives). Tokyo: Sobunsha, 2001.

——, *A History of the Early Islamic Law of Property*. Leiden: Brill, 2004.

Studies of Religion in Japan and the Philosophy of Religion

Abe, Masao, *Zen and Western Thought* [ed. William R. LaFleur]. London: Macmillan, 1985.

——, *A Zen Life: D. T. Suzuki Remembered*. New York: Weatherhill, 1986.

——, *The Emptying God: A Buddhist-Jewish-Christian Conversation* [edited by John B. Cobb, Jr. and Christopher Ives]. Maryknoll, N.Y.: Orbis Books, 1990.

——, *A study of Dogen: His Philosophy and Religion* [ed. Steven Heine]. Albany: State University of New York Press, 1992.

Hatano, Seiichi, *Time and Eternity* [trans. Ichiro Suzuki]. Tokyo: Printing Bureau, Japanese Government, 1963.

Hisamatsu, Shin'ichi, *Zen and the Fine Arts* [trans. Gishin Tokiwa]. Tokyo: Kodansha International, 1971.

——, *Critical Sermons of the Zen Tradition: Hisamatsu's Talks on Linji* [trans. Christopher Ives and Gishin Tokiwa]. Basingstoke, 2002.

Kadowaki, Kakichi, *Zen and the Bible* [trans. Joan Rieck]. Maryknoll, NY: Orbis Books, 2002.

Kiyozawa, Manshi, *December Fan: The Buddhist Essays of Manshi Kiyozawa* [trans. Nobuo Haneda]. Kyoto: Higashi Honganji, 1984.

——, *Zenshu* (Complete Works). Tokyo: Iwanami Shoten, 2003.

Muto, Kazuo, *Shukyo Tektsugaku no Atarashii Kanosei* (New Possibilities of the Philosophy of Religion). Tokyo: Sobunsha, 1974.

Nishida, Kitaro, *Intuition and Reflection in Self-consciousness* [trans. Valdo H. Viglielmo]. Albany: State University of New York Press, 1987.

——, *Last Writings: Nothingness and the Religious Worldview* [trans. David A. Dilworth]. Honolulu: University of Hawaï Press, 1987.

——, *An Inquiry into the Good* [trans. Masao Abe and Christopher Ives]. New Haven: Yale University Press, 1990.

Nishitani, Keiji, *Religion and Nothingness* [trans. Jan Van Bragt]. Berkeley: University of California Press, 1982.

——, *The Self-overcoming of Nihilism* [trans. Graham Parkes with Setsuko Aihara]. Albany: State University of New York Press, 1990.

Onodera, Isao, *Seirei no Shingaku* (Theology of the Holy Spirit). Yokohama: Shumpusha, 2003.

Smith, Wilfred Cantwell, *Faith and Belief*. Princeton: Princeton University Press, 1979.

Suzuki, Daisetsu, *Zen and Japanese Culture*. London: Routledge and Kegan Paul, 1959.

——, *Living by Zen* [ed. Christmas Humphreys]. London: Rider and Co., 1982.

——, *Studies in Zen*. London: Unwin Paperbacks, 1986.

——, *Japanese Spirituality* [trans. Norman Waddell]. New York: Greenwood, 1988.

——, *Mysticism: Christian and Buddhist*. London: Routledge, 2002.

Takeuchi, Yoshinori, *The Heart of Buddhism: In Search of the Timeless Spirit of Primitive Buddhism* [trans. James W. Heisig]. New York: Crossroad, 1983.

Tanabe, Hajime, *Philosophy as Metanoetics* [trans. Takeuchi Yoshinori with Valdo Viglielmo and James W. Heisig]. Berkeley: University of California Press, 1986.

Uchimura, Kanzo, *How I Became a Christian: Out of My Diary*. Tokyo: Keiseisha, 1895.

——, *Representative Men of Japan: Essays*. Tokyo: Keiseisha, 1908.

Ueda, Shizuteru, *Die Gottesgeburt in der Seele und der Durchbruch zur Gottheit: Die mystische Anthropologie Meister Eckharts und ihre Konfrontation mit der Mystik des Zen-Buddhismus*. Gütersloh: G. Mohn, 1965.

——, *Luther und Shinran—Eckhart und Zen* [ed. Martin Kraatz]. Köln: In Kommission bei E. J. Brill, 1989.

Uemura, Masahisa, *Shinri Ippan* (A Glimpse of the Truth). Tokyo: Keiseisha, 1884.

Wach, Joachim, *Introduction to the History of Religions* [edited by Joseph Kitagawa and Gregory Alles]. New York: Macmillan, 1988.

Yagi, Seiichi, *Basho Ron to shite no Shukyo Tetsugaku* (Philosophy of Religion as Topology). Kyoto: Hozokan, 2006.

INDEX